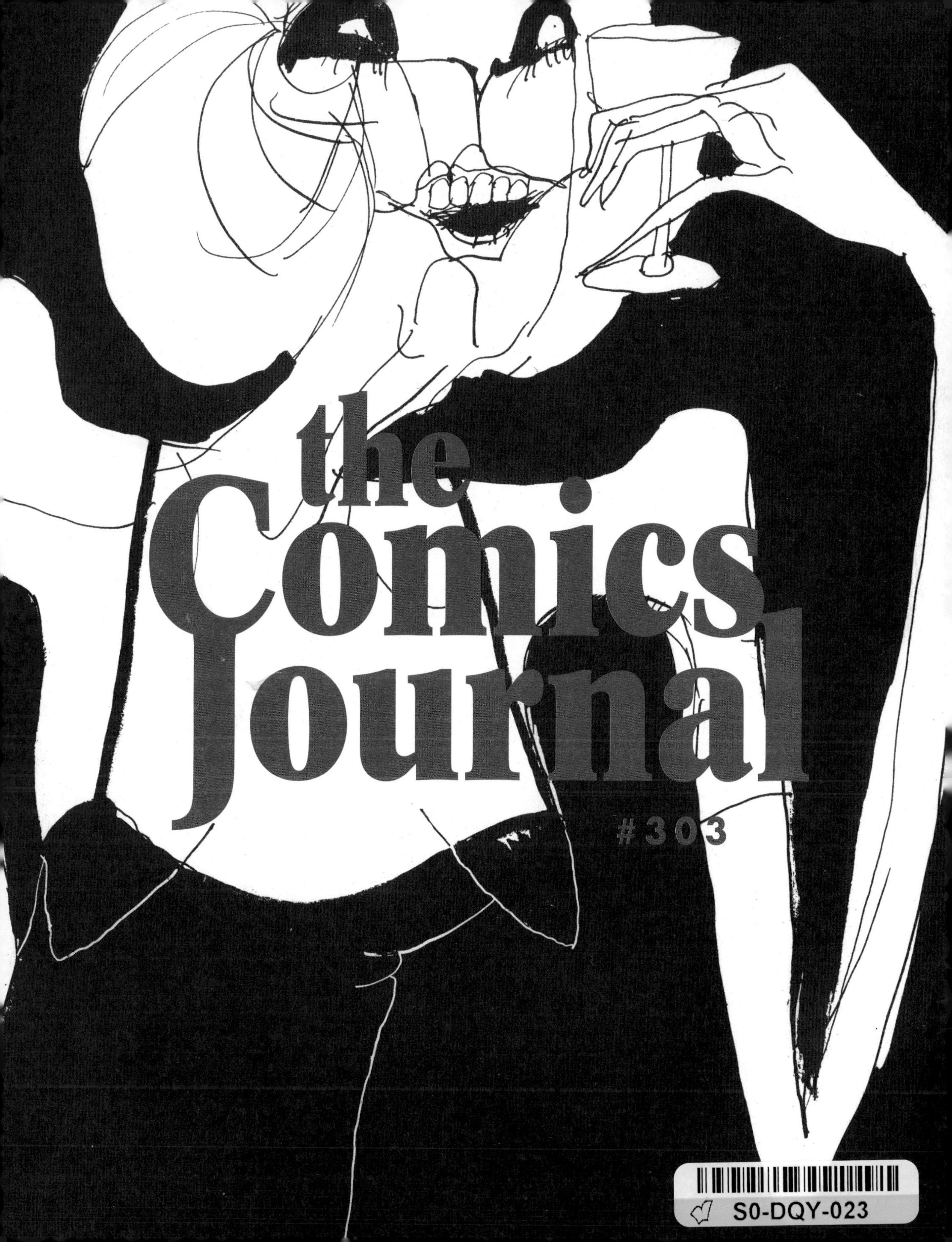
the Comics Journal
#303

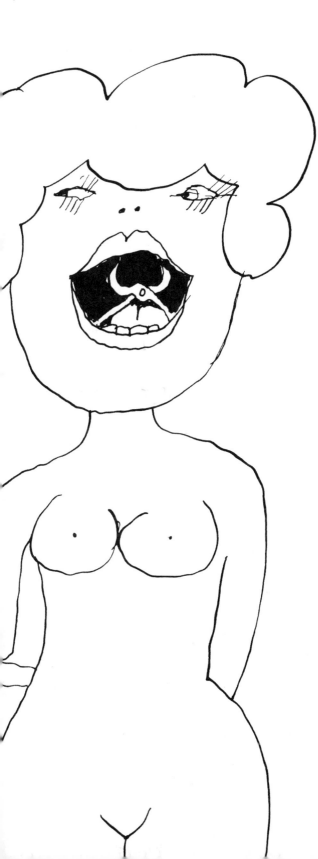

Contributors

Fantagraphics Books, Inc.

7563 Lake City Way NE

Seattle, WA 98115

Fantagraphics.com

Facebook.com/fantagraphics

Twitter: @fantagraphics

First Printing: February 2019

ISBN: 978-1-68396-171-0

Printed in: Korea

COVER: From *The Three Robbers,* by Tomi Ungerer, 1961.

TITLE PAGE: From *The Party,* by Tomi Ungerer, 1966.

CONTENTS: From The *Underground Sketchbook,* Tomi Ungerer, 1964.

4

ANTOINE COSSÉ is a Parisian-born cartoonist and illustrator living in London. His comics have been published by Breakdown Press and Retrofit, and his commercial art has been featured in the *Guardian* and *The New York Times*.

INÉS ESTRADA is a cartoonist from Mexico City. She currently lives and works in Texas, making comics and running her online shop Gatosaurio. Her graphic novel *Alienation* comes out from Fantagraphics in 2019.

KIM JOOHA is a writer living in Toronto, Canada. Jooha is the editor of Alexis Beauclair's *Vanishing Perspective* (2018, 2dcloud) and an upcoming Lale Westvind collection for 2dcloud.

DR. SHEENA C. HOWARD is an Associate Professor in the Department of Communication and Journalism at Rider University; co-writer of the Lion Forge series *Superb* and an Eisner Award-winning author of *Black Comics: Politics of Race and Representation* and *Encyclopedia of Black Comics.*

CHRIS MAUTNER is a social media producer for PennLive.com and writes for Drexel University's *The Smart Set* and TCJ.com. He is also the co-host of the podcast *Comic Books are Burning in Hell.*

MANNIE MURPHY is a cartoonist and armchair historian born and raised in Portland, Oregon. Murphy was also the recipient of a 2008 Xeric Grant, the editor of the Ignatz Award-nominated anthology *Gay Genius* and is featured in the Eisner Award-nominated Fantagraphics anthology *No Straight Lines.*

BEN PASSMORE is an Ignatz Award-winning cartoonist currently living in Philadelphia. His comics *Daygloayhole* and the Eisner Award-nominated *Your Black Friend and Other Strangers* were published by Silver Sprocket. Passmore is also a regular contributor to *The Nib*, and his collaboration with Ezra Claytan Daniels, *BTTM FDRS*, will be published by Fantagraphics in 2019.

ALLY RUSSELL is an Australian-born journalist and cartoonist living in London. She is currently writing a comprehensive biography of comics writer Stephen Perry and works in entertainment publicity.

Editors' Note

The original incarnation of *The Comics Journal* was created in 1976 to champion the idea that the medium should be evaluated by stricter aesthetic standards than it generally had been and perceived as true art.

The Comics Journal pushed and prodded creators and publishers alike in an attempt to elevate not only the work itself but also the culture and discourse surrounding it. The comics landscape was more barren then, and this rallying cry truly had an effect. The magazine's motor, and the enthusiasm and anger that served as that motor's pistons, hoisted comics criticism and the art form's place in literature more broadly. Partly due to the effort of *The Comics Journal*, comics now hold a higher value and have greater merit.

We need a new motor. Comics are now consumed by the general public. Graphic novels are regularly reviewed by tiny blogs as well as the most prominent media outlets. Movies and television shows based on comics are setting record box office numbers and multimedia conglomerates are raking in billions. But where are the creators in all of this? Where is that higher value and greater merit for the artists behind these comics? Many have been lost in the shuffle or simply put out to pasture with no platform.

The magazine in your hands, the new *Comics Journal*, and the motor running it, will be focused on the artists. Sure, we'll still carry on the high standards of criticism that was cultivated in the past, and we'll probably still include our fair share of righteous indignation, but we will be motivated by giving the comic creator that missing platform. This *Comics Journal* will be a place to consider modern and historical artworks, politics, ethics, technology, economics, innovation and comics' and artists' place in society at large. Not just the hyper-specific pop culture niche ditch that comics sites and magazines have been dredging for years; *The Comics Journal* will attempt to take on larger, more crucial matters. We hope you'll join us.

Editor in Chief: **Gary Groth**

Managing Editors: **RJ Casey** and **Kristy Valenti**

Designer: **Sean David Williams** and **Justin Allan-Spencer**

Production: **Paul Baresh** and **Preston White**

Promotion: **Jacq Cohen**

Editorial Assistance: **Kassandra Davis, Conrad Groth, James Ganas, Eric Huberty, Sara Podwall, Reniel Sagcal, Emily Sawan**

Advertising: **Matt Silvie**
For advertising information, email silvie@fantagraphics.com

Special thanks to **Sammy Harkham**

For more thoughtful criticism and reviews, visit **tcj.com**

BLOOD & THUNDER

A lot has changed in comics, and in the world at large, since our last issue in 2013. With that in mind, we asked a number of influential comic creators from across the medium's spectrum what they would like to see from *The Comics Journal* going forward. Here is what they think the *Journal* should look like in its new incarnation …

Illustrations by David Alvarado

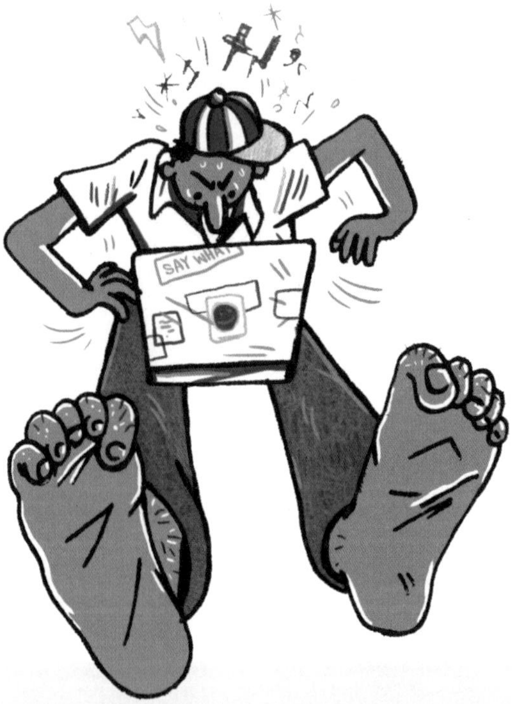
SAY WHAT

YOU GUYS KNOW what you're doing. Bring thoughtful art criticism to comics. Keep shitty artistic intentions in check. Involving more women with strong editorial input – to match their presence on the creative side – is always a good idea.

Good luck with it!

Hartley Lin

I DON'T HAVE ANY GREAT ADVICE, but here goes nothin'…

- R. Fiore always contributed lively letters.
- It'd be great to read Gary's writing each issue … about whatever, not even necessarily comics.
- Less snottiness; more considered and thoughtful arguments and critiques.
- In-depth reviews that cover several thematically related books at once and places them within a greater context.
- In general, avoid reviews that read like college term papers.
- A commissioned, short comics piece each issue would be nice. Could be journalistic, historical, aesthetical, whatever. These could be from a variety of cartoonists. (Note: not me.)
- I don't think that the *Journal* needs to cover or review mainstream comics; there are already a million websites that cover that stuff. Maybe try to focus on what's actually good in comics rather than taking easy pot shots at all the crappy stuff.
- Commission pieces from authors that don't typically write about comics. Throw us some curveballs and offer unexpected takes on the medium from intelligent individuals that can look at it with an unsentimental eye.

I dunno, that's all I've got.

Ivan Brunetti

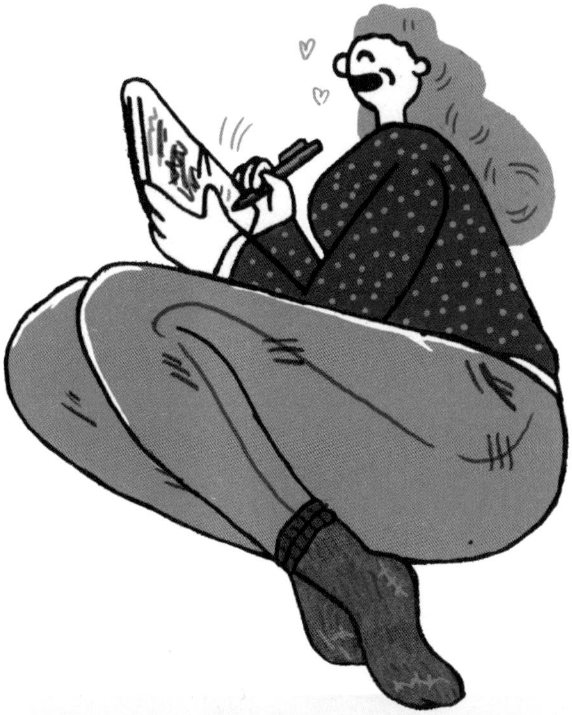

GLAD TO SEE GARY took my advice and is getting back in the game.

There is a great need for comics discussion, advocacy, interviews, reviews, criticism and enlightenment all in one place, and what better place than this publication? Here's my incomplete idea list for now:

- Women! Do a better job at inclusion.
- Comics perspective, history and scholarship from historians, researchers and archivists.
- Use resources like comic libraries, archives and private collections.
- A "Collector's Corner" for people who want to buy artwork or have artwork to sell.
- A feature like "Pro Tips" and/or anecdotes from creators celebrating the print medium.
- A classroom asset. Something I could use in my classroom to supplement curriculum.

Thanks. I look forward to seeing the remarkable new you!

Carol Tyler

I DON'T HAVE MUCH TO SAY about what I think the new *Comics Journal* should be, but I can suggest that an un-retouched smiling image of my face should be on every cover and all the reviews should only be raves about my comics.

Gilbert Hernandez

I ALWAYS LOVED the lengthy interview/profiles and the minicomic reviews that Austin English used to do. I've saved a lot of copies of the magazine because of some of those inspiring interviews. Maybe also include minicomic inserts in the middle of the magazine as a prize inside. Upgrade from the newsprint paper!

Rina Ayuyang

I JUST WANT TO SEE in-depth creator interviews with pictures of the creators and maybe their workspaces. It's something that's been sorely lacking for so long. The main news sites for comics are so heavily controlled by the major companies that everything is just a puff piece and doesn't really say anything. I want to get to know these people.

Ryan Stegman

I WANT ATTENTION GIVEN to webcomics! End-of. The history, the new stuff and their part in revitalizing comics!

C. Spike Trotman

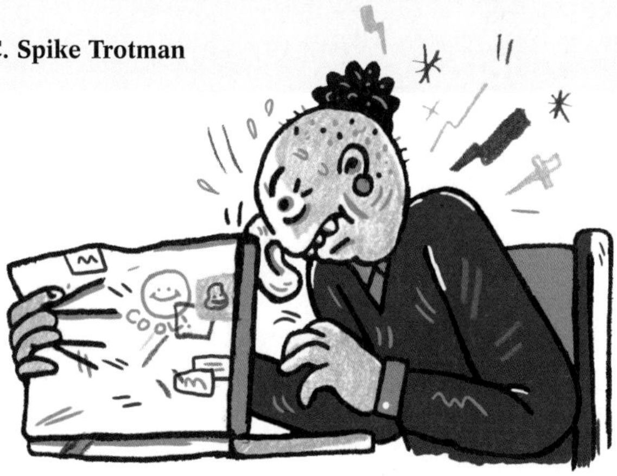
COOL

MORE KRISTY VALENTI!

Sophie Yanow

WELCOME BACK to print, *Comics Journal*! This is great news that you are back. Speaking as someone who has read just about every print issue of *The Comics Journal* (and has also been closely following the website), I can tell you what my expectations are for you:

- Striking visuals that include examples of sequential art, but no lengthy excerpts from graphic novels.
- Strong opinions about the merit, or lack thereof, of various works.
- Deep, probing interviews.
- Queers. Only good can come from having an abundance of queer contributors.

Erik Nebel

SO WHAT WOULD I LIKE to see more of going forward?

- More substantive book/minicomic reviews – especially ones that are willing to dig deep.
- Features on comics history: both well-known and lesser-known figures, including cartoonists as well as other industry professionals.
- More on international comics scenes as well as comics subcultures (genre specific, regional, identity/culturally based).
- Features or discussions on the economics of comics. Pieces on making a living (or not), distribution, publishing, education/schools, conventions/festivals, marketing/social media, work/life balance, etc.
- More short comics pieces. Even features or essays in graphic form.

Very excited to see this back in print!

Whit Taylor

MY FAVORITE ISSUES of the old *Comics Journal* magazine were the ones edited by Helena Harvilicz and Carole Sobocinski, since both women brought what to me was a much-needed air of irreverence to the magazine. This was particularly true in regards to the world of mainstream comics, since they both seemed to share my indifference toward what those hacks are up to (though this latter point may not be a good business model for you).

I'd also urge you to avoid adapting any kind of groupthink when it comes to aesthetic or political opinions. Let your contributors be as "wrong" as they want to be.

And finally, while I'd urge you to be as brave as possible in your criticisms, don't ever let it devolve into feuds. Of course, your targets are gonna be pissed, and possibly overreact. Allow for that, and move on.

Good luck!

Peter Bagge

I THINK THE NEWLY back-in-print *Comics Journal* should feature a Gary Groth centerfold. Every issue if possible.

Gina Wynbrandt

8

I THINK WE CAN ALL AGREE that the *Journal* at its best, when we look back in hindsight, was intellectually rigorous to the point of being heads and shoulders above anything else going on around it. Always somewhat irreverent and forever down for a dumb argument. For each of us, that means different eras in the magazine's history, colored by both when we started reading it and the issues most closely aligned to our own pursuits and passions. But those traits are found throughout any quality run of the mag – Spurgeon's, Heintjes's, George's – despite every managing editor going in different aesthetic directions.

So, thinking of the *Journal* going forward, I don't really care what's covered. At this point in my life, I am interested in like six cartoonists, five of which are dead, so as long as what's covered is done at a high intellectual level, I can read about any topic or book. (Not so much interviews – I'm past the point of being interested in someone just because we both have the same job.) Groth set a standard, but there was no one to really maintain or continue that standard beyond momentary fits and starts, like with Todd Hignite's *Comic Art* magazine and online with the Comics Comics blog. Comics reading is high, but since most of those readers turn over every five to 10 years and remain in that late-teen/art-school period, almost all the criticism is reactionary, idiotic or entry level. *The Comics Journal* should assume its readers know their shit, not just in comics but that they have a high standard all around. They know the value of having something of record that operates at a higher intellectual frequency. It is necessary for the intellectual and aesthetic growth of every artistic medium for some sense of standards to be formed, for new bars to be set, and right now, there is none. Dopey books get taken seriously because they are written up by halfwits for major papers who can't tell the difference between sophistication and the veneer of it. It's great for sales, but it's terrible for the medium. Someone needs to call out this bullshit (and on the other side of the scale, give real consideration to the great works that don't have publicity budgets behind them that are just being entirely ignored, of which there are far too many).

If a high critical standard is impossible, which is most likely since the *Journal* will have no way of consistently attracting quality writing without money, I say please at least fill it with the easy, good stuff: cartoonist Top 10 lists, photos of their studios and original art and sketchbook selections. A fanzine, basically. The value of a print *Journal* over a virtual one is quality images, so that's always a good crutch. Also, please god in heaven, hire a good designer and stick with them.

Good luck,

Sammy Harkham

DEAR EDITORS,

The things I'd love to see in the return of *The Comics Journal*:

· More Dennis Fujitake covers.
· More Noah Van Sciver-conducted interview comics.
· Serialized M.K. Brown comics. A new page or more per issue.
· A new, in-depth Jose Muñoz interview.
· Groth vs. Chaykin: Round Three.

Michel Fiffe

What's in Store for Us

Ben Passmore

I'VE BEEN DRAWING COMICS for a living since I was 26. Like a lot of people, I'd been making them since I was a kid and fantasized about "breaking in." I was huge fan of *Hellboy* and *B.P.R.D.* and sent pitches to publishers many times with no success. I realized that no one was going to publish my weird stories, so, like a lot of scrubby indie cartoonists, I figured out how to print

my own comics and get them in stores. I wasn't that great at internet sales so I spent a lot of time emailing and snail-mailing shops around the country to see if they would take a risk on a self-published floppy comic about porn addiction or violent punks. Most shops weren't into it, but there were a few generous enough to take the plunge and they paid my rent a couple times.

I'd always have the best luck selling books to shops if I went to the store myself. I put patches on my clothes, carried around a smelly bag and traveled around a lot, so going to shops for an initial face-to-face was more possible for me than most other cartoonists. I noticed pretty quickly that the owners or workers wouldn't believe at first that I'd made the comics I was trying to sell them. They weren't hostile – almost never – but I was treated as a rare, if not exciting, anomaly. For a while I just thought people weren't used to punks, but even now – as a very square 30-something – I'll go to my local shop in Philly that carries the more "indie" titles and have to sit through long explanations of the comic form. I realized that the people at the comic shop didn't think black people like comics. Superhero comics, maybe, but surely no brown man would "get" Daniel Clowes.

It's something it took me a while to consider because I'm black and I like comics, especially all the arty non-superhero stuff. A black neighbor gave me my first comic ever. When I was in college, my group of friends, the majority of who are black, read and talked comics voraciously. I don't blame the comic shop owners for thinking that comics is mostly a white thing – it can really appear that way. A 2017 New York Comic Con "Insider Sessions" survey revealed that 69 percent of comic purchasers are white, though this doesn't account for informal markets, such as torrenting. Black ownership of comic shops is very low, with the very first East Coast store owned by a black woman opening in 2016, according to CNN. In eight years of being a freelance comics creator, I can count the number of non-white editors on one hand. This in a country whose non-white population is a little less than half of the overall population and growing. Why is this significant? Well, if you haven't noticed, the nerds are in charge now.

Comics and the related movie industry are making billions and reaching even more viewers each year. Arguably, the types of stories comics tell have never had more influence on the way people think about themselves, their lives and their fantasies. While comic shops aren't exactly the tip of the comic industry's spear these days, they still play a role as a gateway and meeting place for comics fans. While I'm mostly interested in talking about stores that cater to indie comics, I do think that it's important to remember that even our sort of fringe industry is affected by the larger mainstream one. I mostly want to talk about indie comics shops, stores that prefer to carry titles published by individuals and small-to-medium-sized presses, because that's where I have the most personal experience – and I also think these businesses have the most potential for progressive change. While the superhero comics industry seems able to comfortably employ "comicsgaters" and alt-right types like Nick Spencer and Ethan Van Sciver, the constellation of small press-oriented stores, festivals and publishers constantly rep a consistently left-leaning attitude. For example, shortly after Donald Trump's presidential election, Gabe Fowler, owner of Desert Island Comics and producer of the comics anthology *Smoke Signals*, published a vicious anti-Trump edition of his anthology.

My early relationship to comics and comic shops was very Dickensian. As a dusty little kid from a microscopic, white majority town, I didn't have a local comic shop and had to settle for reading one of the few titles the drugstore carried until the manager threw me out for loitering. Later, in college, comic shops were my gateway into the world of indie comics and manga, and away from

"We may encounter many defeats, but we must not be defeated." –MAYA ANGELOU
RESIST!
FREE!
Published by
DESERT ISLAND
540 Metropolitan Avenue
Brooklyn. NY 11211
A WOMAN'S PLACE IS IN THE REVOLUTION!
GAYLE KABAKER is a cover artist for The New Yorker. She lives in Ashfield, MA.
All the contributions here are copyright the individual artists and were provided without monetary compensation. This is a selection from over 1,000 submissions that were sent in from across the world to WWW.RESISTSUBMISSION.COM. Visit our website to see more.

OPPOSITE: From *Daygloayhole* #1, 2015.

ABOVE: The "Resist!" edition of *Smoke Signal*, a free newspaper, from 2017, edited by Françoise Mouly and Nadja Spiegelman and published by Gabe Fowler.

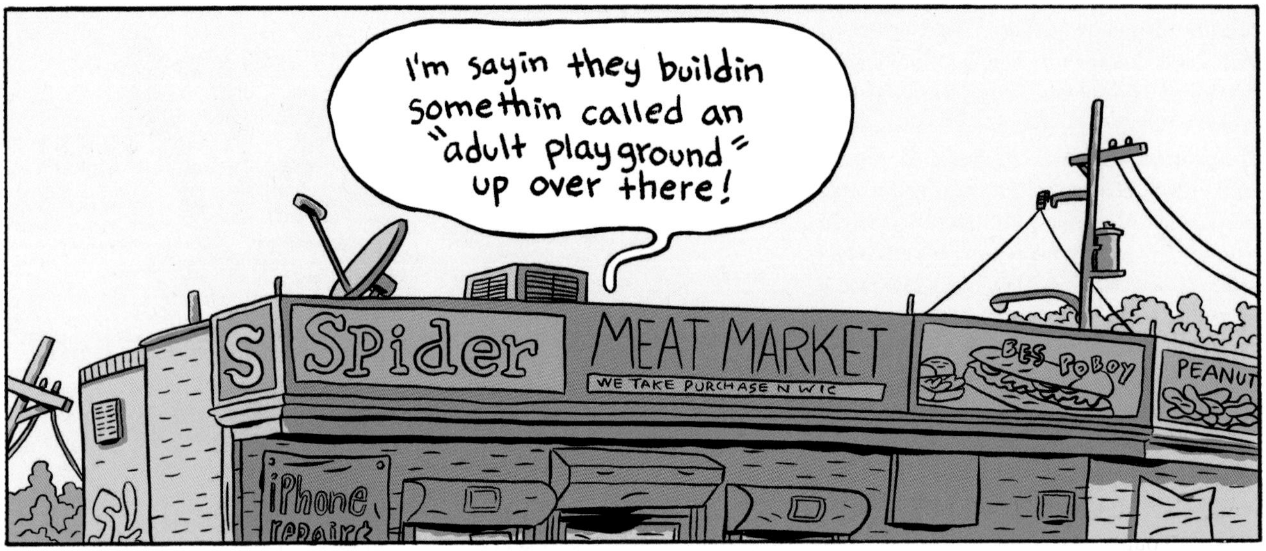
I'm sayin they buildin somethin called an "adult playground" up over there!
S
Spider
MEAT MARKET
WE TAKE PURCHASE N WIC
BES POBOY
PEANUT
iPhone

ABOVE: Panel from Passmore's story in *Now: The New Comics Anthology* #3, 2018.

the superhero stuff that felt childish after some years of being locked up in an institution for being a teen felon. I spent a lot of my 20s haunting comics shops like Atomic Books, Quimby's, the Beguiling and Desert Island, drooling over books I couldn't afford and fantasizing about the day my own work could be up on the shelf alongside my idols.

Last year, when I went back to the corner my college comic shop had been on, I realized it had been turned into a real estate office. I was genuinely sad for the store and for the kids that won't have the same experience I'd had there. Many comic shops are businesses that wind up functioning as community spaces. They host readings, creator signings and special events. The narrative many store owners present of their business is reflective of how comics creators and fans see themselves, slightly embattled nerds and weirdos deeply into something the world won't really understand. This idea of ourselves can be something we use to develop camaraderie with one another, but also serves as factionalism. In 2018, we saw the rise of "Comicsgate," Gamergate's smaller – but just as racist – cousin. In response to comic publishers', creators' and commentators' push for more representative titles, white comics fans have harassed and boycotted said titles in the name of some kind of dated comics purity. In an era when our president is constantly caping and courting latent and overt white supremacy in our society, calls against "diversity" are particularly pointed. As an industry and community, we can be blinded by protectionism and lash out. We can also fail to recognize our complicity in the oppressive aspects of our society. We're on the Trump Train now; but long before Trump, there's been rampant gentrification in predominately impoverished non-white neighborhoods.

“Among the businesses that pop up in redeveloping neighborhoods, coffee shops, brunch spots, grocery stores with weird-looking vegetables in them and comic shop/book stores are often first in line.”

Among the businesses that pop up in redeveloping neighborhoods, coffee shops, brunch spots, grocery stores with weird-looking vegetables in them and comic shop/book stores are often first in line. Of the comic shops I've named, all were established during the early periods of gentrification in their neighborhoods. Quimby's in Wicker Park, Chicago. Atomic Books in the Hampden neighborhood of Baltimore. Desert Island in Williamsburg, New York. The Beguiling

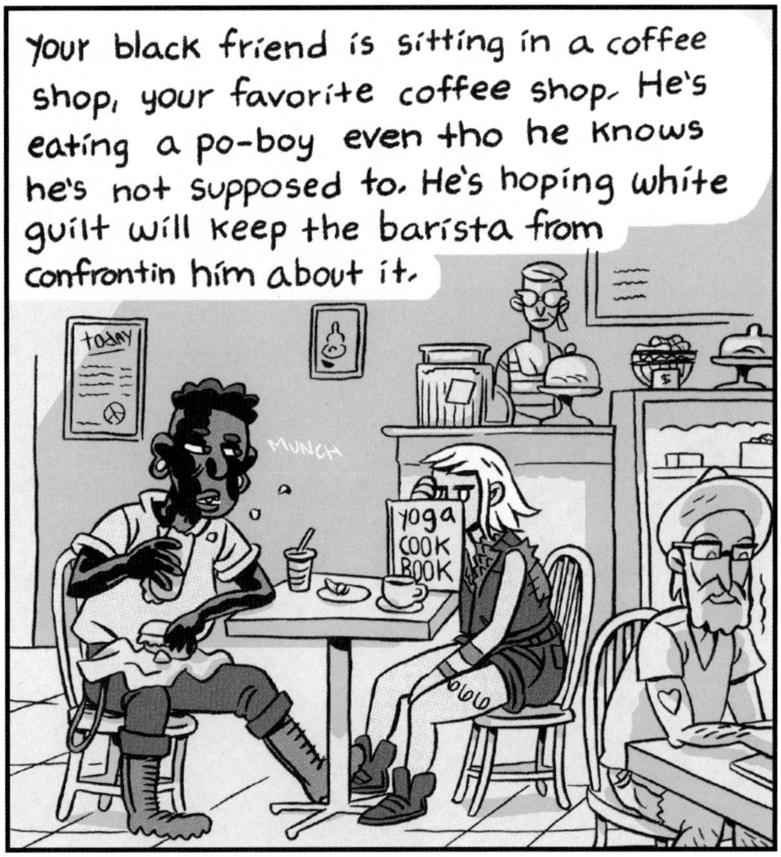
Your black friend is sitting in a coffee shop, your favorite coffee shop. He's eating a po-boy even tho he knows he's not supposed to. He's hoping white guilt will keep the barista from confrontin him about it.
today
MUNCH
yoga COOK BOOK

ABOVE: From *Your Black Friend and Other Strangers*, 2018.

in Toronto, Canada. Wicker Park, Hampden and Williamsburg were all named by *Forbes* in 2012 as "America's Hippest Hipster Neighborhoods." All four neighborhoods saw at least a 20-thousand-dollar increase of average annual income of its residents from the period their comic shop was established to 2013. This doesn't prove anything other than the comic shops were able to weather increases in property tax and demographic shifts while other businesses were not. It doesn't prove that these comic shops intentionally speculated on poor neighborhoods and intended to cater to the newer, whiter and more economically privileged inhabitants. I think what is more likely is that they hadn't accounted for the displacing tendency of redevelopment at all.

This is not to say that comic shops are the forerunners of gentrification, but, in many ways, they are the proxy for our community in the broader sense, especially if we're sold on thinking of them as community spaces more than businesses. It might be useful to get straight about what I mean by gentrification. Gentrification is the systematic displacement of impoverished communities (most often people of color) by local government and businesses. This often requires the explicit or unintended participation of more economically or culturally upper-class people, often white, through moving into recently vacated homes and becoming a patron of new, pricier businesses. Another prominent aspect of gentrification is the introduction of culturally upper-class white things at the expense of the cultural norms that have been established by the long-standing community there. This all ends up reflecting age-old white colonialism, but this time it's bike polo and food trucks. The struggle for people of color in this neighborhood is not only to figure out how to continue to afford their homes, manage increased housing regulations and maintain safety under heavier policing, but also to maintain a feeling of place in a neighborhood that increasingly excludes them.

I don't want you to get the impression that what I'm saying is that I want stores to only fill their shelves with titles by brown people, in part because that won't work and also because I like plenty of comics by white folks. Adding "color" to your shelves isn't going to challenge the damage gentrification leaves in communities. Repositioning stores from being complicit in gentrification to being antagonistic to it will.

If gentrification establishes privileged white enclaves in poor non-white ones, then the answer is to rearrange the logistical advantage whiteness gives you and use it as a tool. White people are the only ones that can challenge the material advantage of whiteness. What I'm calling for is a drastic rethinking of what comics shops are, from privately owned businesses to actual community-oriented organizations. If 2018's arrest of two black men in a Starbucks for the crime of sitting around without buying something proves anything, it's that neutral public space is desperately needed in redeveloped neighborhoods. Cornerstones of black social life, like barber shops, churches and street corners, are often the first to go during the process of gentrification. What would it look like for comic shops to allow space for people to socialize or hold public events, to offer sections of their weekly schedule to organizations or individuals committed to literacy and art education in the city?

In New Orleans, where the bulk of art education and funding is from private companies, the library system and the New Orleans Comic and Zine Festival (full disclosure and flex; I'm one of its organizers) runs free comic and zine workshops for kids across the city. As their neighborhoods gentrify, non-white residents are not likely to find employment in the new businesses that open up, if a 2003 National Bureau of Economic Research study is any indication. The NBER study showed that individuals with names not traditionally associated with white people were 50 percent less likely to receive call-backs from potential employers. What if – rather than being a business owned by one or two people – comic shops were cooperatively owned, allowing some residents of the neighborhood access to equal and equitable employment? Cooperatives may seem like an obscure Commie idea, but the U.S. is home to approximately 30 thousand cooperative businesses that collectively pull in over 650 million dollars in annual revenue. And I know that many of these comic shops aren't making buckets of money, but I would rather be kind of broke doing something I love rather than something I hate. I'm a cartoonist, after all.

You might be wondering why comics should even bother – though, I imagine that if you really feel that way you would've stopped reading by now. The fact is that we are in a unique time – not just because a racist orange is our president, but because we are seeing massive displacement of communities all for the sake of real estate speculation. White people are not moving to black neighborhoods because there's a kale famine; they're moving because they can. No one is neutral in this; you are making a choice even if you're not aware of it. So, the question is, what do you want your community to be? ☼

BELOW: Passmore's poster for the 2014 New Orleans Comic & Zine Festival.

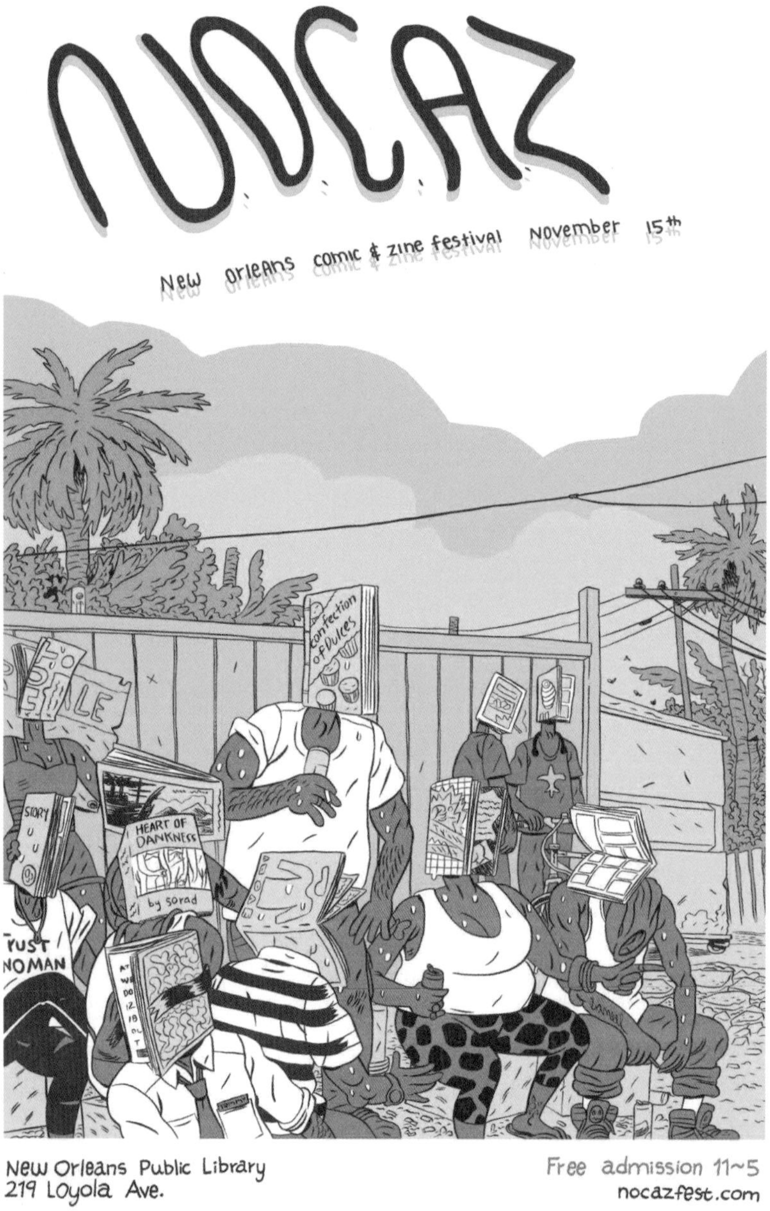
NOCAZ
New Orleans comic & zine festival November 15th
SALE
confection of Dulces
STORY
HEART OF DANKNESS
by sorad
TRUST NO MAN
New Orleans Public Library
219 Loyola Ave.
Free admission 11~5
nocazfest.com

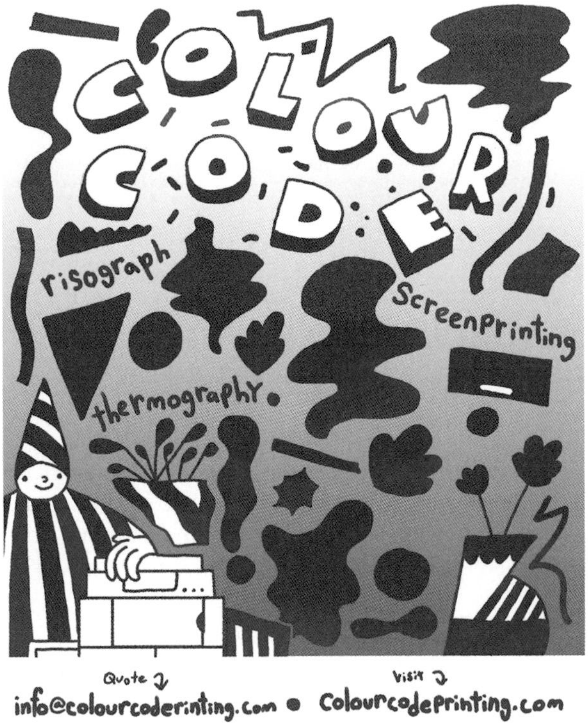
COLOUR CODER
risograph
screenprinting
thermography.
Quote
Visit
info@colourcoderinting.com • colourcodeprinting.com

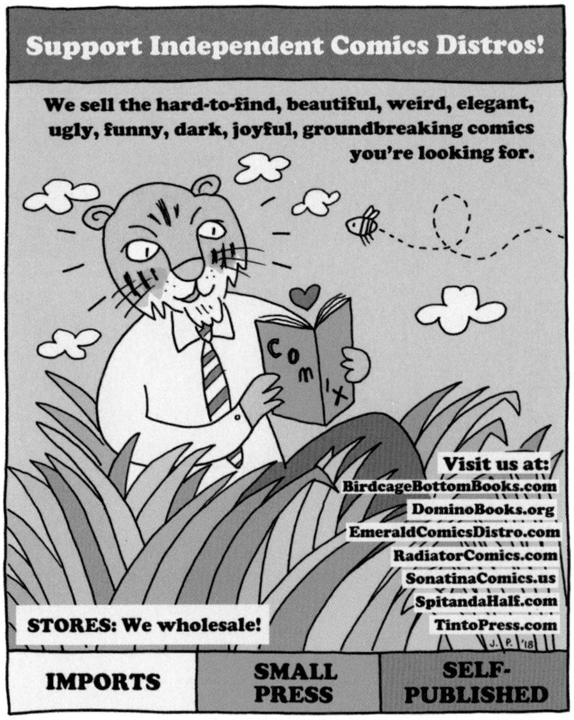
Support Independent Comics Distros!
We sell the hard-to-find, beautiful, weird, elegant, ugly, funny, dark, joyful, groundbreaking comics you're looking for.
Comix
Visit us at:
BirdcageBottomBooks.com
DominoBooks.org
EmeraldComicsDistro.com
RadiatorComics.com
SonatinaComics.us
SpitandaHalf.com
TintoPress.com
STORES: We wholesale!
J. P. '18
IMPORTS
SMALL PRESS
SELF-PUBLISHED

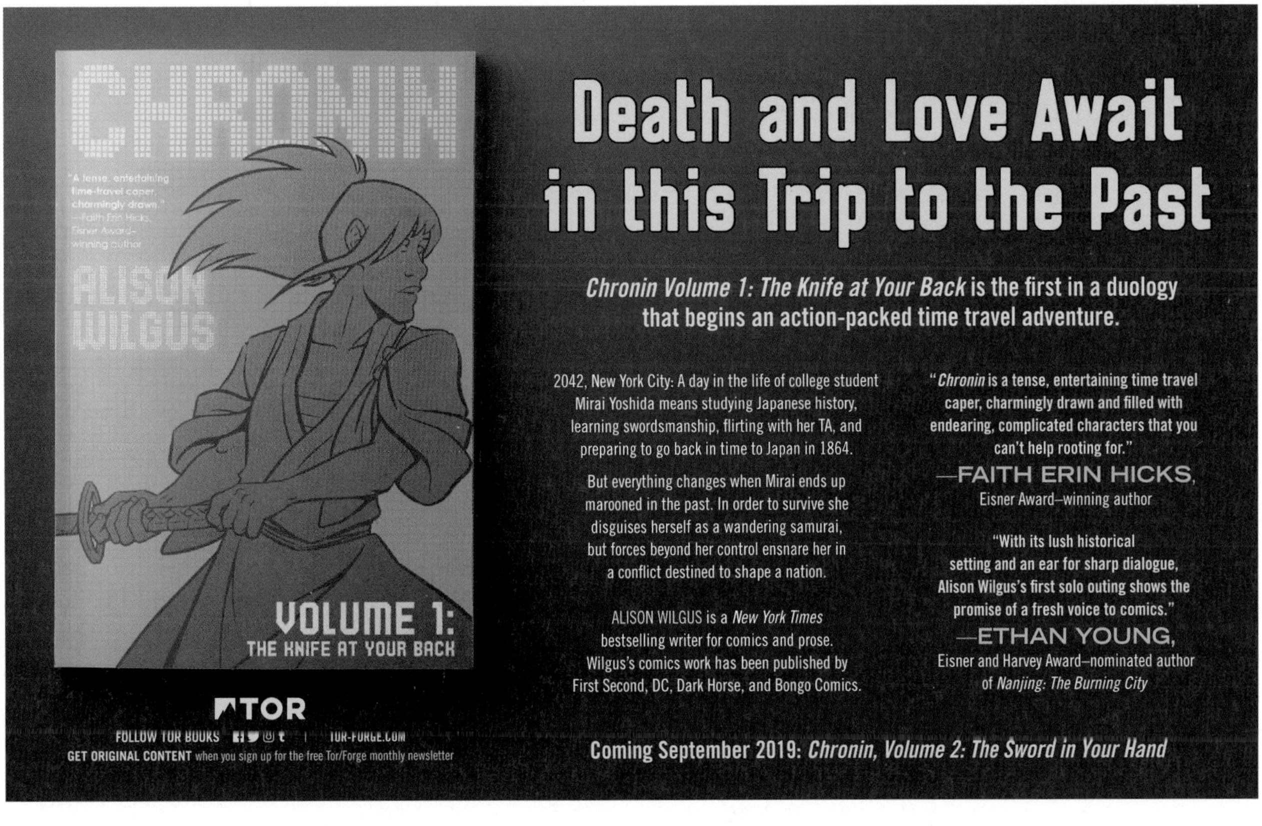
CHRONIN
"A tense, entertaining time-travel caper, charmingly drawn." —Faith Erin Hicks, Eisner Award–winning author
ALISON WILGUS
VOLUME 1: THE KNIFE AT YOUR BACK
TOR
FOLLOW TOR BOOKS | TOR-FORGE.COM
GET ORIGINAL CONTENT when you sign up for the free Tor/Forge monthly newsletter
Death and Love Await in this Trip to the Past
Chronin Volume 1: The Knife at Your Back is the first in a duology that begins an action-packed time travel adventure.
2042, New York City: A day in the life of college student Mirai Yoshida means studying Japanese history, learning swordsmanship, flirting with her TA, and preparing to go back in time to Japan in 1864.
But everything changes when Mirai ends up marooned in the past. In order to survive she disguises herself as a wandering samurai, but forces beyond her control ensnare her in a conflict destined to shape a nation.
ALISON WILGUS is a New York Times bestselling writer for comics and prose. Wilgus's comics work has been published by First Second, DC, Dark Horse, and Bongo Comics.
"Chronin is a tense, entertaining time travel caper, charmingly drawn and filled with endearing, complicated characters that you can't help rooting for."
—FAITH ERIN HICKS, Eisner Award–winning author
"With its lush historical setting and an ear for sharp dialogue, Alison Wilgus's first solo outing shows the promise of a fresh voice to comics."
—ETHAN YOUNG, Eisner and Harvey Award–nominated author of Nanjing: The Burning City
Coming September 2019: Chronin, Volume 2: The Sword in Your Hand

GEN CON ®

AUGUST 1 – 4, 2019
JULY 30 – AUGUST 2, 2020

60,000 gamers

500 game companies

Sun King Beer Garden

Free concerts

Fun costumes

Kids 10 & Under Free

gencon.com

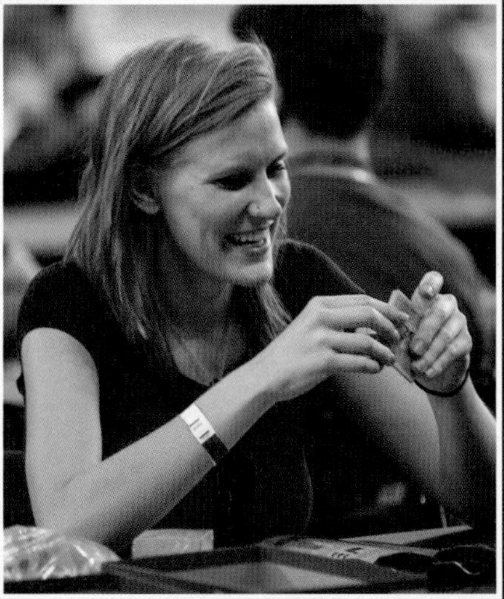

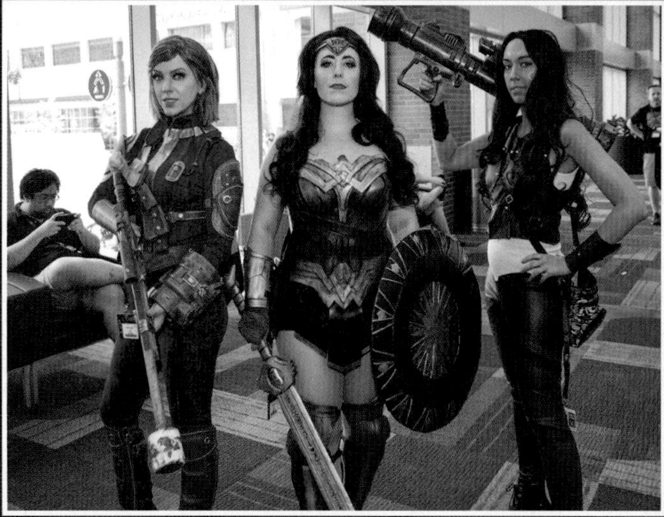

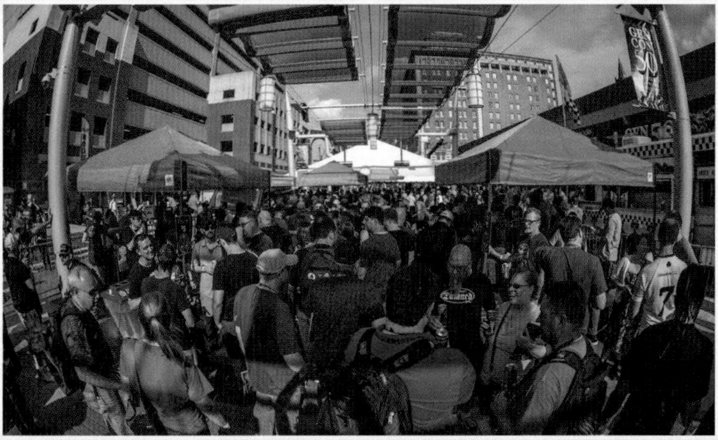

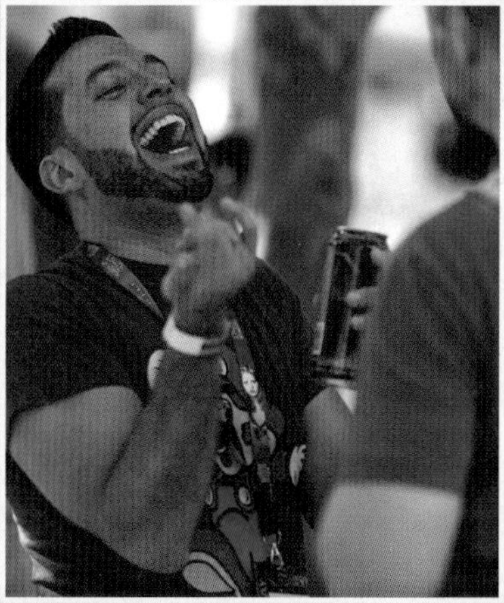

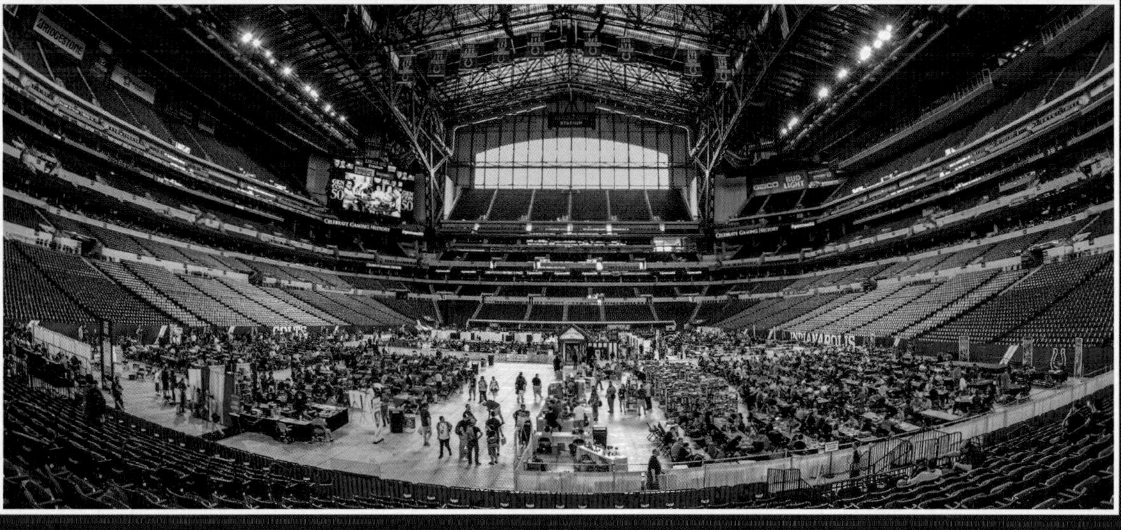

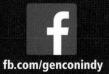

fb.com/genconindy

@gen_con

@gen_con

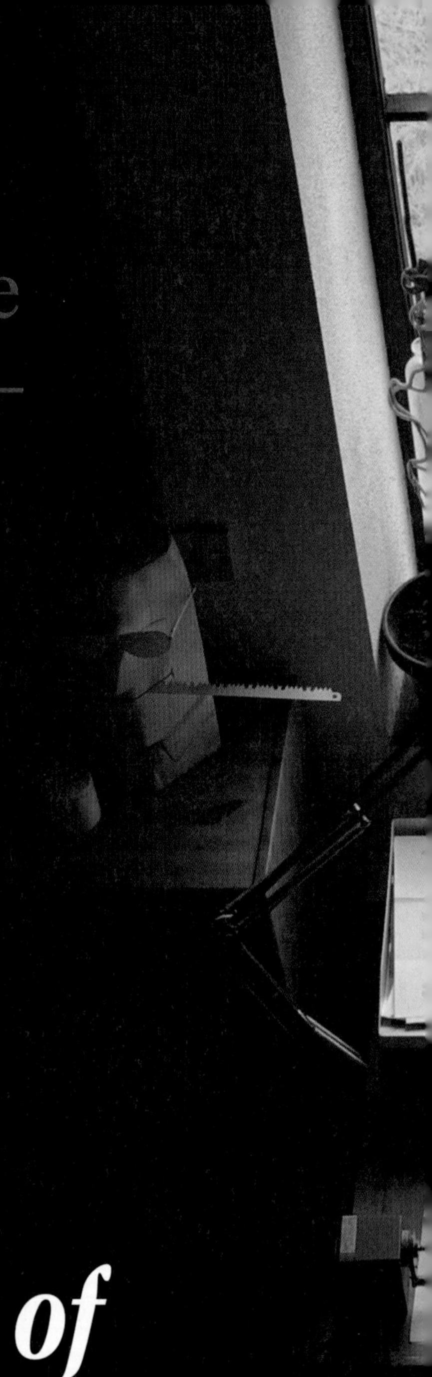

“Every artist should have some cause to fight for – or fight against.”

The Fear & Anger of Tomi Ungerer

Interview by Gary Groth

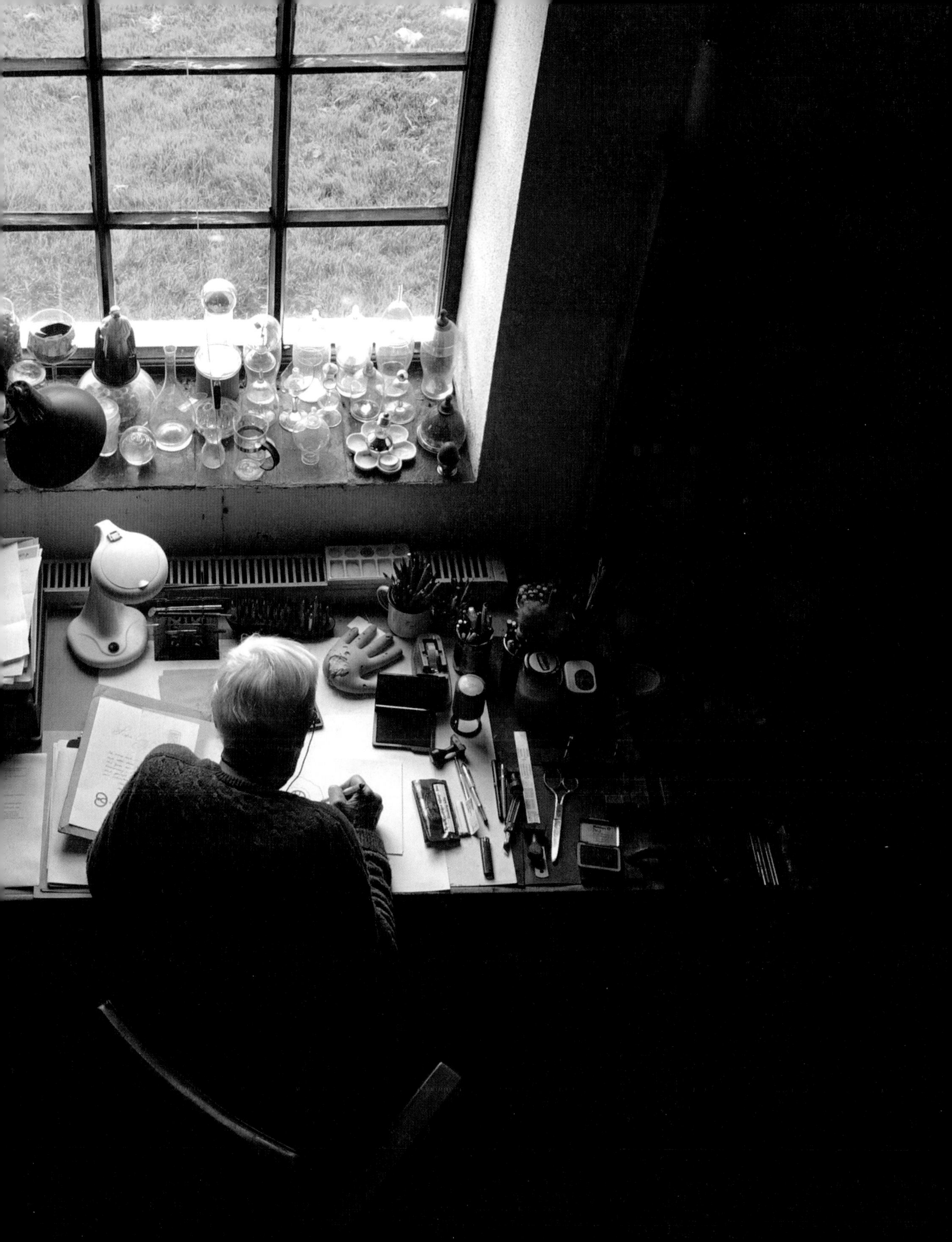

PREVIOUS: Ungerer in his studio, 2018.

RIGHT: "The Abbé Glory, my godfather Pam, my brother Bernard and Papa holding my hands, Mama and my sisters Edith and Vivette." Photo taken circa 1934.

TOMI UNGERER HAS BEEN an artistic force of nature for more than 60 years – a cartoonist of international repute, a best-selling children's book author, a painter, a prose writer, a sculptor, a political dissident and a sexual revolutionary. He has, by his own account, published over 140 books.

If you are an American reader and have not heard of him – or are only glancingly aware of his work – you are not alone. He has apparently been persona non grata in North American publishing circles for nearly 50 of those 60 years – although, to be fair, the feeling may have been mutual. He has been published consistently in Europe by his long-standing publisher, Diogenes, throughout much of this time – but rarely in America. (Phaidon has, over the last half decade, republished many of his children's books.) It is, frankly, shocking to think of an artist of Ungerer's stature and achievement being so little known in the country in which he originally made his mark, but it's true. I welcome the opportunity to introduce him to new readers and to rejuvenate an appreciation in those who have known his work for decades.

Ungerer was born in 1931 in Strasbourg, in the Alsace region of France, as close to the German border as you can get. The region was described by Ben Macintyre in *Rogue*

Heroes, his history of the SAS during World War II, thusly:

> From 1871 until the First World War, the Vosges Mountains had marked the border between France and the German empire. Alsace-Lorraine, wedged between the Vosges and the Rhine, is a half-German, half-French hybrid, and some of the most fought-over territory on the planet; the region was annexed by the French Republic in 1918, but then seized back by Hitler's troops in 1941.

Ungerer's early childhood was fraught. When Ungerer was 3 years old, his father, Theo, died. Nonetheless, he loomed large in Ungerer's personal mythology – perhaps larger than if he had lived. His father was, Ungerer wrote, a "pure aesthete, obsessed with beauty in nature and art." Theo co-owned, with his brother, a factory that produced astronomical clocks. "He was a true renaissance man: inventor, historian, writer (in German, French and Alsatian), engineer, historian, painter, illustrator and bibliophile." His father's masterpiece, Ungerer believes, is a public clock designed for the campanile in the square of Messina, Sicily.

After his father's death, the family consisted of his mother and three siblings–his brother Bernard (who told him, "Be tenacious" and instilled in him integrity, honesty, endurance, discipline, concern for others) and his two sisters, Vivette and Edith. His mother was a "stunning beauty," class conscious, bourgeois, a poet, an essayist and a source of anxiety: "My mother's uncontrolled displays of affection were for me terribly annoying, especially in public, and the effusion of kisses – particularly the wet ones – revolted me. All of this, and a repertoire of endearing expressions: my sunshine, my little tiger, darling sparrow, little goldbug…Even now, when I hear those words, I feel like crawling and hiding under the nearest table, which, as a matter of fact, I often did as a child …" He grew a beard as soon as he was capable of doing so in order to mitigate his resemblance to her (why, he asked, did he not look more like his father?). His mother's exhibitionistic affection haunted him for the rest of his life. On the other hand, he writes, "My talents were welcomed with enthusiasm at home, and I was constantly encouraged to draw and write by my mother, brother and sisters."

The Nazi incursion changed his life. Ungerer was 10 years old when they rolled in and took control of Alsace; he lived under their fascist regime for five of his most formative years, which he chronicled with emotional and factual perspicacity in *Tomi: A Childhood Under the Nazis.* One day everything was normal; the next day, the Nazis simply marched in. "Imagine my surprise – I was standing in the front yard when a motorcycle with a sidecar drove by." French residents were required to learn German in three months and speak no French in the meantime, nor own French books or even a beret; those who were caught speaking their native language were sent to internment camps. Ungerer learned the necessity of courage and guile, which would serve him well as an artist for the rest of his life.

The Germans did their best to indoctrinate him. He was bombarded with propaganda – "It was total, systematic brainwashing, every day." He and his schoolmates listened to Hitler over the radio. One of his homework assignments was to draw a Jew. In order to attend school, you had to join the Hitler Youth, which he avoided, thanks to the ingenuity of his mother. His name was changed from Tomi (Jean Thomas) to Johann. Mail was censored. Jazz, modern art and comic strips were considered degenerate art and were forbidden. Children were encouraged to inform on their parents.

He drew from an early age, influenced mightily by the Alsatian illustrator Hansi (Jean-Jacques Waltz), who wrote and drew

LEFT: "The arrival of the Wehrmacht, the German army, as I saw it in 1940."

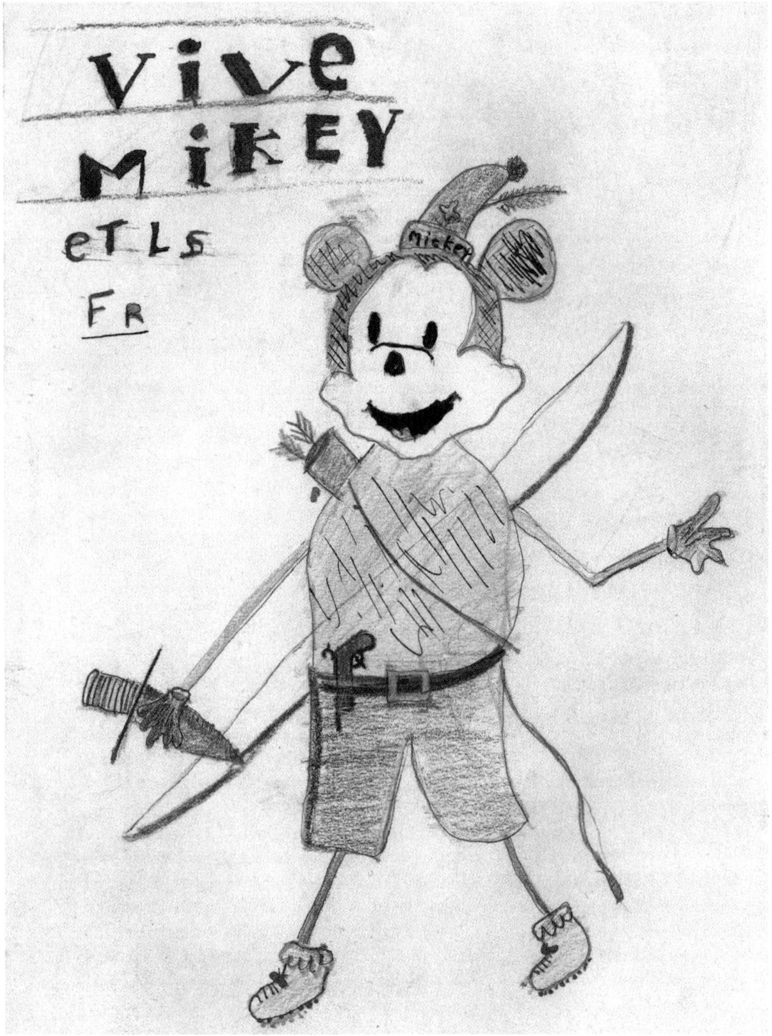
Vive
MiKEY
eT LS
FR

ABOVE: "A drawing of Mickey Mouse that survived Uncle Heino's raids."

The History of Alsace Told for Young Children. Ungerer drew Mickey Mouse over and over. He read the proto-comics of *Münchener Bilderbogen*, illustrated broadsides produced in Munich featuring the work of Wilhelm Busch, Lothar Meggendorfer and Adolf Oberländer, among others. Other Alsatian influences include the 15th century painter and engraver Martin Schongauer and the more contemporary painter and illustrator Léo Schnug. Eventually, he would chronicle the depredations of the Nazis in a series of crudely expressive drawings for which he would have been severely punished if they had been discovered.

The liberation on February 2, 1945, brought relief but not joy. Neither the French – who reclaimed Alsace – nor the Americans behaved well, in Ungerer's view. "We were disenchanted with the Americans," he wrote. "They seemed to behave like well-fed babies, chewing gum, and didn't seem to care whether they were in France or Germany. Our celebrations and enthusiasm left them cold. They would throw chewing gum and chocolates on the ground and watch us scramble to get a morsel. They weren't really arrogant, just aloof. To them we were part of a 'zoo of savages.'" The French were no better. After they had reestablished civic order, schools reopened with French teachers who, Ungerer writes, "would laugh at our German accents and punish us for all the French grammar we'd forgotten. They treated us as if we were second-class citizens – even collaborators." He was 14 years old.

After high school, he continued his education, spending many hours at the Musée Unterlinden, where he saw Matthias Grünewald's *Isenheim Altarpiece*, which affected him as deeply as any single work of art: "Grünewald has without a doubt exerted the greatest influence of any painter on my artistic career." He went hitchhiking across Europe – in Iceland, Norway, Yugoslavia and Greece, worked on cargo vessels. When he was hitching in Lapland, he walked 20 kilometers to the Russian border, crossed the bridge to Russia, went to the bathroom and fled into the woods – chased by the Russian police, who did not catch him. In 1951, he hitchhiked to North Cape, Norway, and tried to sell stories about his trip to newspapers. In between his travels, he earned a living as a window dresser and advertising artist for local Alsatian businesses such as Feyel Foie Gras and Dopff au Moulin wines. He drew his first poster in 1954 for Schwindenhammer Stationary.

In 1952, he joined the French Camel Corp in Algeria, where he served in the Zerakla Camp, but was discharged due to pleurisy. He studied at the École des Arts Décoratifs [Municipal School for Decorative Arts] in Strasbourg between 1953 and 1954, but he was restless and was soon expelled for being "subversive and perverse." A charge to which Ungerer replied: "The professor who wrote that comment was either a complete fool or perceptive beyond his wildest imaginings."

Ungerer made a habit of visiting the American Cultural Center in Strasbourg where he befriended American Fulbright students and became interested in artists like James Thurber, Charles Addams and Saul Steinberg. He felt a kinship with and wanted to join them in America. The last paragraph Ungerer wrote in *A Childhood Under the Nazis* is a summation of his experiences thus far, and could serve as his life's credo; it seems especially poignant insofar as it reflects the adventurous and questing spirit that would propel him to a new country that would become his home for the next 15 years.

> I packed my rucksack and walked into life, stepping over prejudices and jumping over a lot of conclusions. These excursions into the real world taught me that we are each of us born with a life sentence (which is easier to survive with a smile), that a conscience is more effective when tortured and that we rid ourselves of prejudices only to replace them with other ones. I learned to transfuse my fear, insecurity and anger into my work – trauma can fuel talent, if you have any. The pragmatic vision that I developed, concerning the good and evil in myself and in others, has no definite borderlines. I learned from relativity, which is food for doubt, and doubt is a virtue with enough living space for every imperfect, sin-ridden, life-loving creature on Earth.

Welcome to New York

UNGERER FAMOUSLY ARRIVED in New York in 1956 with $60 in his pocket and two trunks of drawings and manuscripts that he intended to show to publishers. What finally spurred him to move to New York, he has said, was jazz: "I was a big jazz fan, I thought I would be able to see some jazz." He was disappointed in the jazz scene he found there, but he nonetheless took Manhattan, and for the next 15 years wrote and illustrated children's books and drew countless images for posters, magazines, advertising and satirical books.

He made the rounds of publishers in 1956 and initially carried around his drawings in a paper shopping bag. Caught in a downpour one day, he retreated to the nearest store, which happened to be a pharmacy at Broadway and 43rd. Taking pity upon this poor, recently arrived aspiring artist, the store gave him a box to protect his soggy drawings. He gratefully accepted it without noticing that it was a wholesale container for Trojan condoms. Like so many fortuitous moments in Ungerer's life, this was fitting: "I kept the box until I had enough money to afford a proper portfolio. It became my own trademark and with its subversive contents, fitted the fabled Greek epic: The Trojan Horse disgorging its consequences."

Art directors and editors, he said, "were very frank with me. I went to Golden Books and the guy there was very nice. 'This is not like our stuff at all. The only person who would publish anything like this is Ursula Nordstrom at Harper & Brothers.'" Harper & Brothers was founded in 1817; it became Harper & Row in 1962, and, finally, HarperCollins in 1990, each corporate merger reflecting a diminution of integrity. But, at the time, it was a publisher of independence and quality, and Nordstrom was a renowned children's book editor who had pioneered a shift in children's books from one of stifling moralism to those that respected children's imaginative faculties – such as E.B. White's *Charlotte's Web* (1952) and Crockett Johnson's *Harold and the Purple Crayon* (1955). She had also been working with the young Maurice Sendak for several years, and recognized aesthetic quality when she saw it. (Ungerer and Sendak would become close, lifelong friends. "We met," Ungerer has said, "by our shared taste for German Romantic illustrations and drawings. We used to go to Third Avenue and hunt for secondhand books. I used to go to The Strand with Maurice Sendak all the time.")

THE MELLOPS
GO
SPELUNKING
by Tomi Ungerer
by
Hans Christian
Andersen
Prize Winner
PHAIDON

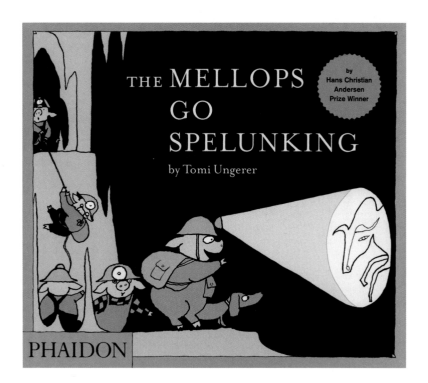

ABOVE: *The Mellops Go Spelunking*, 1963.

Ungerer had contempt for most American children's books being produced at the time. "I had been exposed much to American children's books and I was shocked when I arrived at the level of them. I thought they were absolutely ghastly in their styles and everything." According to Ungerer, he showed his portfolio to Nordstrom who was impressed and told him to come up with a children's story. He invented the Mellops family – mother, father and sons Isidor, Ferdinand and Felix – all anthropomorphic pigs. The first Mellops story he brought her was "a horrible adventure where they were kidnapped by a butcher who was going to turn them into sausages." She suggested he try again. He did, and the result was *The Mellops Go Flying*, quickly followed by *The Mellops Go Diving for Treasure*, both published in 1957, both enormously successful.

Susan Hirschman, who worked at Harper from 1955 to 1964 as both Associate Editor and Managing Editor under Nordstrom, provides a somewhat different version of Ungerer's arrival at the publisher's office – detailed and vivid and bursting with great feeling for Ungerer:

In '57 it was my job to see anyone who arrived at the office with a portfolio and wanted to be seen, whether they had an appointment or not. Ursula believed very strongly that everybody ought to be seen. And Tomi arrived straight off the boat from Alsace and poor and tired and sick! And he had a perfectly wonderful dummy of a book about a very large dog and a boat that he kept afloat. And it was very, very, very close to a book that William Pène du Bois had written in the '30s that I had grown up on that I loved. I'm sure that Tomi had never seen it. It was one of those flukes that happen. He was clearly enormously talented and I said, "Could I keep the dummy?" and made an appointment with him for the next day to see Ursula Nordstrom. I brought in the Pène du Bois book, and Ursula and I agreed that it was too close. Tomi came in and Ursula said, "Dear, this is one of those publishing flukes," and Tomi, who was sick and hungry, I think, burst into tears. Men didn't cry in offices in those days! And Ursula said, "Miss Carr" – that was me – "shut the door." And then said to Tomi, "Stop crying. You have nothing to cry about. We will give you a contract today and a check for an advance on your first Harper book. Here's a Kleenex, and you have nothing to cry about."

So he stopped crying and went home. He went to the hospital and came out of the hospital and sent us the dummy of *The Mellops Go Flying*, which was his first book. He was young and terribly excited and I never, in all my years of work, met anyone who worked harder than he did. He didn't walk, he ran. [*Laughs.*] And he saw everybody there was to see in advertising and that kind of thing in New York in those days. And his ads were on the trucks of the *New York Times*. Great, huge posters. He was wonderful. And he did great books for us.

The Mellops series were adventure stories told in a light, leisurely, whimsical manner in a series of crisp and striking visual compositions. They were not revolutionary for their time. The children's book scholar and historian Leonard Marcus cites many predecessors, including *A Head for Happy* (1931) by Helen Sewell, *Otto at Sea* (1936) and its companion volumes by William Pène du Bois, *Calico the Wonder Horse* (1941) by Virginia Lee Burton and *Crocodile Tears* (1956) by André François (who was the closest in sensibility to Ungerer). Indeed, by the standards of Ungerer's later children's books, they would look conventional. Each story follows a similar arc of the Mellops family accidentally stumbling upon the possibility of an adventure, launching themselves full throttle into it, ending with nothing to show for it but the thrill itself, and arriving home to savor a cream cake baked by Mrs. Mellop. (The cream cake was an invention and not something he recollected from his own childhood: "I should have said meringue pie or something.") He was learning how to create books.

About his new editor and ally, with whom he worked nearly until her retirement in 1973, he said, "Ursula Nordstrom was really the only one who was different and had the guts to fight all the mushy sentimentality, all semi-realistic, with smiling children and pink cheeks."

Although there were exceptions to Ungerer's general condemnation of children's books– Ludwig Bemelmans and Dr. Seuss come to mind, not to mention Maurice Sendak – he was essentially right, and he became one of the artists who did something about it, which was to create books for children that respected their intelligence and imagination and attained the same standards as fiction for literate adults. Ungerer was raised on Grimms' fairy tales (presumably the originals and not the sanitized versions) and Perrault's fairy tales. He shared Sendak's belief that stories for children should not be sugarcoated, that, in fact, children should have to wrestle with the reality that awaits them, which will include fear and loneliness and pain. "Why am I the pedagogues' nightmare," he once asked. "They think I traumatize children. They think children should be loved and protected. But if you do only that, they're not ready for life."

Between 1957 and 1973, he wrote and drew 22 children's books, as well as illustrated numerous children's books he didn't write. (He would not create another children's book, at least not one published in English, until 1997). He was impossible to pigeonhole as a children's book author; some books were conventional adventure stories (such as the Mellops series). *Ask Me a Question* (1968) was a series of visual puns. *Snail, Where Are You?* (1962) was a *Where's Waldo*-style visual puzzle book – 25 years

Snail, Where
Are You?
Tomi Ungerer
PHAIDON

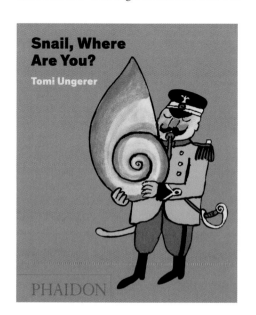

LEFT: *Snail, Where Are You?*, 1962.

RIGHT: From *Ask Me a Question*, 1968.

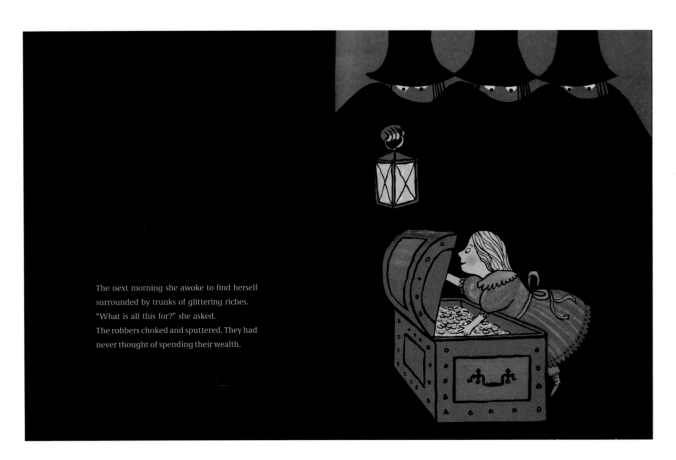

The next morning she awoke to find herself
surrounded by trunks of glittering riches.
"What is all this for?" she asked.
The robbers choked and sputtered. They had
never thought of spending their wealth.

ABOVE AND OPPOSITE: From
The Three Robbers, 1961.

before *Where's Waldo*! Many of his stories involve fear, disappointment, fatalism, resignation, perverse detours into Dadaesque weirdness and occasionally redemption and triumph.

His first bona fide masterpiece, in my view, is *The Three Robbers* (1961). The three eponymous robbers are highwaymen who attack travelers and steal their possessions. The only "possession" in one carriage they stop is a little girl named Tiffany – so they take her and put her to bed in their cave hideout. The next day she discovers their trunks of stolen goods – "gold, jewels, money, watches, wedding rings and precious stones." "What is all this for?" she naively asks, an echo of the 1939 sociological classic *Knowledge for What?* by Robert Lynd. They had never considered the question, but once they do, they use the money to buy a castle, and start an orphanage to give homes to parentless children. "Evil can be the most fertile ground for good, and the good can learn

from the cleverness of evil," Ungerer said of the theme of the book. It was his most visually sophisticated book to date, the first to have been composed using the two-page spread as a consistent design unit and exploiting the predominantly black-drenched characters against great swathes of rich colors. The drawing took on a much heavier, chunkier, more ominous graphic tone – quite distinct from his earlier books, even his previous one, *Emile*, which he drew still using a delicate line *à la* Sempé's.

And it may have the distinction of being the first time he clashed with one of his publishers. Ungerer attained a respect for language (he knows three fluently – English, French and German) and has a corresponding appreciation for a rich and idiosyncratic vocabulary. One of the robbers carried a blunderbuss, he wrote on the first page of the story, a somewhat archaic term for a kind of large-bore shotgun, but, of course, a much juicer and more intriguing term. His

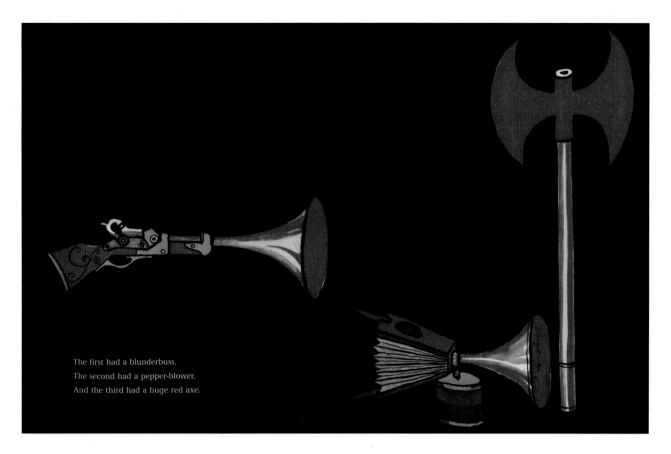

The first had a blunderbuss.
The second had a pepper-blower.
And the third had a huge red axe.

U.K. publisher took special aim at it when he wrote a critique of the story: "We have a boy in the back room who wrote a much better version of your story, and he certainly didn't use the word blunderbuss." Ungerer was proud of his use of "blunderbuss" and, in fact, opposes those educational experts – to whom most publishers of children's books pay strict obeisance – who believe that vocabulary should be scientifically calibrated to children's ages. "This was a big fight in the old days," he said in 2015. "Still to this day, the Americans say you should use a vocabulary that the children already have and understand. And I say, no. Children should be given a challenge with new words. My wife and I read our children stories every night – way ahead of their age. I never had this problem with Ursula Nordstrom at Harper. She was the only one who didn't give a shit about this. But when *The Three Robbers* came out, they wanted me to take out the word blunderbuss for the gun. But blunderbuss – isn't that a beautiful word? My God! Blunderbuss!" Elsewhere, he effused about language and children: "I'm in love with language. Between the ages of three and seven, children can learn three languages a year. If you're not teaching them another language, you can always develop their vocabulary. Make them ask, 'What does that mean?'"

His next landmark children's book was *Moon Man* (1967), a portrait of alienation, loneliness, persecution and transcendence – all of which Ungerer knew something about. Fascinated by and envious of the joyful revelry he sees on the Earth, the lonely Moon Man grabs the tail of a comet one night and lands on Earth with a thud, expecting to dance the night away. Instead, he is hunted and jailed. "Government officials were alerted. Statesmen, scientists and generals panicked. They called the mysterious visitor an invader." He escapes from jail and comes upon a costume party where "the Moon

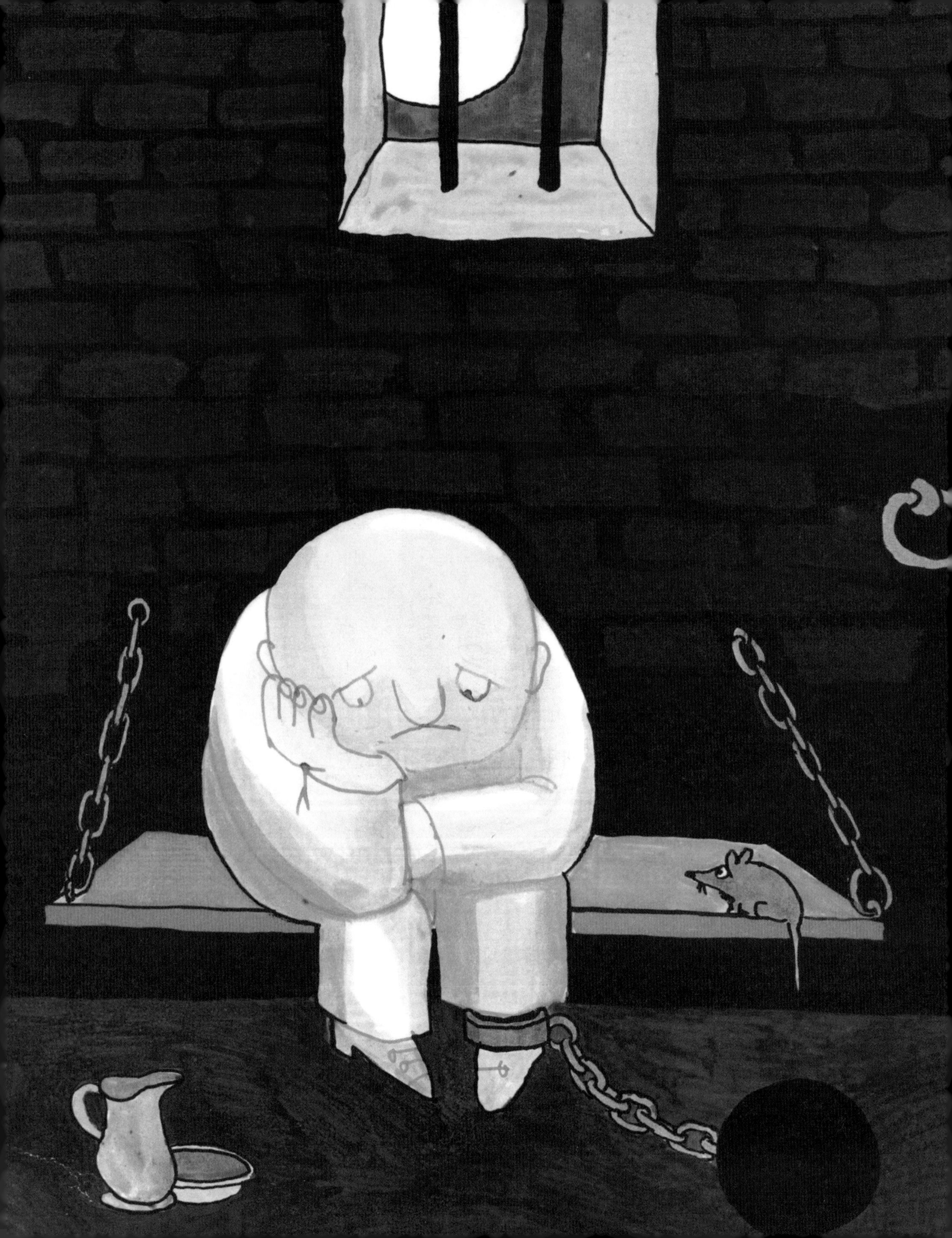

Man danced blissfully for hours," fulfilling his dream. But, once again, the police are in hot pursuit and nearly catch him when he discovers and seeks refuge in an "ancient castle" where the "long-forgotten scientist Doktor Bunsen van der Dunkel" had just coincidentally "been perfecting a spacecraft to reach the moon." And so the doctor packs up the Moon Man and sends him back to his home.

Aside from the transient gaiety of the partyers and the generous nature of the good professor, the humans are mostly depicted in *Moon Man* as exploitive, fearful, paranoid, violent and malicious. About the deeper impulses behind the story, Ungerer wrote, "In a way, I've been an immigrant all my life – I was born in Alsace. I went away to America, then I went to Canada and then I went to Ireland …. I was an outsider wherever I went. When I landed in New York from Europe, it was like the Moon Man landing on Earth."

There are other standout books in this period: *Zeralda's Ogre*, published a year after *Moon Man*, about an ogre who snatches little children from the local village and eats them, but who is brought around by Zeralda, who tutors him in culinary delights other than small children. *The Hat* is a story in which, like the films *Winchester '73* or *The Yellow Rolls Royce*, the drama unfolds as an inanimate object changes hands, although in Ungerer's telling, the hat changes hands only once (with the hint that there are further adventures awaiting our hat and its new owners) and becomes animate, doing good deeds and bringing good luck and even romance to the protagonist Benito Badoglio.

I Am Papa Snap and These Are My Favorite No Such Stories (1971) is as inventively conceived as it is titled. A series of vignettes mostly told over a succession of two-page spreads (with occasional single pages), it is bleak, fatalistic and weird, starring characters with names like Uncle Rimskey, Zink Slugg, Arson Twitch, Spiffy Loin and the four Tremblance Brothers – Fester, Foster, Faster

OPPOSITE: From
Moon Man, 1966.

BELOW LEFT: From
Zeralda's Ogre, 1967.

BELOW RIGHT: From *I Am
Papa Snap and These Are My
Favorite No Such Stories,* 1971.

and Foster. One of the two-page spreads reads in its entirety:

> Every day
> Rain, shine or overcast
> He walks down to the shore.
> He sits on a rock to read or dream,
> He has no friends, no enemies.
> He lives in peace.
> No one knows anything about him.
> Not even his name.

It's a children's book that reads as though it were conceived by the combined sensibilities of Alfred Jarry and Samuel Beckett. I doubt there has been a children's book like it before or since.

Ungerer was not content to devote his talents exclusively to the creation of children's books, though. Or perhaps it is more accurate to say he was too creatively and dispositionally restless to contain his talent to a single niche. Ungerer could be not inappropriately compared to the musical composer and bassist Charles Mingus, an artist Ungerer admires, who was ferociously independent and creatively protean, who rejected the jazz label just as Ungerer rejects the cartoonist label, and who resisted being contained in a single aesthetic idiom. When asked why he expresses himself in so many different ways, Ungerer replied, "I would be bored otherwise. It nearly gives me an inferiority complex when I see other artists who have one style and just build it up. I am a jack-of-all-trades, I go in all directions. I am interested in this and that. On one day, for example, I can start working with sculptures, the telephone rings and it gives me another idea for a story so I have to write it down, then I go back to another project afterwards." (I refer to Ungerer throughout, with apologies, as a cartoonist, because I do not see it as a pejorative; quite the opposite, in fact.)

Three years after Ungerer's first Mellops book appeared, he created two books of a decidedly adult nature: *Inside Marriage*, subtitled "Wedding Pictures," and appropriately published by Barney Rosset's Grove Press; and *Horrible: An Account of the Sad Achievements of Progress*. *Inside Marriage* is a commentary on romance and marriage cleverly disguised as a narrative of the mating ritual, and although it is composed of a series of beguilingly charming Thurberesque drawings, and it ends sweetly, a closer look indicates a more conflicted view

INSIDE MARRIAGE
By Tomi Ungerer
EVERGREEN C-1 $1.00

RIGHT: *Inside Marriage*, 1960.

a new home
and a new prison.

BELOW: From *Inside Marriage*, 1960.

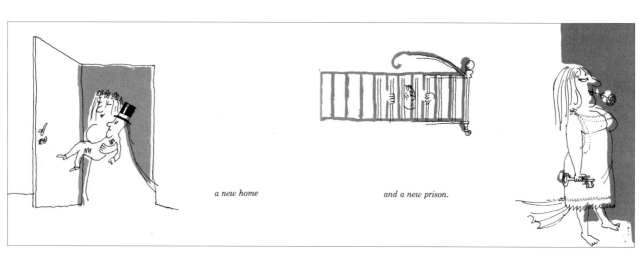

of romantic relationships: the book is littered with imagery reflecting what is at the very least barbed ambivalence or, more likely, recondite hostility. The marriage ceremony, for example, is depicted as a duel with the bridegroom on one side with a pistol and the bride on the other with a machine gun. It's as if he started out trying to create a lighthearted, crowd-pleasing little book about the joys of marriage but couldn't contain his satirical impulses. This isn't surprising from someone who, 20 years later, mused on love: "We are, after all, alone in this world. And the greatest luxury two human beings can have is to be alone together." *Horrible* is a gentle and ingenious satire on consumerism, gadgetry, gluttony and excess as expressed through a series of visual puns that often juxtapose

the mechanical delights and modern product design of mass-produced goods with the organicism of the human and animal worlds.

If *Inside Marriage* reflects a sensibility that hadn't quite coalesced and *Horrible* one that is more bemused than repelled by what the artist sees around him, his later cartoon collections reveal no such ambivalence – rather, they have a sensibility uncompromisingly at war with the most grotesque depredations of human folly. *Underground Sketchbook* came out in 1964, and it is a masterpiece of visual conceptual ingenuity. The back cover describes it as a "chronicle of the automated inhumanity of modern man" and refers to its subject matter as the "maladies of the modern world." In his introduction, Jonathan Miller wrote, "those who read this volume as it should be read, in one sitting, will have enjoyed a sulphuric moral experience." To say the least. The book is a relentless rage against avarice, consumerism, alienation, the exploitation of everything, the mechanization of experience and the public acquiescence to the worst

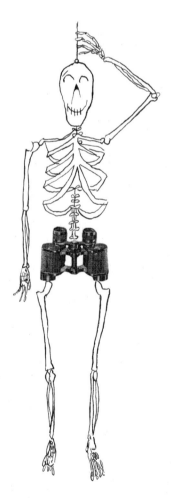

LEFT: From *Horrible*, 1960.

RIGHT: From *The Underground Sketchbook*, 1964.

Mrs. Ursula Rottenham at dinner with Mr. Julius Grunt, irrepressible Pittsburgh financier

ABOVE: From *The Party,* 1966.

instincts that create a modern economy. It is the first book by Ungerer in which anger is the motivating force; the artist has often said that anger served as a catalyst for his work. "Political drawings are something I've done all my life," he once explained. "If I didn't have my work and my creativity, I'd be fit for the insane asylum – most artists would. So, I've been very lucky that everything I felt – especially getting angry–I can get out of my system by putting it on paper. This explains my engagement."

Underground Sketchbook isn't merely a series of morally outraged cartoons, though. The drawings range from the playfully absurd to the most disillusioned portraits of dehumanization, often cohabiting within the same drawing, creating a vertiginous and emotionally disturbing response on the part of the viewer. It is the first book in which Ungerer's sly, subversive wit, visual perspicacity and profoundly black humor is on full, unfettered display. In one drawing entitled "The Example," a couple watches two cars on top of each other, and it takes an important second to realize the cars are fucking; a man is skewered on his day calendar; a military officer's uniform is proudly decorated with a miniature hanged man. *Underground*

Sketchbook feels like a warm-up to his next book two years later, *The Party* (1966). Whereas the disparate drawings in *Underground Sketchbook* were originally drawn out of an inner need and never intended for publication, *The Party* was conceived as a single book– it could even be considered a proto-graphic novel. It has an Altmanesque narrative, of sorts – the conceit of which is that it provides snapshots of the goings-on among the participants at a party in the East Hamptons. "There are so many people present and so much to see that it was impossible to mention them all, who came to enjoy a most, most wonderful party," is the author's jocosely facetious introduction; following is a series of extemporaneous portraits of the idle rich, the ruling class, the power elite, the one percent – call them what you will – a succession of smug, bloated, drooling, libidinous, ostentatious monsters. Each drawing is accompanied by a hilariously incongruous caption, lettered – or scrawled – in the author's hand, providing the name and a brief deadpan description of his or her high social standing, creating an irreconcilable dissonance between image and text. "Mrs. Noula Rottenham at dinner with Mr. Julius Grint, irrepressible Pittsburgh financier" is,

ABOVE: From *Compromises*, 1970.

for example, juxtaposed against a drawing of Julius dementedly slathering his tongue up Noula's arm while Noula stares at the reader in a comatose ecstasy. It may be the most acid book of Ungerer's career, each drawing depicting the outer manifestation of a rotting soul. The book was the result of his visceral reaction to such parties that he witnessed.

Ungerer's first residence in Manhattan was a "dingy, dark basement room in the West 70s." But with the enormous financial success of his children's books, as well as his lucrative commercial assignments, he bought a brownstone in the Village (formerly Aaron Burr's home), but he also lived for a time in a huge house in East Hampton, a rich enclave, which he drove to and from in his (used) Bentley. It is unclear why someone with an aversion to the rich would live among them, except for that very reason, and one can imagine that he took a perverse delight in doing so. But by living there he witnessed high-toned parties given by his neighbors. It sounds apocryphal, but Ungerer said that he enjoyed shooting a Remington rifle over the heads of the nearby partygoers. "It was mischievously that I triggered my whizzing bullets over the ducking guests," he said. "I always kept a silver one for Peggy Guggenheim," he added in jest, or perhaps not, referring to the socialite and art collector, "but didn't know what she looked like."

In 1970, *Compromises*, a collection of 100 drawings commenting broadly on the human comedy, was published. Chosen, the jacket copy informs us, from "thousands of drawings made during the past five years," these sketches look more spontaneous than those appearing in previous collections, as if they'd come barreling straight out of his subconscious and landing onto the page. It's a rich and rewarding selection of drawings that tackle many of his usual preoccupations: male-female relationships, hypocrisy, futility and the paradoxes of life.

His creative output during what I will call his American Period – roughly from 1957 to 1971, when he was between the ages of 26 and 40 – was staggering, so voluminous that it's virtually impossible to wrap one's head around. In addition to the children's books he wrote and drew entirely himself, he collaborated with the children's book author William Cole on eight books; illustrated at least 26 books by other writers, appeared in the *New York Times* and such mass circulation magazines as *Esquire*, *Life*,

Harper's Bazaar, the *Village Voice*, *Holiday* and *Ramparts*; was published in small circulation literary magazines such as *Paris Review* and *Evergreen Review*; drew advertising illustrations, conceived entire ad campaigns, including posters, for myriad commercial clients, such as the Ice Capades, Aqueduct Raceway, the New York State Lottery, the Electric Circus (a nightclub in the East Village), the U.S. Park Service, Kent Cigarettes, Swissair, Air India, Pepsi and many others. He drew film posters for Stanley Kubrick's *Dr. Strangelove*, the documentary *Monterey Pop*, Otto *Preminger's Skidoo* (a wackadoodle cinematic abomination that features a prominent cameo of Ungerer's anti-war Kiss For Peace poster), and at least two Broadway plays: Terence Frisby's *There's a Girl in My Soup* and Gore Vidal's *The Best Man*. "Everything I do is with a bit of joy," said Ungerer, and this was no more evident than in his posters for the Ice Capades, which were stunning examples of graphic design, exquisitely capturing the exuberance of speed of the skaters in a perfect cartoon idiom–sketchy, spontaneous, yet masterfully controlled.

Although Ungerer's political commentary is more cultural and visceral than ideological and programmatic, his anti-war posters during America's Vietnam adventure are the closest he's gotten to a purely political protest. According to Jack Rennert, who edited a 1971 collection of Ungerer's poster art, "In 1967, Tomi was approached by a group of students and faculty members, mostly from Columbia University, to create a series of anti-war posters. He agreed to do so, but subsequently found it frustrating and maddening to deal with the maze of bureaucracy of peace organizations. Finally, rather than see all his drawings remain in his sketchbook, he decided to publish them himself. With the help of his friend, Richard Kasak, he printed and arranged for the distribution of the posters … As many of the original sketches as their finances allowed were turned into posters."

There was a surfeit of protest art in the '60s – much of it earnest and well-intentioned, some of it angry, but the vast majority blunt, inarticulate, witless – but Ungerer's images rocked the viewer back on their heels by the sheer ferocity of their eloquence and moral outrage. The only other contemporary artists of such purely graphic power that I can think of who compare are Gerald Scarfe (whose political targets are more focused) and Ralph Steadman (who shares many other affinities with Ungerer). Ungerer's expression was as cruel and scalding as the war itself, and therefore a perfect rejoinder to it. "As brilliant as the kids' books are," said Jules Feiffer, "and as brilliant as his other work, when I see them reproduced still I find those political posters from the '60s shocking to look at." He's right: they are shocking to look at. It's as if the bile rose in Ungerer's throat and he spat it directly at the warmongers. Explaining how he was able to

BELOW LEFT: Poster for *Dr. Strangelove*, 1964.

BELOW RIGHT: Detail from a 1965 Ice Capades poster.

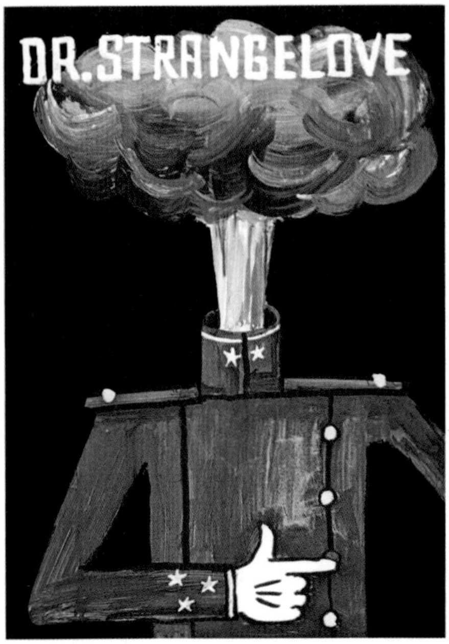
DR.STRANGELOVE

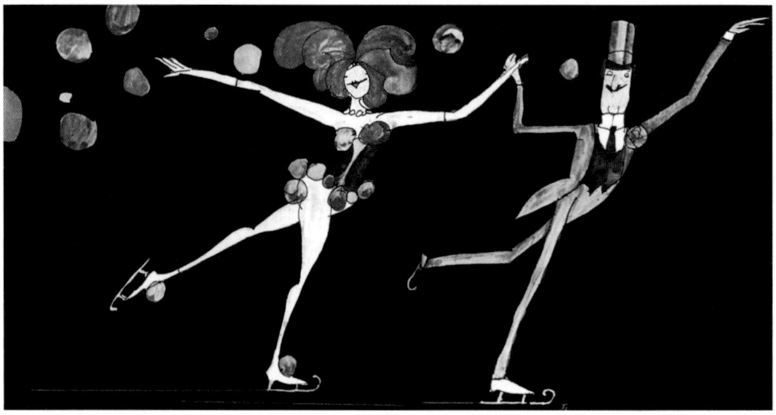

channel such moral outrage into effective propagandistic images, he said, "The Nazis woke up the anger in me, but on the other hand I was exposed to the propaganda of the greatest genius ever, which was Dr. Goebbels. The best way to fight your enemies is to fight them with their own weapons. So, in a way, my Vietnam posters used the same kind of shock effect that I was brought up with. It's really quite ironical that I should say such a thing."

There are drawings of a Vietnamese person fleeing a poster of Uncle Sam, having the statue of liberty stuffed down his throat so that he forcibly has to kiss the Statue of Liberty's ass; of an American airman painting pictures of Vietnamese children on his plane; of a U.S. soldier nonchalantly lighting a cigarette as he watches a village burn; a doctored photo of General Westmoreland wearing an apron covered in blood. And in a more general critique, he drew a Nazi saluting the American flag, which may be more chillingly resonant now than when it was drawn in 1968. Certainly, living under Nazi occupation and seeing, up close, the consequences of barbarity during war inflames his consciousness in a way that one who hadn't suffered that experience can't possibly understand. "I'm very, very thankful for all the things that happened to me because they shaped me and they shaped my opinions which have stuck to me all my life," he said. "Frankly, we've seen enough war to hate it. Not to hate it but to loathe it. I hate hate." He rejected hate as a motivating force, but if any of his expression comes close, it's his anti-war art. "I realized," he elaborated, "that if you live with hate, you actually suffer more than the hated one because it's obsessional. I was just able to get rid of it. I may dislike strongly or may feel absolutely disgusted but … "

He was personally involved in two harrowing events of a political nature that bookended the 1960s, incidents that he has recounted numerous times and that would weigh heavily on him for the rest of his life. The first occurred in 1960. Ungerer applied for a visa to visit China as a reporter for *Newsweek*. At that time, China was demonized in U.S. foreign policy circles almost as much as the Soviet Union – as a Communist state bent on taking over the world, one domino at a time – which theory would rationalize our entry into Vietnam a couple of years later, beginning with "advisors," then escalating with ground troops.

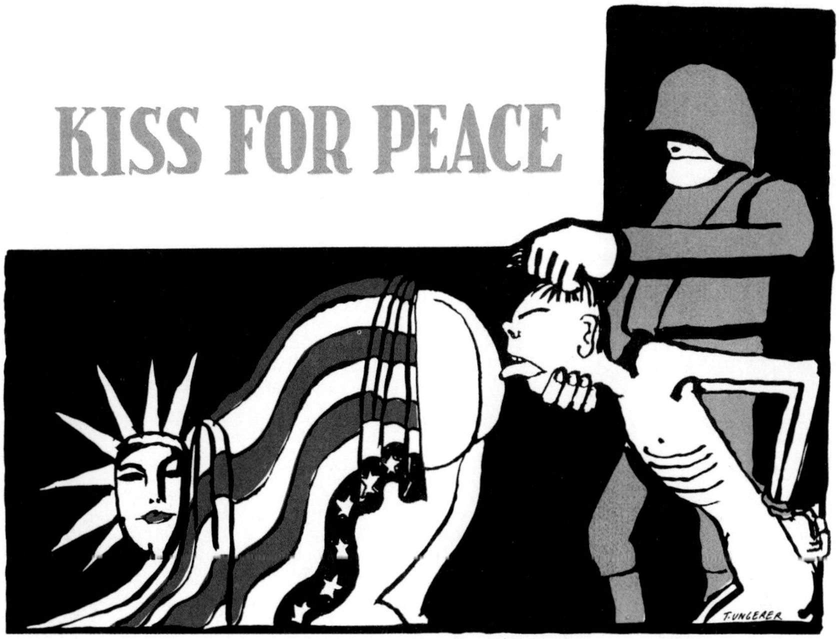
KISS FOR PEACE
T. UNGERER

LEFT: Anti-Vietnam War poster, 1967.

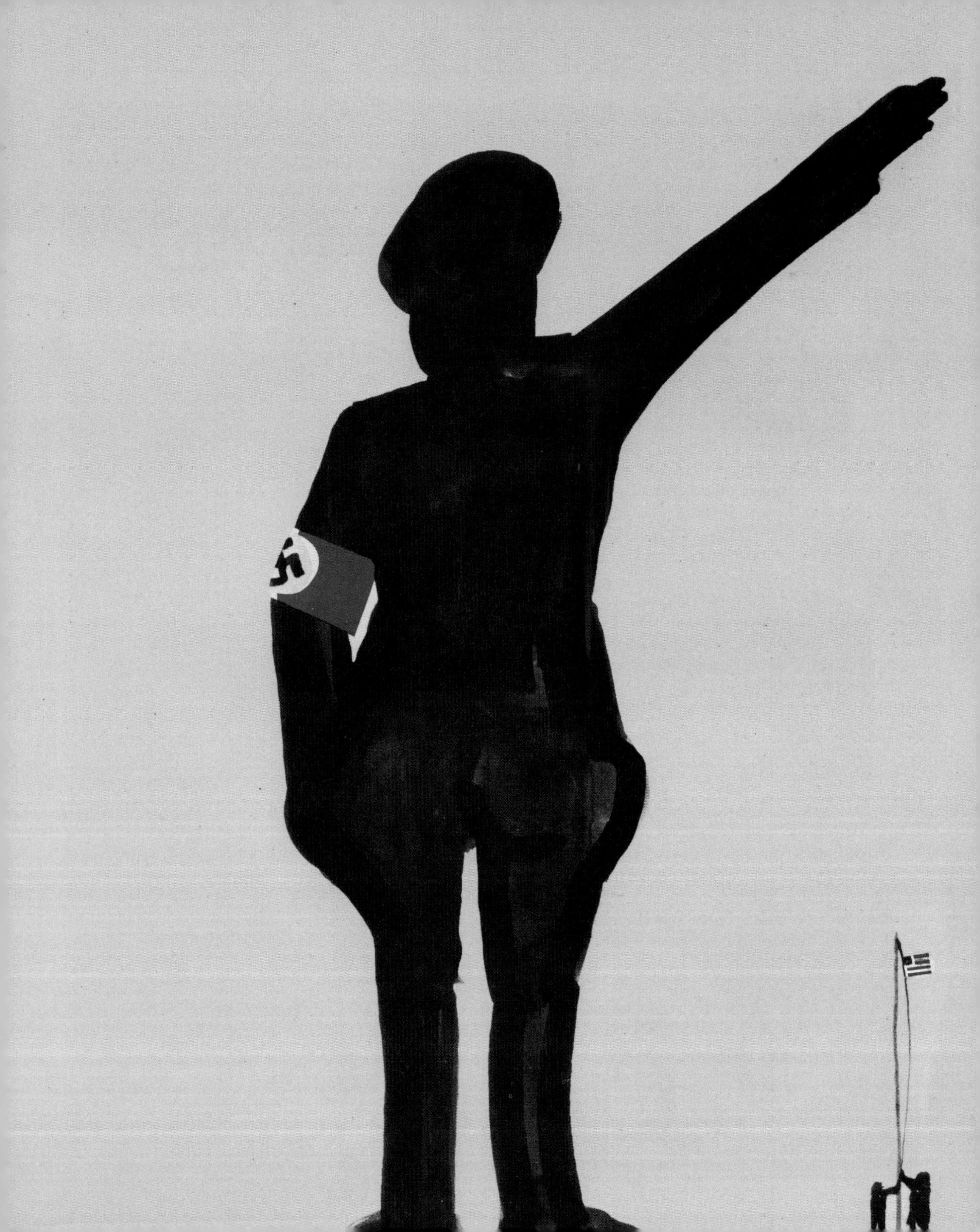

Ungerer describes what happened: "I went from New York to Paris, and then came a telex saying if I went to China I would not be allowed back into the U.S. It was a witch hunt in those days, and wanting to go to China made me a Communist. So I gave up on my trip. But when I arrived in New York, I was arrested and kidnapped, just like in the movies. They grabbed me. There were three men in the hallway, and one said, 'Drop your suitcases quietly.' The guy behind me grabbed my suitcases, and then they whisked me off in a car. Then they grilled me, they even opened the soles of my shoes, and after that my telephones were tapped and my mail was opened. The message was: 'Get out of here.' And then Kennedy was elected, and I wasn't tapped anymore, but it was the beginning of my problems. Even before the erotica, I'd been pegged as a Communist, and that's when it really started. Then came the erotica."

A public speaking gig at a 1969 American Library Convention proved to be a pivotal event in Ungerer's life. He has told the story numerous times with very little variation. The most succinct and coherent account may appear in a 2015 *New Yorker* article by Robert Sullivan, the premise of which is how Ungerer was blacklisted in the American library system due to this ALA confrontation. Sullivan writes:

> Ungerer was sent away, really, his books banned, removed from libraries, and not reviewed in, for instance, the [*New York*] *Times*, after he was deemed too offensive as an artist. It was a break that was not his fault, though he certainly didn't help matters and still seems to blame himself for it ... Ungerer remembers the break as having begun at an American Library Association conference in 1969. "You can really pinpoint exactly the moment that my multiple activities came out into the open," he says. "It all happened in this one evening, at a children's-book convention, and I had to say a few words."
>
> When Ungerer stood at the podium on that fateful (in his mind) day, he was suddenly hit with questions that, one has to think, he knew were coming. "And somebody in the audience attacked me," he recalls ...
>
> Ungerer crossed a line at the ALA event, as the crowd pushed him – asking how dare he draw *Fornicon* and children's books. "They really went after me," he recounts [from the documentary *Far Out Isn't Far Enough*], seemingly over the moment until he adds, "Really, like a pack of bitches." What he says happened was – and a librarian who knew others at the event confirms his story – he got angry. "When I really blow up, then I'm blind, really blind – blind with anger," he says. "Stupidly, I use the word that you certainly shouldn't use anyway, especially in those days, and I said to defend myself, 'If people didn't fuck, you wouldn't have any children, and without children you would be out of work.' And that went, of course, very badly, especially with the word F-U-C-K."
>
> His punishment was to be effectively blacklisted in America, his books taken from libraries, his children's publishing career in America over. His penance was to leave town."[1]

He left town in 1971.

But not before giving what feels like a parting gift to America – the notorious *Fornicon*, published in 1970 (a year after his ALA encounter!). I was disappointed, given its reputation, when I finally got my hands on it; it's not pornographic at all – not if pornography is defined as something that stimulates the sexual impulse. It is impossible to know what will accomplish that in any given person, of course, sexuality being the most subjective of human experiences, but this would surely activate the libido of

OPPOSITE: Sketch for poster, 1968.

1 Although there is little doubt that this ALA event – or such an event at a children's book convention – occurred, I could find no independent corroboration that Ungerer was literally systematically blacklisted from American libraries.

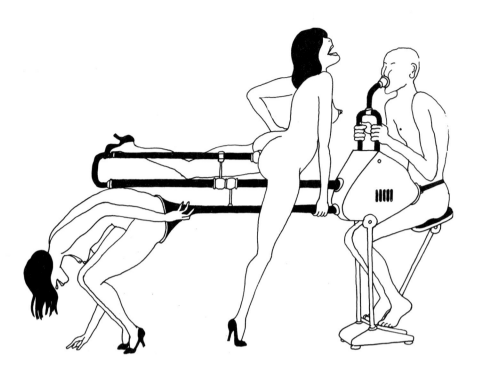

ABOVE: From *Fornicon,* 1969.

a distinct minority of viewers, if any. It is composed entirely of sexual imagery, but of a purely satirical nature. It could even be seen as anti-pornographic and pro-sensuality. It is a critique of the increasing mechanization of society, using sex as a metaphor and, if it's about sex at all, it's also, presumably, an animadversion against the sexual tactician, sex as an instrumental force, divorced from the cultural, social, aesthetic matrix, from any deeper meaning. The images represent another imaginative tour de force – men, women and even animals, organically attached to all manner of perverse, presumably pleasure-giving mechanical devices.

His production of children's books did not come to a complete stop during this period, but it slowed down considerably: He published two more children's books with Harper in the '70s: *I Am Papa Snap* (1971) and *No Kiss for Mother* (1973). He also published *The Beast of Monsieur Racine* with, curiously, Farrar, Strauss & Giroux in 1971. *A Storybook from Tomi Ungerer*, a collection of illustrated folk and fairy tales chosen by Ungerer, came out in 1974 (from Franklin Watts, New York). He did not create another children's book published in English until 1997.

Why he specifically left the U.S. is unclear. Ungerer obviously became disenchanted with the land of the free and the home of the brave. "After 16 years – blacklisted in the American customs register, my books officially banned from all public libraries – like a rat," he said with no little bitterness. (It was around this time that he met, on the subway, the woman who would become his third wife in 1970, Yvonne Wright, who coincidentally worked for the Children's Book Council.) After the ALA confrontation, he had an exhibition of his paintings at the D'Arcy Gallery in Cheltenham: no sales, no reviews, he says (which means that the contagion had spread to the U.K.). He exhibited images from *Fornicon* at the Waddell Gallery in Manhattan: "Same flop, not a peep …. I asked a friend, a reputed art critic, why he wouldn't write about my show. 'Tomi,' he told me, 'if I did I'd lose my reputation.' I stopped painting." Finally, when he was once asked why he left New York, he replied vaguely, "I had this big huge villa in Long Island and I was fed up with all this upper-class society. I was really an angry man." About moving, he wrote: "Yvonne and I left New York City in 1971, head over wheels. We were suddenly

TOMI UNGERER

THE BEAST OF
MONSIEUR RACINE
TOMI UNGERER

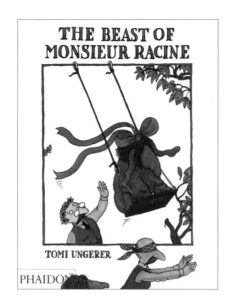

LEFT: *No Kiss for Mother, 1973.*

RIGHT: *The Beast of Monsieur Racine, 1971*

BELOW: *Far Out Isn't Far Enough*, 1983.

fed up with city life, racing along, our lives had run out of fuel, stalled, so we struck out on foot on the first side road, not even expecting the unexpected."

Where do you go if you're an angry, fed-up man living in a huge villa in Long Island? If you're this angry, fed-up man, you move to a small fishing village "on the Wild Atlantic Coast of Nova Scotia"– as far as you could get culturally and socially from New York City.

He spent over five years in that village and recounts those years with brio, sensitivity and dark humor in an illustrated diary/ memoir *Far Out Isn't Far Enough*. Ungerer is one of those rare cartoonists who is as good a prose writer as he is a drawer, and *Far Out* is proof of this. I can think of only a handful of cartoonists about whom this can be said: James Thurber, Shel Silverstein, Jules Feiffer, Ralph Steadman, Edward Sorel, Jim Woodring. (Is it generational? Or am I missing a cartoonist under 60 who qualifies?) The book is filled with hilarious and terrifying incidents, steeped in local color and vivid, eccentric characters, with occasional and unobtrusive forays into philosophical and aesthetic observations. It is mostly about the people and the life. What struck me most forcefully was the casual violence Ungerer records that runs like a turbulent, subterranean river throughout the book, from which he himself was not immune. He depicts the people who lived there – his neighbors, as it were – as both decent and monstrous, without, weirdly, any necessary contradiction. Isn't this all too often the case?

One of his "earliest friends and neighbors" was Strap Tinsel (one of the many peculiarly beguiling charms of the book is that it is populated by people with names like Flack McGully and Slinky McWire – and, of course, Strap Tinsel). "Strap," Ungerer writes, "came

Far Out isn't Far Enough
Life in the Back of Beyond
Tomi Ungerer
PHAIDON

from a cluster of houses situated outside the town limits, oddly nicknamed 'Dodge City.' Strap and his brothers and little sister were left fatherless and their mother took to drink. They are a pretty reckless bunch in Dodge City, but we have always been on good terms with them. One thing I made clear from the beginning: 'If you get drink in you, don't come near here, or I swear I'll shoot you.' That was plain and clear and we were never bothered." He continues:

> One day Strap plugged one of his brothers with a few mind-soothing bullets …
>
> So, I asked him:
>
> "Strap, why did you shoot your brother?"
>
> "Oh, once a year you got to shoot it out."
>
> His older brother just died, drunk; he gagged on his own vomit. Strap goes fishing on trawlers and we do not see him very much anymore.

There is violence that is more casual. "I wonder if pain is nonexistent for certain people?," Ungerer muses. The reason behind this question stems from this anecdote of an impromptu conversation between he and a fisherman:

One day I was having a little stroll by the harbor and met this fisherman, so we started a bit of a chat about the weather and lobsters…

"There's only one third of the lobster there usetah be."

"So, bad, eh?"

"Well, we gets paid more for 'em, so we just put out more traps."

"But more traps means less lobsters next year."

"Nothin' teh worry about, there's always unemployment money." So we keep on talking for a while, and he finally says, "I'd better be going now and do som'th'n about it …"

And he shows me his hand, stigmatized by a fish-hook that has gone right through the palm.

On the ground a pool of blood testifying to the length of our yarns …

Or this more personal brush with violence: "Yvonne and I were in search of a nice Christmas tree in a wooded piece of property we used to own. There we were, when gunshots started punctuating the silence all around us. It was the first time in my

BELOW: From *Far Out Isn't Far Enough*, 1983.

life that I have felt hunted and I still have nightmares about it."

The place was called Gull Harbor, population 2,000. It had three fisheries, the largest employers in town. It wasn't exactly lawless, but, "there are no local police; the last town cop was beaten up and gave up his job." They bought a "wrecked house" on a peninsula two miles from "town" and fixed it up. Tomi and Yvonne entered a new life, raising chickens, ducks, geese, goats, cows, pigs and horses. "We liked them, we killed them, we ate them," he writes (meaning, probably, all of them but the horses).

Ungerer adapted to his new life with a pedagogical zeal. He learned to slaughter a pig and discovered, by doing so, a spiritual dimension: "I'm really proud of being a good butcher. What I love is discipline. To lay out a carcass, to dispose a carcass is something you really learn. It's quite creative and it's architectural. When you empty out the guts and you look at the chest, it's gothic. It's like you're looking into a cathedral."

The book is not merely well-written; it is written with great flair and distinctive literary style. By style I mean a subjective interpretation of reality rendered by the uniquely purposeful use of language. His language is like his pen line, singularly and eloquently expressive. The book is epigrammatic, capturing the regional vernacular not merely of how these people – and not excluding Tomi and Yvonne – talk but how they live, the lives they inhabit. Although he is often funny in a blackish way (Ungerer's preferred mode of percipience), he's not blind to the narrowness and aridity of the culture either. Describing the insipid reportage in a local newspaper, he delivers a perfect example of style and content: "A life of unmolested mediocrity in a world

BELOW: From *Slow Agony*, 1983.

RIGHT: From *America*, 1974.

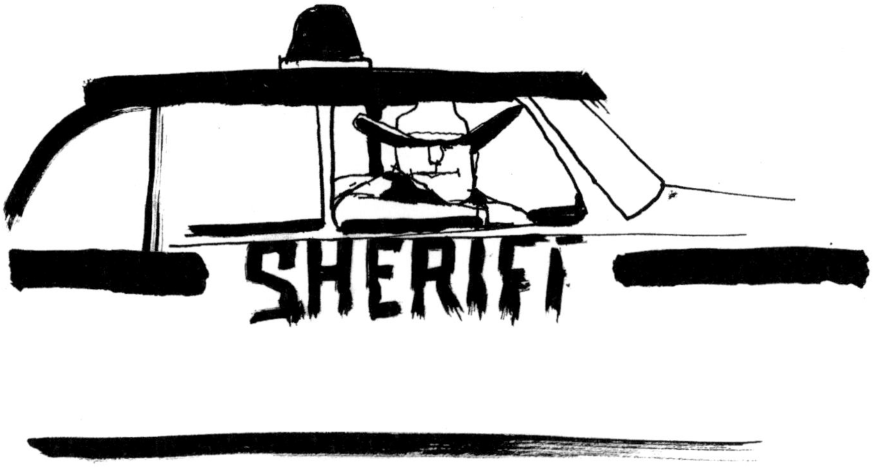
SHERIFF

where everything is molested by mediocrity." Here's a description of a friend's car in which he was driven from the airport: "The transmission oil started leaking away; the suspension was so soft it felt like we were being driven inside a rotten watermelon." This observation should be familiar to every sequential comics lover: "This house has a lot of windows, all divided into small panes, as if segmenting the landscape into that many postcards. Out at sea a boat or in the sky the clouds will move from one postcard to another."

He felt moved enough by his experience to transubstantiate it into a series of paintings, published in a book with the title, free of the irony, detachment and humor of his journal, *Slow Agony* (1983). The book is also entirely free of people; it depicts houses, buildings, boats, cars – all dilapidated, weathered, broken down, rotting, rusting out, half-destroyed. They are moving because there is nothing condescending about their portrayal. Quite the contrary, their images exude a love and respect for what nature wreaks upon all these man-made objects.

The experience of living there was obviously fascinating, brutal, revelatory – but unsustainable. In typical Ungerer fashion, there was an existential moment when he realized it was time to go. The farm was earlier beset by an attack of wild dogs that succeeded in killing several sheep ("One sheep in agony, her stomach ripped open, her intestines unrolled all over the place, another one disemboweled inside the corral; some survivors are huddled in a mess of blood and torn wool … "). Shortly afterward, he attempts, arduously and at length, to deliver ewes, resulting in not only the death of all three baby ewes but the mother as well. Reflecting upon it, he writes: "I feel stupid, criminal, vain…. The dogs' raid and Salome's wretched death marked the end of this part of our lives. We closed the farm down."

To the best of my knowledge, with an occasional, rare exception, his books did not appear in the U.S. again until Phaidon began reissuing his children's books in 2009–a 36-year exile from American publishing (though possibly a self-exile). He was, throughout those 36 years, published primarily in Germany, France and England, though undoubtedly in many other countries as well – just not in the United States. One might assume that Ungerer's productivity would diminish while living in Nova Scotia, at least slightly – the distractions of wild dog attacks and operating a working farm eating into one's art-making time – but I'm not so sure. His official bibliography cites 18 books published between 1971 and 1976 – on average, three books per year! (This number includes books he illustrated written by others.)

During this period, he published a number of books about which I know nothing: *Spiegelmensch: Ein deutsches*

Wintermärchen (Mirror Man: A German Winter Fairy Tale) in 1973; *Kneipenlieder (Pub Songs)*, 1974; *Alumette (Matches)*, 1974; *Id*, 1975; *Kinderliederbuch*, 1975; *Hopp, Hopp, Hopp: Liederliche Liederskizzen*, 1975; *Totempole: Erotische Zeichnungen (Totem Pole: Erotic Drawings)*, 1976; *Ben Witter: Liebesdienste (Ben Witter: Love Services)*; *Der erfolgreiche Geschäftsmann: Ein Stundenbuch für Managers (The Successful Businessman: A Book of Hours for Managers)*, 1976.

I have not seen any of these books, but one can infer from the titles the vast range of their subject matter and of Ungerer's interests, from adaptations of fairy tales to original children's books to erotica to – well, what could *The Successful Businessman: A Book of Hours for Managers* even be? He also contributed drawings to the successful 1972 election campaign of Willy Brandt (whom he met in 1962) for the Chancellorship of Germany. He worked on various advertising campaigns, at the behest of Robert Pütz, the owner of an ad agency in Cologne, Germany, for companies that produced vegetable "products," computers and printing supplies. *Das grosse Liederbuch (The Great Song Book)*, a collection of 60 of the "best loved songs in the English language" ("The Farmer in the Dell," "Oh My Darling, Clementine," "Rock-a-Bye Baby," etc.) accompanied by almost 100 watercolor illustrations by Ungerer appeared in 1975.

He published two big collections of thematically unified drawings: *America* and *Adam and Eve*. The images in *America* are clearly based upon individuals he saw and incidents he witnessed during his stay in the States. The drawings run from the harshly satirical to straight portraiture – and everything in between, by turns sensitive, respectful, harshly judgmental. There are drawings of the working class, lascivious office predators, exhibitionistic and slatternly women, urban dwellers, football players and jockeys, grotesquely smiling bourgeois couples, businessmen brimming with rapacity, nudists, farmers, motorcycle cops and small town sheriffs, cowboys, jails, gas stations,

big luxury cars, slot machines. Every page is a distillation of something uniquely and quintessentially American – many of the portraits exude smug self-satisfaction, vulgarity, opportunism. His most loving portraits are those of black Americans and prisoners (the latter of which are mostly white), which is not surprising. He was deeply affected by the segregation prevalent in America at the time he arrived. "The biggest shock for me when I came to America," he has said, was "the irony that the Americans fought the Nazis to get rid of racism and fascism, which I suffered in my own way … and then I come to America and my first father-in-law was the sheriff of Amarillo, Texas, and when I went down there I realized there was still segregation. It was so shocking that I don't think I ever got over it." There is no question where his sympathies lie. There is something sadly contemporary about this book, published in 1974. There is not a single image that could not have been drawn, with slight changes in fashion and style, yesterday. Paging through it, one is tempted to believe that nothing changes; that there is no such thing as progress in human affairs – or at least in American ones.

ABOVE: From *America*, 1974.

Romantic relations come in for a severe drubbing in *Adam and Eve*. Ungerer's "scurrilous wit," the back cover tells us, "is aimed at the human comedy, the droll and devious war between the sexes … " That's putting it mildly. It is a relentless assault on all the lies, hypocrisies and quackery about romantic relationships that advertising, movies, television and now, social media, trade in. There are a few images that are sweet, even chivalric. Most are not. Women are usually portrayed as bullies, harpies, manipulators. One drawing depicts a man and a woman in a boxing ring, with the man clearly getting the worst of it. "Mozart!" screams a woman holding a cat o' nine tails as a schlumpy little man trudges, and certainly not for the first time, to a piano and a swivel chair with spikes sticking out of the seat. But, being an equal-opportunity satirist, Ungerer depicts men mostly as single-minded, one-dimensional, shallow, clueless louts or simply as saps. A man is harpooning the great white whale, composed of a woman's buttocks; a man is gleefully skulking away with the genital portion of a schematic diagram of a woman sliced horizontally. Ungerer's general view of humanity might be summed up

ABOVE and RIGHT: From
Adam and Eve, 1976.

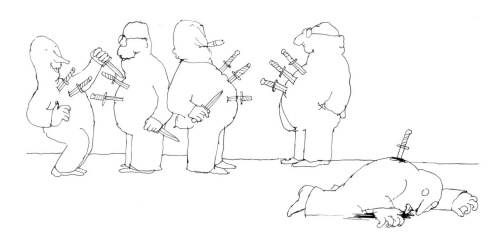

Tomi Ungerer
Tortoni Tremolo
THE CURSED MUSICIAN
Tomi Co

Otto
The Autobiography of a Teddy Bear

LEFT: *Tortoni Tromolo: The Cursed Musician*, 1998.

RIGHT: *Otto: The Autobiography of a Teddy Bear*, 1999.

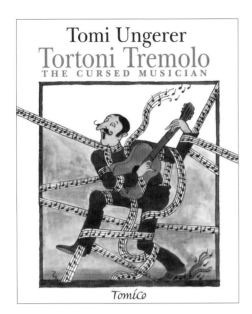

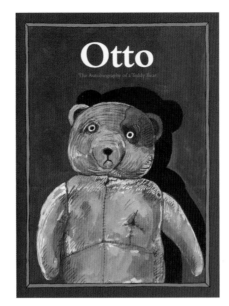

in a cartoon of five old bonhomie-filled men cheerfully knifing each other or a panorama of a couple of dozen men with their heads in the sand being systematically executed. The closest he gets to depicting marital bliss is a drawing of husband and wife sitting on either side of a table with their right and left hands nailed to it – together forever. It is an unrelentingly bleak and jaundiced picture of romantic love. It is a far cry from *Inside Marriage*, published 16 years earlier.

In 1976, with a week's notice, six suitcases and Yvonne pregnant with their first child, they moved to Ireland, where he finally found peace – or what passes for peace in Ungerer's world. (Ungerer's two other children lived with their mothers.) In Ireland, he said, he "needed to discover a new sense of measure .... It's the one place I've found that I fit in. It is a country without arrogance and behavioral distinctions between social classes .... It's the quality of the people we found there, the right kind of spirit-minded people .... Also, it is coastal. The strongest memory in my life is when I saw the ocean for the first time in Normandy." He bought a 200-acre property with a view of the coast.

His productivity from the time he moved to Ireland in 1976 to today has not slackened. During this period, he has written and drawn 53 books and illustrated 22 books written by others. I have tried to familiarize myself with as many of them as I reasonably could; what follows is a brief, selective survey of the books I found most interesting. I'm sure I have unintentionally omitted many worthy ones, but I hope this serves as a good overview of many of the highlights of Ungerer's oeuvre of the last 40 years.

Ungerer continued to create children's books, sometimes in collaboration with others: *Les Histoires farfelues de Papaski* (*The Wacky Stories of Papaski*), 1977; *Abracadabra* (with Robert Pütz), 1979; *Adelaide, das fliegende Känguruh* (*Adelaide, the Flying Kangaroo*), 1980. I cannot find another children's book until 1998 when he published two books: *Flix* and *Tortoni Tremolo*: *The Cursed Musician* (both published in the U.S. by Roberts Rinehart Publishing Group, the latter of which won the Hans Christian Andersen Award); *Otto* in 1999; and *Fog Island* in 2013. Two children's books–*Die Blaue Wolke* (*The Blue Cloud*), 2000; and *New Freunde* (*New Friends*), 2007 – were published in Germany but not in English.

To my eye, Ungerer's later children's books became more overtly autobiographi cal, more political, just this side of didactic. *Flix*'s distinctly political message is that of promoting human comity and opposing bigotry in all its guises. Two cats, Zeno and Colza, have a child who just happens to be a dog, which they name Flix. There are two segregated communities of dogs and cats, and Flix endures the prejudices of being the wrong species in the wrong community. But after he saves a cat from drowning, he is accepted in the cat community. Flix marries, goes into politics, creates a new party – the CDU (Cats and Dogs United) – and campaigns "for a joint administration of the two cities, mixed education, shared language, mutual respect and equal rights"– echoing Ungerer's own work in this vein, when he served as councilor in the inter-ministerial Franco-German Committee and as the Charge d'Affaires in the French Ministry of Culture; he was awarded the Commandeur de l'Ordre du Mérite "in recognition of his lifelong efforts to fight prejudice by artistic and political means, and in particular his work for Franco-German relations."

Otto is a story about the eponymously named teddy bear, created in Germany who serves as a witness to the persecution of the Jews in Germany and the war itself. By happenstance, he is taken to America, where he is ultimately reunited with his childhood owner. Its depiction of violence and brutality is unusually stark for a children's book and obviously drawn with great conviction. "*Otto*," said Ungerer, "is about the trauma of the Second World War. You see war on television, and I think children should be exposed to what war is like as early as possible," a view not likely held by many American readers, but in fact a corrective to the glorification of war and the worship of the military that increasingly surrounds children growing up in America. He elaborated: "*Otto* is about the Shoah, about persecution, making friends, about acceptance of immigrants in a neighborhood … "

The subtle satirical jab of *Tortoni Tromolo* is aimed squarely at television. A fortune-telling neighbor, unhappy with his nocturnal playing, puts a curse on the musician Tromolo (whose name changes throughout the story due to the curse: Tremolo Tortino, Telmoro Notrito, Lotemro Inotrot, etc., a delightfully pixilated touch). Henceforth, when he plays any instrument, the notes take tangible form and start flooding out of the sax, piano or trumpet, at first causing disarray wherever he plays, later harnessed into commercial success. But when he achieves enough popularity to appear on TV, his notes cascade out of TV sets all over the country, causing chaos and the consequent disappearance of TVs. "With no more TeeVee, families returned to their old ways of entertaining themselves. They told stories, read books and played games. Dinner tables were brought back, and home-cooked meals were served every night." In other words, a utopian children's book.

Fog Island is surely one of his most accomplished children's books, lighthearted but scary, atmospheric, enchanting and one of his most visually dazzling. The story opens at a family farm in a charming, storybook fishing village. The family's father gives his two children, Finn and Cara, a currach (a specific kind of handmade boat to us landlubbers), but with an ominous admonishment: "Never leave the bay, and stay clear of Fog Island! It's a doomed and evil place, surrounded by treacherous currents. Those who have ventured there have never returned." You'll never believe this, but the kids wander off course and get stranded on, yes, Fog Island, where things aren't nearly as dire as their father warned them they were, and, indeed, where they meet the Fog Man, a kind, playful, wizened prankster. They subsequently engage in a fantastical and surreal adventure.

During this time, Ungerer published at least nine cartoon books that dealt with adult themes, most of which, at least, were visual polemics, commenting on both interior demons and social ills. He came out in rapid succession with three tours de force of satirical assault: *Babylon* (1979), *Symptomatics* (1982), and *Rigor Mortis* (1983). They could be seen, collectively, as Ungerer's most pungent criticism of modern life. Although they are each distinguished by different visual stylizations – different techniques, different

OPPOSITE: From *Fog Island*, 2013.

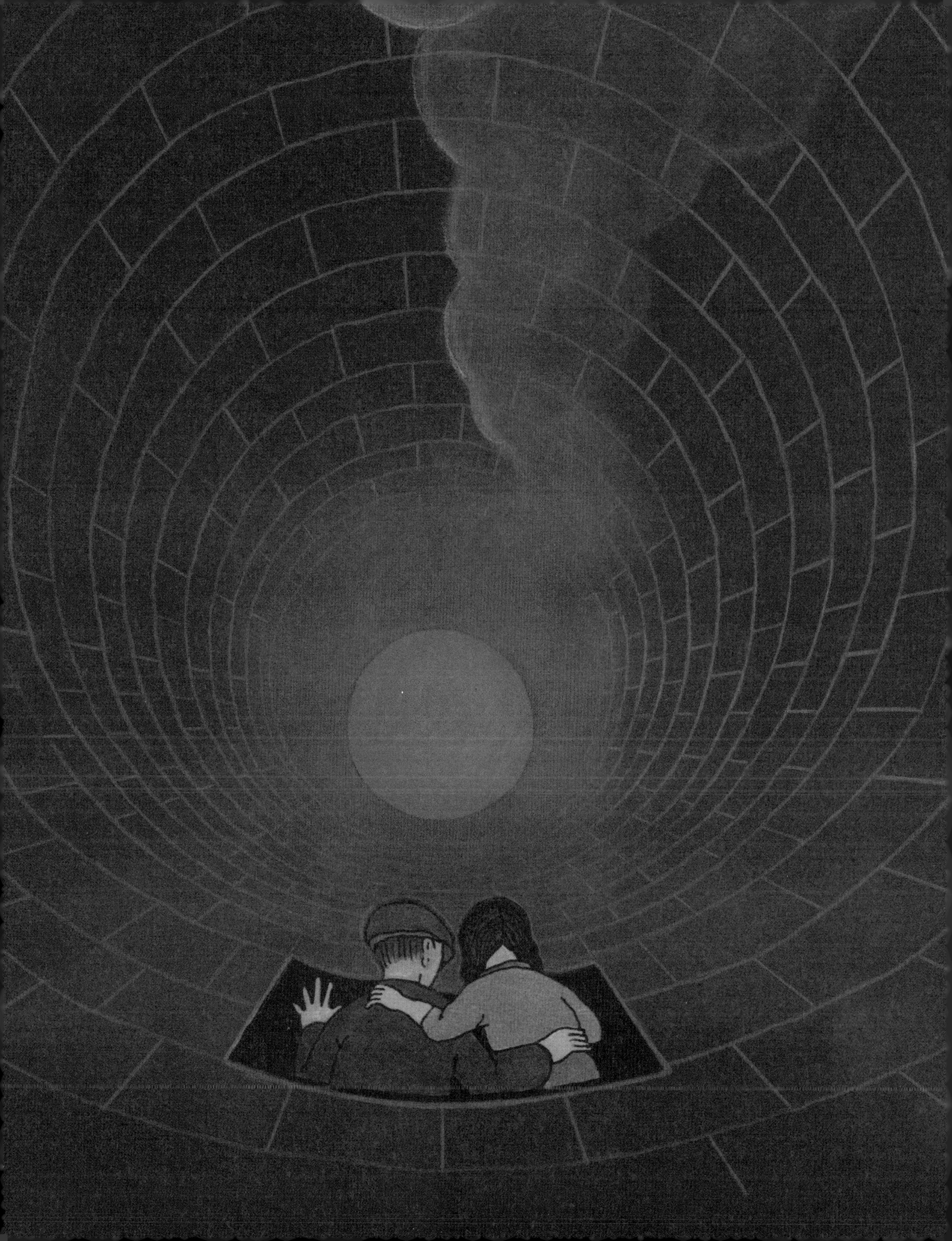

media, each one executed with breathtaking mastery – the thematic differences among them are pretty nuanced. Like all great artists, Ungerer has his obsessions that he returns to again and again. Like Charles Schulz, he can express the same or a similar sentiment with slight shifts in perspective and with freshness and different coloration each time he revisits it – in Schulz's case, it is the result of the most nuanced narrative variation, in Ungerer's, it is the sheer force of his visual imagination.

Babylon may be the most sobering of the three, as if Ungerer could not step back from the abyss he was peering into and leaven his pessimism with humor; indeed, this is the blackest of black humor. Drawn entirely in pencil, these fully formed images, reproduced in lush, dense, gray tones, rival the satirical vitriol of his anti-war posters of the previous decade: they fairly radiate repellence at what human beings can do to one another

BELOW: From *Babylon,* 1979.

in supposedly civilized circumstances. (The book, he says, although published when he lived in Ireland, was drawn in Nova Scotia.) His contempt for the ruling class is etched on virtually every page. He depicts the bourgeoisie as vassals of the ruling class – malevolent members of a voyeuristic tribe who accept their position as the natural order of things and take glee in the subordination of those beneath them and the exploitation of those who make their position possible. "The secret burden of the bourgeoisie" depicts a couple enjoying watching a tiny prole in a birdcage. "Smile!" depicts a vulgar tourist snapping a picture of a suffering black man. The most mundane consumer activities are portrayed as grotesque affronts – going to the grocery store, working out at the gym, waiting at the laundromat. Men are drawn as human cash registers. France's motto, *"Liberté, égalité, fraternité"* is a hypocrisy, illustrated by a self-satisfied rotund man in

a heavy coat walking a naked person like a dog. Trendy spiritualism and religious quackery are skewered. Several drawings show people desperately trying to improve their appearance by putting lipstick on or having plastic surgery, clearly a transparent attempt to hide their own inner ugliness – a theme he will return to with even greater ferocity in *Rigor Mortis*. It's as though, throughout *Babylon*, he is saying that there is no decent idea that cannot – and will not– be debased, turned to shit and used as a weapon against all. "There's one thing I can tell you for sure," he once said, "there's no such thing as a sheltering sky." And he means it.

I do not see a contradiction, as many would, between Ungerer's compassion and empathy on the one hand and his fatalistic outlook on the other. The one is borne of the other, and in his case, his ability to eat his cake and have it too is a virtue, not a defect. Clearly, political oppression, whether of the capitalist variety or the totalitarian (if you care to make a distinction) leads to human suffering, and it's human suffering that he chronicles. This is no more on display than in *Symptomatics*, which addresses Sisyphean futility, failure, loneliness, alienation, fear, inner conflict and, on a larger social scale, the ongoing Taylorization of the planet. The world is depicted as a minefield; competitiveness as nothing less than a *circus maximus*; individualism crushed beneath the wheel of impersonal social systems, as Hesse might have put it. These images comprise a bleak, cautionary vision of man's inhumanity to his fellow man and to himself.

Rigor Mortis could be a sequel to 1966's *The Party*. It is filled with grotesque examples of the beautiful and the damned – men and women of leisure depicted as cripples, deformities, skin-draped husks, often skeletons literally stripped of their superficially lovely façade. The bourgeoisie is, once again, depicted as a fetid, loveless lot, scheming against each other in a *Lord of the Flies* world of our own creation. A naked couple embrace, each with a knife in his and her back; a ramrod-straight skeleton resides proudly in a wheelchair with an Iron Cross

medal pinned to his chest; a speaker is manipulating his audience with puppet strings attached to their throats. It is a bleak vision of humanity for which Trumpism is the *reductio ad absurdum* and therefore not a hypothetical construct but a prescient reminder that our humanity can be easily forfeited if we are not vigilant. And, Ungerer seems to argue, we are not vigilant.

Reading these three books back-to-back in one sitting, as I did, is an overpowering experience. They comprise, along with *The Party*, *Compromises*, and *Adam and Eve*, among the most unrelentingly coruscating and unforgiving portraits of man's

ABOVE: From *Babylon*, 1979.

BELOW: From *Symptomatics*, 1982.

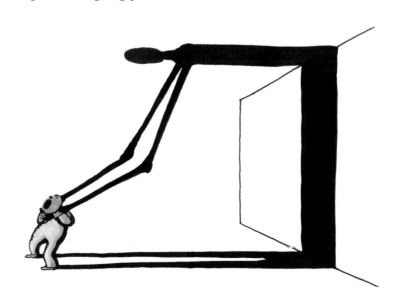

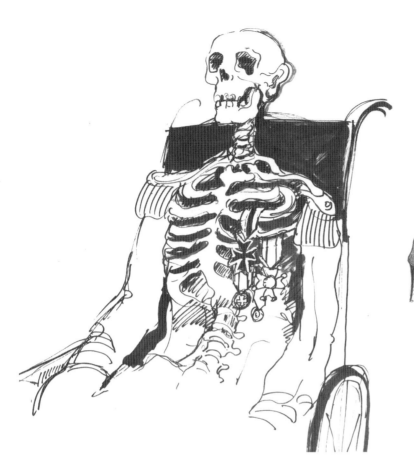

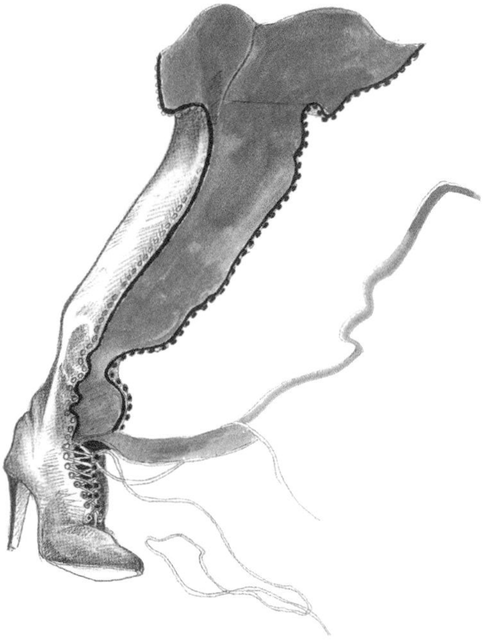

LEFT: From *Rigor Mortis*, 1983.

RIGHT: From *Schutzengel der Hölles*, 1986.

OPPOSITE: From *Cats as Cats Can*, 1997.

inhumanity to his fellow man ever penned by an artist.

He also published other "adult" cartoon books during this same period that I have not seen, and about which I could find little to no information: *Schnipp-Schnapp* (*Snip-Snap*), 1987; *Tomi Ungerers Tierleben* (*Tomi Ungerer's Life*), 1990; *Tomi Ungerers Erzählungen für Erwachsene* (*Tomi Ungerer's Tales for Adults*), 1992; *Hallali*, 1999; *Cœur à cœur* (*Heart to Heart*), 2004, apparently, a volume about love and relationships; and *Europolitain*, 1998.

In 1986, he published a book that was one of his most personally satisfying: *Schutzengel der Hölle* or *Guardian Angel of Hell*, a collection of interviews with dominatrices in a bordello in Hamburg, where he lived briefly. He sees the prostitutes here as part of the underclass, unfairly and hypocritically looked down upon by respectable society, victims of injustice who should be given full rights as legal and legitimate workers. He described

the circumstances for making the book: "A friend of mine introduced me to Domenica, who was considered the empress of prostitution in Germany. She welcomed me and said I could stay there. Fine women. Fine ladies. I lived on and off in the street…and the houses are all run by women. I did a book on the dominas with the greatest respect, as they do the work where the psychiatrists stop. They are never touched by men–they only administer torture. I had the greatest compliment with this book when a woman told me it was the only book that had ever made her throw up." The drawings accompanying the interviews are the opposite of erotic: realistic and discrete portraits of the women and their professional accouterments.

Other highlights during this period include two books of erotica (*Femme Fatale: A Victorian Sketchbook*, 1984; and *Erototoscope*, 2001). I have seen neither, but unlike *Fornicon*, which was "a rebellion against a mechanization of our lives, not only of sex," these appear to be genuine erotica. About his attitude toward the erotic, he said in 2015, "I've been very misunderstood in those days. I was definitely part of the sexual revolution. The things I used to say are normal now. I was always more interested in the woman than in myself. I was fascinated by women's fantasies. For me, eroticism was always about staging a fantasy according to the partner's taste. It is really Even Steven. Women have a right to sexual fantasy just as men have."

Less known than his satirical bent and his children's books is his love of animals and the opportunity they provide for drawing: *The Animals of Tomi Ungerer* was published in 1990 and *Vogel*, apparently, a collection of drawings of bird life, in 2004. And if you thought it was impossible to create a book of cat drawings that wasn't banal, think again. I did, and had to. *Cats as Cats Can* (1997) is a startlingly inventive series of cat drawings, displacing the previous champ, B. Kliban, and making Ungerer the preeminent cat drawer. The book is elevated by its stylistic and imaginative virtuosities working in harmony. There are a few beautifully realistic renditions of cats, but the book ranges all over the aesthetic landscape in terms of both style and media: modernist, minimalist, abstract, traditional gag drawings, visual puns, mixed media, found objects, pen and ink, watercolor – this little book is the dizzyingly bravura performance one has come to expect from the artist.

In 2015 and 2016 he published two illustrated prose books: *Besser nie als spät: Neue Gedanken und Notizen* (*Better Never Than Late: New Thoughts and Notes*), a collection of apothegms divided into chapters with titles like "Knowledge and Doubts," "Children and Adults," and "War and Peace"; and *Warum bin ich nicht du?: Philosophische Fragen von Kindern Beantwortet von Tomi Ungerer* (*Why Am I Not You?: Philosophical Questions of Children Answered by Tomi Ungerer*), a compilation of columns that ran in the German *Philosophie Magazine* in which he answered questions from children.

This is, mind you, an incomplete summary of Tomi Ungerer's publishing career – those works that I discovered and considered, by either reading or inference, the most significant. I'm sure I missed many that deserve comment. But there is also more to Ungerer's creative output than his books. He is a sculptor, who also creates three-dimensional

67 STRASBOURG ROBERTSAU
1.12. 96
B. RHIN

T.UNGERER

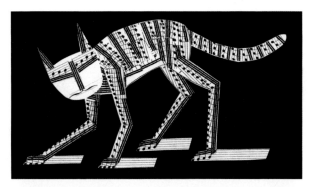

ABOVE: The *Kindergarten Die Katze*, designed by Tomi Ungerer and architect Ayla-Suzan Yöndel and constructed in 2011.

objects using, according to his website, found objects, repurposed farm implements and material such as wood, rust and Barbie dolls. He designed, with the architect Ayla-Suzan Yöndel, the building in Wolfartsweier Village near Karlsruhe, Baden-Wuerttemberg, Germany in the shape of a cat, where the mouth below a whisker-lined nose is the door, the eyes are windows and the belly of the beast serves as classrooms. The cat's tail is a slide that children can play on. His website lists over 120 public exhibitions between 1960 and the present. Two documentaries have been produced about his life and art: *Far Out Isn't Far Enough: The Tomi Ungerer Story*, directed by Brad Bernstein, and *Tomi Ungerer vs. America*, directed by Tania Rakhmanova. (Of the two, *Far Out Isn't Far Enough* is the one to see). He's received numerous awards – perhaps the source of ironic satisfaction to a perennial outsider like Ungerer – among them, the Jacob Burckhardt Prize, awarded by the Goethe Foundation; and the Commandeur de l'Ordre National du Mérite and Commandeur de la Légion d'honneur, both given to him by France.

Ungerer is one of the most internationally renowned artists and cartoonists alive, as well as one of the most prolific, yet he's virtually unknown in America, where he initially made his name and reputation, even among cartoonists and the cognoscenti consisting of comics critics, amateur scholars and academics. He was instrumental in shifting children's books to a more challenging and literary level.

"No one, I daresay, was as original," said Maurice Sendak. "Tomi influenced everybody. We helped change the scene in America so children were dealt with like the little animals we know they are."

Ungerer's satirical drawings and political art is among the most incendiary ever conceived. He should serve as an inspiration to all cartoonists (indeed, to all artists working in any of the visual and literary media) of any age. At 87, he is still furiously creating art, though mortality is clearly on his mind, at least on occasion. "My address book is like a cemetery," he said in 2017, "and soon it will be my turn."

I HAD WANTED TO INTERVIEW Tomi Ungerer ever since I saw his *Underground Sketchbook*. It was such a singular work of the visual, the existential and the polemical – not infrequently in a single drawing – that I casually tracked down a few more of his books. I was never disappointed. But I didn't know just how vast his creative output was until I began seriously researching his career for this interview. I wanted to talk to him in person at least for the first interview, but because he lives in Ireland and still maintains a full workload, it was difficult to coordinate our schedules. Fortuitously, the Kilkenny Animated, a festival of animation, cartooning, illustration and performance, was scheduled for the weekend of February 23 last year, and the festival organizers invited me to interview Tomi on stage after a showing of his documentary *Far Out Isn't Far Enough*. I happily accepted. It was the perfect opportunity to meet Tomi, put my research to good use and get at least one interview under my belt. (I got two.) I'd like to thank Paul Young and Naoise Nunn at Kilkenny Animated for inviting me.

This interview was conducted in three sessions and stitched together: in person February 24 and 25, 2018, and over the phone in May 2018.

The best thing about both documentaries is Tomi, talking. In person, he was exactly as he was in those documentaries. He radiates both warmth and neuroses, the latter mitigated by a resigned self-awareness and a wicked sense of humor that has clearly served him well throughout his life. The warmth is accompanied by a guilelessness, an honesty, and an unfettered irreverence. He is voluble and his conversation tends to careen all over the place.

I cannot attest to the accuracy of his memory when it comes to his life and experience, but his memory of artists and writers, especially those he admires, is astounding. One of the highlights of our conversation, in my opinion, was talking about American literary figures and jazz musicians. Physically, Tomi walks slowly with a cane, but he is also, oxymoronically, loose-limbed and animated. I am grateful that he agreed to spend as much time with me as he did and hope I have upheld my part of the bargain. My thanks, too, to his daughter, Aria, and her partner, Herman Baily, for helping to make this happen and for being so hospitable and helpful in Kilkenny.

Gary Groth
August 2018

BELOW: Ungerer in his studio, 2018.

ABOVE: Ungerer in his studio, 2018.

Childhood: Mother, Father, Nazi Occupation

GARY GROTH: My dilemma interviewing you is that your career is so vast.

TOMI UNGERER: And I'm not very candid. I don't know who I am.

My job is to find out who you are. It seems to me that so much of your art has been shaped by your living under the Nazi occupation and your early childhood experiences where you learned how to acquire courage.

Survival.

You admired your father, even though…

I was forced to admire him.

He was a big influence.

I did a book on my father called *Once Upon My Father*. I did a lot of research with my brother and sisters. They took half the stuff out.

Why did they do that?

Because it was so negative. Nobody's perfect. But for them, he was perfect. My older brother and sisters knew my father and adored him and worshiped him. My mother worshiped him. I was brought up in father worship. Everybody was telling me all the time, "Oh, those were wonderful days with your father. All was beautiful," and all of that. I found this huge trunk with every letter my mother wrote. I made a copy of the letters she wrote and the replies. Everything was recorded and I discovered some very unsavory things, like the dirty laundry in every family. And the thing is that at first I was marked by having no father. OK, that's all right, that's one thing. But then I was the youngest, and all my mother's love came down just like a Jewish mother.

Smothering.

Yeah, it was a love slaughter. I had to fight on every level. I was just born different. I think you can only explain that by the fact that I was a born rebel. As a child, I couldn't stand any social injustice.

Was it living under the Nazi occupation that made you a rebel?

No, it was even before that. Before that was even worse. The Nazis saved me. Because I had to go to the local school. My mother just dumped me. You read my book, [*Tomi: A Childhood*] *Under the Nazis*?

Yeah.

You read through all this Protestant shit and all that stuff. I think I was a born rebel. And my mother was actually already a born rebel in her own way, so it's not that it came out of nowhere. But for me, there were already, at an early stage, some moral standards by which I would abide the rest of my life, which were not the moral standards I found in my family and in my mother.

Can you elaborate on what you found disconcerting about your familial morality?
I can tell you an example. One day, we were on the bus – it's not in my book – and an elderly woman came in and I got up to give my seat to her. And my mother wanted me to stay in my seat because this was a

lower-class woman. We were very poor, but bourgeois poor.

Your mother was very class conscious.

Incredibly. There's a word for it in my language, which we call *gratl* in Alsatian. Totally class conscious. Class-conscious and religious – all the Catholics went to Hell. I was brought up and educated with hate. Hatred of the neighbors, hatred of the Germans, hatred of the Catholics, it was nothing but hate, hate, hate. And I do believe I was born a man of peace, I really was. I've always wanted peace.

I even carried it on at the Ministère de la Culture. I had this plan. I had this whole commission to commission children's books to teach children respect of [people without] money, respect of all these different things, and we had the whole thing going on. I did my book, *Making Friends*. But I was like that. I was completely appalled by this Protestant hypocrisy.

How old were you, do you think, when you attained the consciousness to rebel against that?

Well, when I was 6 years old, I dutifully went on my knees before I went to bed to sleep and I prayed to God. And there was never any response, so I said, "Come on, Jesus!" [*Laughter.*] And my uncle was an evangelist. I was brought up with this and I just discarded it. And the whole thing was just … I had been a big Protestant, I had the confirmation. I don't know … What were you brought up as?

Catholic.

Catholic. Well, we had confirmation. We didn't have first communion, but confirmation. Confirmation was at 14 years old. It was after the War and it's where you take the bread and the body for the first time. And I realized–I said, "No, I don't believe in God, I'm not taking it," and instead I was lined up with all the other kids and I walked out of

ABOVE: Young Tomi and mother, 1935.

church. But I got my presents anyway. And I walked out of church because I considered it a hypocrisy to take … Already, then, I called it spiritual cannibalism. But why should I take the bread and the body of the you-know-what-I-mean if I didn't believe in it? That was that. Out.

How did your mother react to that?

Oh, she was very open-minded.

She was?

Oh, yeah. I mean, even with [the publication of] *Fornicon* and all that. She always said, "An artist and a writer can do anything he wants." Oh, she was very open-minded on those things. About sex, not so much. Everything that had to deal with sex was dirty.

She was somewhat puritanical about sexual matters?

No, my mother was an open-minded individual. I don't remember her ever taking us to the Protestant church. But she had other problems. After my father's death, there was like a pendulum, you know? And Pastor Wolf came. Even the Protestants do exorcism too. I was there, and I still have the document that she signed having been exorcised from the devil. She was possessed by the pendulum. Even asleep, she couldn't get rid of her pendulum. Out of the bed, she had a pendulum all the time to get in contact with my father.

She was superstitious.

Oh, very. She was superstitious, yeah. Like the Protestants, there was one Catholic saint that she absolutely loved. And with good reason too. I have the greatest respect for St. Francis of Assisi. I have the prayer of St. Francis of Assisi in my pocket. It's the most beautiful moral document there is.

But you see it as a secular moral document, right?

It's like, "Oh Lord, make me an instrument of your peace." I always have it on me. It's not as a superstition because it's the most beautiful … I wouldn't say, "Oh Lord," I would just say, "Make me an instrument of your peace."

Fear and Anxiety, Physical and Psychic

One thing, very important: I was born a very sickly child. At 2 or 3, I was not allowed to run because of my heart. I had a heart

failure. And what they called rheumatic fever. My poor mother took the opportunity to baby me, and she used my sicknesses to keep me home. And I fought it very early. I remember we didn't have hot water, but we had a bathtub, and I used to fill the bathtub with cold water and take cold baths to become tough. But then I didn't learn swimming – because I had the chicken breast, because it was a fashion when I was a baby, my mother replaced my milk with orange juice. I didn't have the lime. No, the …

Calcium?

Yeah, not the lime, excuse me. [*Laughs.*] They talk about Lyme disease, it's completely different. I didn't have the calcium for my bones. I had a breast like a boat. And that's flattened over the years. My oldest memories were earaches. All my life has been like that. I had the most incredible accident, and my mother called me "*drôle de corps,*" "strange body." And I'm writing right now a book making fun of all the diseases, accidents, like the Chernobyl accident – all hilarious, absolutely.

Well, you fight despair with humor, I think.

[*Laughs.*] Yeah.

Perhaps all great satirists do.

I'm still terribly sickly. I'm sick most of the time. I have something wrong.

Well, in a lot of the photos I've seen of you and some of the film clips I've seen of you, you look robust.

I never look sick and I never have fever, strangely. But just lately, the whole last year, five months with a tooth infection and then finally microsurgery from above. They operated. I was released in September, then after that I had a purulent sinus infection. I had a mouth full of puss.

Jesus.

I just now had a lung infection. I'm just getting out of that one. And a lot of other things. When you have all these problems, you become self-conscious and a lot of it becomes psychological. That's the trick my mother played on me.

At some point, though, it seems you became quite robust as a young man. In photos I've seen of you, of film clips.

In a way, yes, but I still had all kinds of inflammation. Like I was saying, diverticulitis is something that old people get, but I had my first one at 37. I've had five of them and been taken with ambulances, and now I've found what's wrong.

> " I wouldn't say, "Oh Lord," I would just say, "Make me an instrument of your peace." "

What was that you had?

Diverticulitis. It's like appendicitis. It ends up with peritonitis. And then it was too late when I found out that it was the black grains and buns that opium … What do you call them? I'm sorry. Not the moon flower. The little black grains. They don't get digested.

Poppy seeds.
But your life in Nova Scotia was incredibly hard, physically.

Oh, yeah, very tough.

But you did it.

Yeah, but did you see all the accidents I had? Nobody would believe that story, but my wife witnessed it. We had chickens and there was a fox. So, I ran after the fox, picked up a stone while running, threw it at the fox. It hit him in the head and he fell dead. But on the way, running through bushes, I cut my eye. Which is very painful, to have your cornea cut – just to say. [*Laughs.*]

RIGHT: From *Symptomatics*, 1982.

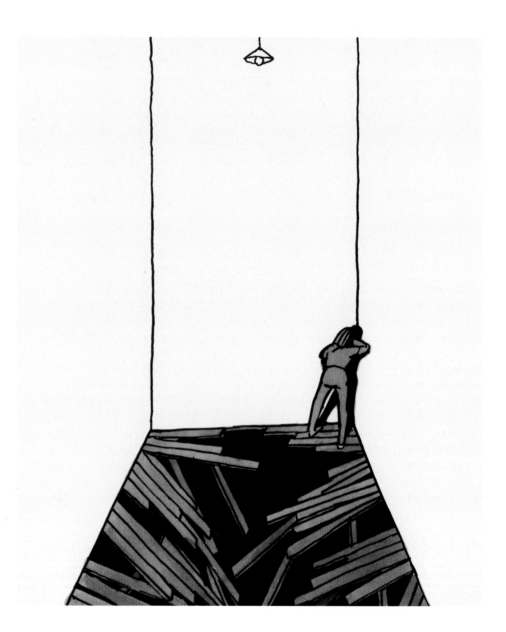

It required a tremendous amount of endurance ...

Look at what I just said. If you saw the burn that I got 10 days ago ... I lost my balance and I fell and there was a hot stove and my hand fell on the hot stove.

Well, that could happen to anyone.

You keep on trucking, you just keep on going. But I hate pain, I hate pain. I can't stand pain any more. I don't want any of it any more.

You're talking about physical pain?

Yeah. Oh, mental pain is much worse.

You make a great distinction between fear and anxiety.

Oh, you spotted that one?

Yes. You said that fear does not compare to anxiety. Anxiety is something much deeper because it sticks to you all the time.

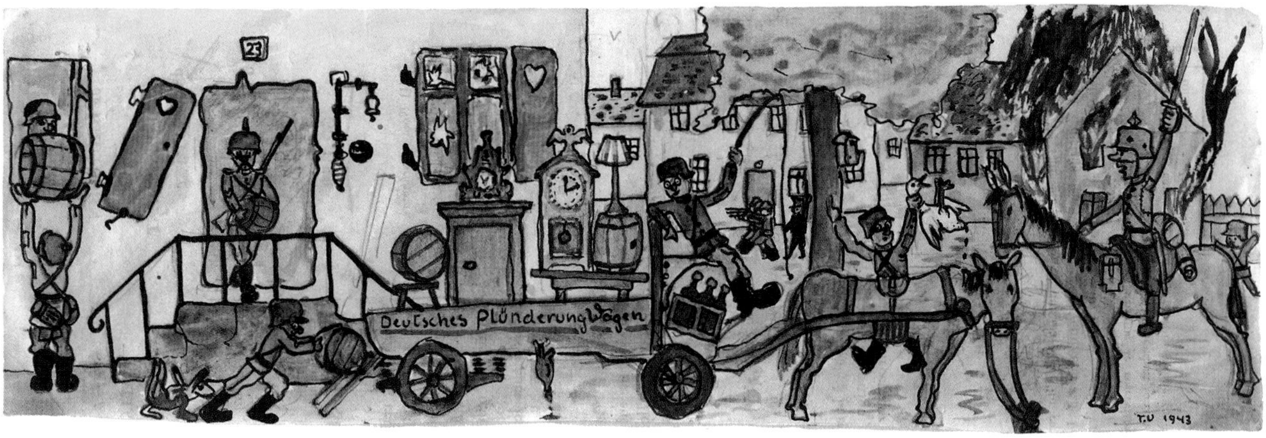
Deutsches Plünderung Wagen
T.U 1943

ABOVE: "My Hansi-inspired imaginary scene of the Germans sacking Alsace. The actual plundering was much more discreet."

Yeah, anxiety is something underlying. It goes back to childhood.

And you told me you were full of anxiety.

Yes, and in my family, there's a great tendency for depression as well. My mother had seven years of depression and she was liberated from her depression by my birth. I already have a tendency for depression and thanks be to God I have my work. This is why my work is so important because it gives an outlet to my anxiety and my anguishes. The Germans have this wonderful word used in psychiatry, which is "angst."

Oh, yes, your work is full of angst.

Sure. I don't think I would have done all my work and all this in my life if it hadn't been just an outlet. My work is my sanatorium. My wife said if I didn't have my work I would have ended up in a madhouse. And she's right. [*Groth laughs.*] Everything that's negative in me, I've turned into my work. My tremendous insecurity, my angers, all that. And through my work I was able, years and years ago, to get rid of hatred. I can dislike something strongly but not hate.

Do you think it was worth it having so much angst and being such a great artist?

Then I wouldn't be what I am if I hadn't had that. I can give you something. Under the Nazis, for instance, if you had to go to the Gestapo, that was courage. You just faced it. But you feared being arrested all the time. But we had a radio and we were listening to Radio London. And right across the street there was a post saying if you had a radio you would be arrested as a spy and shot. Each time you listened to the radio you are courageous by doing so. But you have anxiety of being arrested for it and then thrown to a concentration camp. This is the difference between the fear and the courage and the angst.

Sexual Liberation

You had a great conflict with your mother.

Yeah. Later on. Very heavy.

What was the basis of that conflict? That stuck with you –

Over love. Over love.
She smothered you.

Yeah, she bothered and smothered me, exactly.

Do you think that affected your perception of women and relationships throughout your life?

Oh, definitely. I'm a misogynist, basically. And actually, I would say that freedom from women is in masturbation because there you can do everything. [*Laughter.*]

Without judgment.

Yeah, absolutely. It is safe, there's no venereal disease.

But already very early, I couldn't understand. I mean, I never fell in love. I fell in love only once, when I met my wife. But otherwise, I was always straight with every woman I had a rapport with and, my God, how many? I always said excellent things, because I was straight. I'd say, "Listen. I'm interested in sex, I'm interested in eroticism," or whatever. It's really easy to get a girl if you fall in love and all of that sweet shit and mellow crap and all that stuff. But it was never my game. I never used hypocrisy, never faked anything. It was always straightforward. The only problem is that women fall in love. And when we don't fall in love, I'm very sorry … because it's asking for suffering.

> " The women and men I depicted in my work were always the kind of women and men I did not like. "

You said you never wanted to fall in love. Or you never expected to.

No, I couldn't understand how idiotic my friends were. "Oh, I met this girl. La da da." [*More mocking noises.*]

[Referring to the #MeToo movement]: That's why I'm so happy right now to see that all those pigs that for all these years have been panting like dogs in heat after women and whistling at their tits and all that. A woman couldn't work for him if she couldn't get through the fucking bit and all that stuff. And especially with the Americans or the Italians, when a girl was oh [*whistles*] and all that stuff, that was never my game. I'm so happy now to see that at last women are being respected. I always

thought this was so totally disgusting. Basically, that's why I'm Protestant. Things have to be orderly and ethically right. I have my morals. And there are words that I don't like to use. A word like C-U-N-T, I think that's a disgusting word the way it's used, and I wouldn't use it. In my Malparti book, there's not even a word like "shit." Nowhere do I ever use words like that. I say "defecation," I will even say "pudding" instead. And everybody knows what I'm talking about, but I'm not using the word "fuck," I'm not using the word "shit." It's gratuitous. And nowadays, everything is replaced.

I always looked for a woman as an equal, as a friend, and to have a good time. And then carrying it through and the whole thing. But later on in life, because I'm a slow learner, whenever I'd meet a person, I'd say, "What are your fantasies?" I was interested in a woman's fantasies. And I'd say, "OK, I will stage them." And I tell you … there are some things I cannot talk about.

Did you succeed in finding a lot of women who were open to that kind of honesty?

Well, absolutely, since I had my needs. Always, I'd say, "Well, whatever."

You just referred to yourself rather blithely as a misogynist and you've said this in other interviews too, but I'd like to know what you mean by that.

Well, first you have to see what my mother was. She was over-loving me. And for some reason that I happen to know that I wouldn't mention, at the age of 5-and-a-half she got rid of me and sent me to stay with my uncle, who was an evangelist. It was horrible and traumatic to be over-loved on one side and then to be thrown away. And that has really, in a way, made me a misogynist. But don't forget that I'm a satirist. And I must say that the women and men I depicted in my work were always the kind of women and men I did not like. This gives the impression of being a misogynist. Which I basically am, in a way. But then again, I'm a misogynist with much more respect for the kind of women I like. And I told you already, from very young I always liked girls who were free. And that's maybe what I liked about the American Fulbright students, they were more free. It's always with girls like these that I went hitchhiking and all that. But already then when I was young I was engaged with women's rights and abortion. I remember there was one young student who got pregnant and I collected money so she could have an abortion in Switzerland. And I did that already at the age of 19. If there was one thing I couldn't stand it was especially the girls who are pretty who behaved like bimbos or played up their beauty. And then especially the American mean, crushing wife – I did my best drawing about those bitches.

It seems to me that your attitude towards women is more nuanced than one of misogyny.

Oh yeah, I wouldn't call myself a misogynist because misogynist would comprise all women. I would be automatically against all women, and that's not at all my case. I have the greatest respect for women and the idea that they should be paid the same and all those things … even when I was in Hamburg and I lived in the bordello I tried to have them be able to make their leather outfits tax deductible. They should be recognized as a profession as long as they don't work for pimps.

So, you don't hate women.

No, there's nothing to do with that.

But that's what the term means and is an especially inflammatory one now.

No, and this is why I said I'm not. But as I said as a satirist … I mean, if you take a book like *The Party*, the men are just as ugly

BELOW: From *The Party,* 1966.

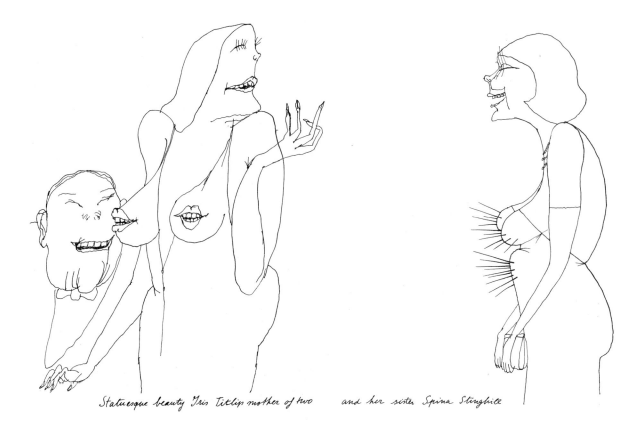

Statuesque beauty Iris Titlip mother of two   and her sister Spina Stinghill

as the women. They're just of a certain class of people that revolts me. That's all.

I'd say you're an equal opportunity satirist.

I'm an accuser. I just show the defects in society. In *Babylon*, I made a list of all the problems of society. *Babylon* is like a lexicon of all the evils, from drugs to everything.

How early did you start drawing erotica? *Fornicon* came out in 1970.

My whole erotic world started in the '60s, actually. Because, as I say, I was a slow learner. When I was young, you couldn't find a girl, you couldn't find anyone.

"By opening the freedom, it's the end of eroticism. This is the end.

And that would have been while you were in New York [1956–1971]?

No, even before New York, with [fellow] students or whatever. It was terribly frustrating in the olden days just to find anyone. I've never been able to play the game of fake love or anything. I'm a straight guy.

When you described this woman coming to your studio, saying …

She was a young girl, she was 18 or 19.

Was that a moment of liberation for you?

Oh, no. You see, when you ask about a woman's or person's fantasies, it means you can play out your fantasies too. It's give and take. Whenever I'd meet somebody whose sexual dreams or fantasies I'd be ready to do, she'd be bound to do my fantasies. And I have some, too, but they develop very slowly. With this girl, I realized that I really liked to tie somebody up. And if I hadn't had this understanding, there would have been no sense for me to go and live with the dominatrixes of Hamburg [a commissioned

reportage for *Stern* magazine and later for the book *Schutzengel der Hölle*] if I didn't know what it was all about. In my fantasies, I like to be the master. But the fantasies can change too. I will adapt to anything. It's a game, it's a game. And it's a freedom, that's all. And now, this big, huge volume came out, *Erotocscope*, by Taschen. Have you seen it?

I haven't been able to get that yet.

Oh man, it's unfindable now. But when this book came out, and I was doing a lot of signings, there were hundreds of people. There were lines of people, and there were more women than men. That's when I knew that I won the battle. My God, if I can have as many women buying my erotica as men, that means that the battle is over. But then it's the end of eroticism too. Because if it's not forbidden, if it's all in the open, if it's all natural, then what are you gonna do with it? Something is only erotic when it's forbidden.

It loses something.

Yeah, exactly. But in *Erotoscope* I wrote a piece for every chapter. And it was barely translated, I don't really remember. But anyway, that was really a case in point. And I think, really, I've been such a staunch defender of eroticism. By opening the freedom, it's the end of eroticism. This is the end.

But, do you think that that fight is ever over? Do you think it's more of a pendulum that keeps swinging back and forth?

I think it's a pendulum. I see for instance with the younger generation, since everything is open and all the girls are available. It's so free now that there's no eroticism anymore. Because nothing is forbidden. In a way we gain on freedom and we lose on eroticism.

Well, *Fornicon* was not really erotic.

Not at all. It's a clinical book. And people like Gloria Steinem really understood that this was a book for the feminists. It's a book which is – well, all those books like [*The Joy of*] *Frogs*, my erotic frog book. This was a satire on all the books telling you how to do it. Which was an invasion in America in those days. Which was understandable. But those books were directed towards the mechanization of sex which, again, I was ahead of my time.

You've consistently advocated for sexual freedom.

Right from the beginning. All my life. All I wanted was a girlfriend who I could befriend and who I could have sex with, with pleasure, on a free, equal basis. Which is what I did, when I was hitchhiking with girls and all that. I always advocated sexual freedom. There's that big, huge volume by Taschen called *Erotoscope*. It's a huge compound of all my erotic books. And when this came out and I was signing, sometimes there were more women with this book than men. I thought the battle was won. Because I've always believed that women should be able to have their own sexual fantasies. And that was always erotically my purpose with a woman, to find out what her fantasies were. And then to stage them. It's like this with my slave. Can you imagine this girl who comes to me and I said, "What would you like to do professionally?" And she said, "I read this book and I would like to be your slave." This is great courage to be able to say something like that. And that's what she became.

Skeptical of Romantic Love

You draw consistently harsh images about marriages, gender relationships, romance and one of the things you said was, "The worst thing that can happen in an affair is to fall in love because then you trip. I think it's better to have a level of friendship without sentimentality. It's about communion, sharing and daring and partaking in a common experience as long as you don't hurt anyone." I thought that that echoed the Ancient Greeks, who did not believe in romance; rather, they believed in friendship.

I wouldn't know about that. I'm a big lacuna with Greek and Latin writers.

They believed love was embodied in friendship; they had no concept of romantic love, indeed, would have rejected it.

It's absolutely that. Because the problem with that kind of love, there's the sense of possession. And the worst thing with love, what have you got? You've got jealousy. And is it worth incurring all this crap? The horrors of my life are all the women who fell in love with me. And I warned them, I said, "Don't fall in love. *Bitte keine liebe*, please no love." You say "falling in love." You trip! And this is what I drew in all those things. In a love affair, I always thought of the woman as a partner.

This is one of my favorite cartoons, "One More Marriage."

I did a painting of that in those days in the Waddell Gallery. A big painting of that subject.

It's such a simple cartoon, but it's so full of meaning. Is this your perception of what marriages are usually like?

Marriage is a completely other thing, you know. My first wife I married for my green card, and my second one I didn't know very well.

Your first marriage was with whom?

With Nancy Dennis.

And your second one was with Miriam.

Miriam, yeah. Nancy Dennis was a Fulbright student in Strasbourg at the time.

You also said, "Greater harmony is possible when you are wary of each other. If a relationship is based on distrust, then you know it's realistic. There's no danger of crushed ideals. The osmosis of distrust is really the secret of love." You said that in 1981. Do you still believe that?

That's a long time ago. I would say so, because you change your mind all the time. I always say I get rid of one prejudice to replace it for another one.

Do you think that it's inevitable that one prejudice is replaced with another?

Yeah, I guess so. We're all bound to have prejudices. That's why we have to fight them. This is where awareness comes in. We're all Jekyll and Hyde. And now we have to decide what we want in us and what we want to get rid of. But the demons will remain, like Goebbels said in his eight-volume diaries, "I have to go back to my demons." He was a good writer. I always said to my wife when we worked out her French, I said, "The best way to learn French is with [crime novelist] Simenon." And the other day at dinner, I said, "The best way to learn German would be with the diaries of Goebbels." Because that stuff is written so simply and clearly, in short sentences. And there was a Jewish lady at the table.

Uh-oh. [*Laughter.*]

Oh, my God. And I had to explain myself. I didn't mean to, but I can easily hurt feelings. Sometimes I mean it, but anyway.

Abstract Expressionists and Bullshit

What did you think of the Abstract Expressionists when they came in?

For me, the only way of judging a piece of work is what I have in writing on my wall. For me, they mean nothing. But I have an absolute adoration for Rothko. I think Rothko is absolutely ... It's all relative, you see.

You love Rothko?

Oh, yeah, and he's an Abstract Expressionist.

Yeah, he is. And you like his Abstract Expressionist work?

Oh, absolutely. Because it just hits my liking, that's all.

But not Jasper Johns?

BELOW: From *Adam and Eve*, 1976.

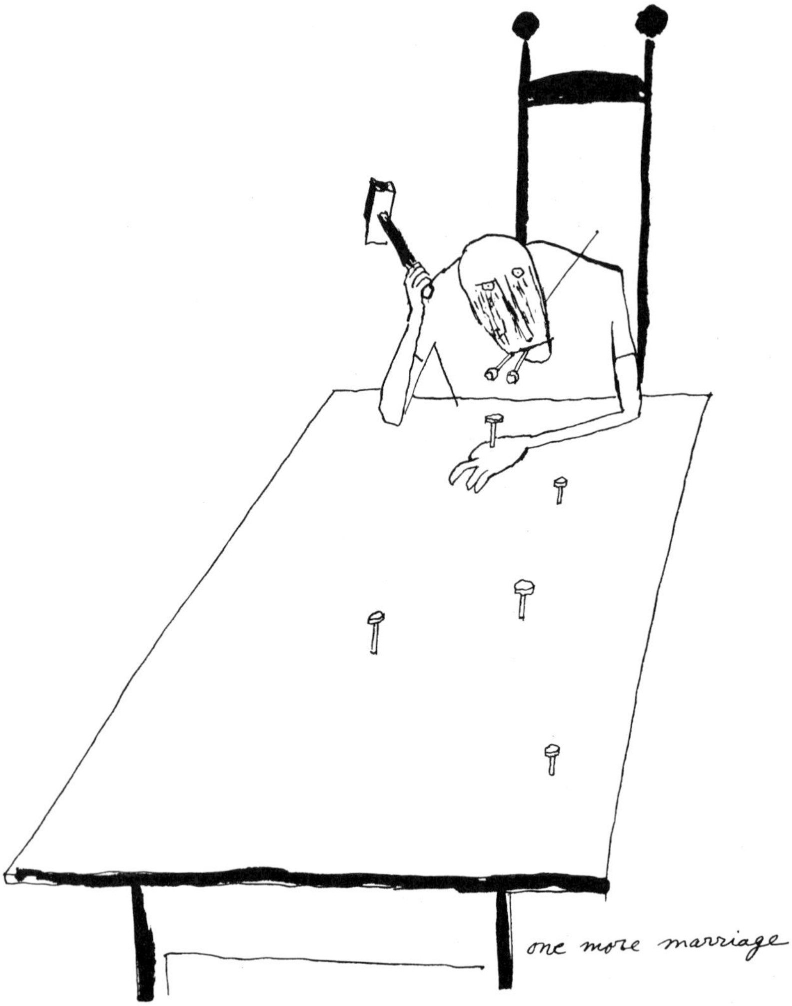
one more marriage

Oh, Jasper Johns I love. Here you're really hitting on the spot. He ended up being under the Pop Art label, which is completely unfair. Because Jasper Johns is Jasper Johns and Rothko is Rothko. And I never wanted to be classified in anything. I really unlabeled myself all my life. Even jumping from one thing to the other.

What do you think of Rauschenberg?

I think it's completely bullshit. Because I do a lot of objects and a lot of sculptures. I just had an exhibition in Kunsthaus in Zurich, which is one of the most fabulous art institutes. And the biggest German museum, too, after the same show of my collages and objects – I don't call them sculptures. But Rauschenberg is bullshit, excuse me. It doesn't mean that I'm putting him down. I'm just not qualified. I wouldn't judge. I would never go into reviewing books unless it's a book I like, because I don't believe in destroying somebody's career. Think of a writer who spends five years on a novel and then he gets panned. It's not fair. I wish everybody had a museum.

But wouldn't you agree that there's a lot of bad work out there?

Nowadays? Yes. I mean, I don't go to exhibitions. Either it's good and I feel, "What am I doing here, one painting is better than everything I've done all my life." And the rest is bullshit. What do you want me to say? All I can do is avoid it and just keep on doing my own thing.

Becoming a Children's Book Author, Rejecting Newspaper Strips

When you came to the United States in 1956 you brought a dummy of a children's book with you.

Yes.

Is that what you wanted to be specifically, a children's book author?

Yes, I wanted to be a children's book author. I had already taken this book to Munich to a publisher at the time and it was turned down. I have the original dummy, which was too cruel. It was Mellops, the same family, and they got into the hands of a butcher and it was quite cruel. But they got away, and finally the butcher ended in the meat grinder or something like that. Ursula Nordstrom saw the dummy and she liked the family and the characters. And she said, "Make another story about those characters." And that's what I did and that was my first book, *The Mellops Go Flying*. And I made a dummy of the airplane to see if it could fly and it actually does fly. And then the book came out and it was an honored book of the Spring Book Festival. My first book had won an award.

What was it about children's books that appealed to you so much that you wanted to do them?
Well, the fact that either you worked for magazines or you worked for books. And I always aimed for working for books, because books are lasting. A magazine is thrown away but a book remains. And I think it's my childishness. I would say that all the children's books I have done would have been books I would have liked to have myself as a child.

Were you familiar with American newspaper strips?

You mean comics?

Well, comics and newspaper strips like *Peanuts* and *Pogo* and *Krazy Kat*?

Oh, I loathe that. To this day, I loathe them all.

What do you dislike about them?

RIGHT: From *The Mellops Go Spelunking,* 1978

I met some of the authors, who were perfectly nice people, like the guy who did *Pogo* at the time, lovely man. But it is a form that … I only go for French comics, which are really artful. But the *Captain Valiant* [*Prince Valiant*] and all this, I always thought it was all hogwash, and just the sight of *Peanuts* absolutely makes me burp a little bit. I don't get it. I don't understand what people find in it. I mean, I never became that American.

> **Just the sight of *Peanuts* absolutely makes me burp a little bit.**

When you were in the States, you probably did not look at comic books.

No, not at all. I was not interested in that at all. And I never did. I was never a comic strip artist. Because one thing is that I don't like balloons. Like in French comics, it's such good artwork but it's always spoiled with this balloon. Now there's one comic strip that I absolutely adore, which is *Little Nemo.* Some of the old ones. I think *Little Nemo* is *génial.* Absolutely, it's genius.

Winsor McCay.

There are a few exceptions.

New York in the '50s, Jazz and Racism

When you arrived in New York in 1956, you had a trunk full of drawings and you started making the rounds to publishers.

It was my old army trunk too. I joined the army, you know that.

Yes, I do.

I loved it, it was a great vacation. [*Groth laughs.*] No, I joined the army because I didn't want to go to Vietnam. The French were fighting in Vietnam and when you joined the army, you could choose your regiment. I chose the Camel Corps, because I figured they'll never use camels in Indochina. That was before the troubles in Algeria, ironically.

You were introducing yourself to the publishing world and I think you met Maurice Sendak in the '50s.

Oh, yeah, yeah.

You never met Saul Steinberg. But he was a big influence on you.

Oh, the biggest, by all means, on everybody of my generation. And Steinberg was a genius, because he was able to put a philosophical concept in a drawing.

o are the other artists that you met?

A lot of them, and I'm still in contact with whoever is still alive. I'm still in very close contact with Jules Feiffer, Bob Blechman. Very good friend. Very good friend. Paul Davis, among others. And then [Shel] Silverstein. I told Silverstein, "You should do children's books," because he was writing songs for children. That was not that close, not that close. But there was one guy who I consider still one of the best *dessinateurs* of the century. That was Bob Weaver. He was a masochist. I absolutely wanted to have his books published. He had wonderful sketchbooks. Look, here's a story: I took him to a publisher and he came with a big portfolio only with one drawing to make fun. And the irony: he became blind, macular degeneration.

Thomas Allen was another. He was more an illustrator. Thomas Allen was really bluegrass, he came from the South. It's through him I got all my contacts with certain bluegrass players. He did wonderful portraits of Jimmy Rushing.

I always found that—let's use the word cartoonists, people who draw in humor, in the humorous vein—I never felt any sense of jealousy among cartoonists and illustrators. And everybody, whenever there was a new magazine, we would immediately say, "Gee, you should go and see this art director and find out what's happening." And I would say this of the French cartoonists and the American cartoonists and German cartoonists, English cartoonists, Ronald Searle and all those people. No sense of jealousy. Really of camaraderie and of mutual respect. And I found this in another profession: Among cooks. In France, the cooks are in contact with each other all the time. They invite each other to meet at one another's restaurants, they partake the recipes and all that stuff.

You found a real sense of camaraderie and community among cartoonists.

Yes, absolutely, just having fun and playing stupid games like spoons. I remember Bob Weaver and I were in a wheelchair at home. He used to sit and play the spastic.

How did you meet Feiffer?

I met Jules Feiffer much later. I actually really met him when he visited me in Nova Scotia. No, I'd met him before, but we were not like meeting weekly.

In a brownstone where I lived in New York, my neighbor next door was Bob Dylan and his daughter used to play with my American daughter that I had with Miriam. But I never tried to meet him or anything. I don't like Bob Dylan. I think he's a good poet, but I don't know.

You don't like his music?

It's all right, it's fine. Maybe he used too many people, you know? He did some downright lifting. I mean, I'm talking really stealing from other musicians in jazz. People wouldn't know because they don't, but I could tell. And I never lifted from somebody else. To be influenced is one thing.

Can you give me a sense of what it was like when you were getting started?

America was not at all what I expected. I thought it'd be like Switzerland or something like that. It was completely overboard. I went to America because of the jazz and the blues. And I was laughed at. It was "race music."

Wasn't New York full of jazz at that time?

Nothing. You couldn't even buy it. There was just the x label by RCA [10 inch records] if you wanted to buy it. There was one shop in New York called The Record Changer where you could exchange records. That's where I met LeRoi Jones [who now goes by Amiri Baraka]. We worked a lot together.

Jimmy Yancey for me is one of the greatest geniuses. I was just doing a film on my jazz records and I came back, I said, "Geez, that's great. Look, I found my old Jimmy

Yanceys." But they're all broken. Precious records, 78s.

Have you ever heard of Lightnin' Hopkins?

Yeah, of course.

Well, I brought him to New York. I organized the concert for him in New York. We were in a small room and there were about 12 people. Nobody. He had the biggest feet and yellow shoes, my God.

> " My biggest shock when I came to America is to realize the racism. I've never gotten over it. "

Wait a minute, you arranged a concert by Lightnin' Hopkins?

Yeah, with a few other friends. You never do things alone.

How did you do that?

Well, I contacted him. I'd met him before.

And this would have been in the early '60s?

Yeah, yeah.

OK, so who were your jazz idols when you got to New York? Who were you listening to? Coltrane?

A lot of people. Some of them are geniuses in jazz. You have to go back. You see, Miles Davis was a genius. So was Jimi Hendrix. Miles Davis was a genius. But there would be no Miles Davis if before you hadn't had Bubber Miley with Duke Ellington and *Black and Tan Fantasy*, for instance. And you wouldn't have had Bubber Miley if you hadn't had Tommy Ladnier. I'm sounding a bit pretentious.

No, you're not. You're just talking about great artists you admire.

Yeah. I would definitely put Jimmy Yancey as one of the great inspirers. You know he played at the age of 12 before the First World War to the Queen of England? And then he came and he got a job in Chicago as a night watchman at the baseball stadium and he just stayed at home. He would occasionally go out and play in the pubs over in Chicago. And everybody came to him to learn. But his sound remains, absolutely. I would say Jimmy Yancey is one of the most forgotten geniuses, though I wouldn't call him a genius necessarily. But absolutely unique. I mean, you hear three chords and you know it's Jimmy Yancey. Very sad. It's urban. You see, the blues originally was country, and then very early I got into bluegrass. I bought my first Johnny Cash record in '59. They were old 45s. My first Johnny Cash in '59: "Don't take your guns to town, son/don't take your guns to town." Then I got really heavily into bluegrass, western, all that stuff.

Did you like Elvis?

No, but I was a blues man.

How about Art Tatum?

Oh, he's good, very good. I saw him in concert. I've never met him. He's not the greatest, but he's solid good.

Then I branched out with modern jazz like you were just talking, like Mingus, all those people. It's absolutely brilliant, absolutely brilliant.

But New York was a disappointment when it came to jazz.

Oh, in those days there was nothing. No, no, there was only The Blue Note Bar where you could get it. I went there. That's where I met ... I used to have some of them come to my place in Long Island, like J.C. Higginbotham.

My biggest shock when I came to America is to realize the racism. I've never gotten over it. I never have. And when I think the Americans fought the fascists, and here they are. Don't forget my first passport wife, Nancy, was a Fulbright student. Her husband was sheriff of Amarillo, Texas.

And that was even worse, wasn't it?

Oh, I went down there the first Christmas. I went down with my first money down there and there were real sheriffs! That's why I have so many sheriffs in my books. Well, I had bad experiences with them too. Arrested. It was a beard! I was refused a drink.

In fact, the racism was so systemic and oppressive that musicians like Sidney Bechet preferred to leave America and go to France.

Oh, yeah, absolutely. He was running a laundry in San Francisco, Big Bill Broonzy. I was brought up before I knew all the words: "If you're white, you're right. If you're brown, stick around. But if you're black, oh, get back, get back, get back." "John Turner's been here and gone" and all those things. My whole youth was blues and jazz.

How were you introduced to blues and jazz? How did you get into those forms?

That just came about after the War. That was just what was playing.

Working with Your Hands

I'm a big diary reader. You're gonna laugh, but three years ago my son just gave me this huge thing, the first diaries in English, in the 16th century? The burning of London and all that. He's fantastic.

Samuel Pepys? Does this fuel your own work?

Yeah, because I work by comparison. This is why I read so many biographies of other artists, of other writers, because actually one compares oneself. And I've realized that what makes me different from all the other artists and all the writers is that I work with my hands. I do all my furnishings, I have my workshop, I've been a farmer. My God, I was on a farm with 600 sheep. Building the fences, building roads, building all that stuff. I mean, some of the things I would never do again because I made the wrong electrical installation and fell from a ladder. It was awful. I could have been killed. I was installing a rod in a high ceiling like this and then the end of the rod actually melted in my hand and I fell off the ladder. All these accidents, but I always tried everything.

Do you derive satisfaction from working with your hands?

Definitely.

Where does that need come from?

I would say it developed. Already when I was littler, I used whatever tools were around. I'm very mechanical. I made a lot of inventions, even in eating. For instance, if I cut the camembert, I cut it always lengthwise, but not going through the middle. So When you put it back in the box, it balances and the cream stays in it. I cut it in slices like that, and then when I put it back in the box, it balances and the cream doesn't run out. And then if I have camembert with bread, if I have a baguette, I cut one side like this and the other side like this. Every piece is long and has a crust. Nothing but tricks like this. My own cooking is nothing but trickery. When I do lamb chops, I cut off the tail of the lamb and I fry them with a lot of garlic in a separate pan. And then in the oil, you put your chops, which can be then rare, because you cannot have chops rare. But then you have too much grease, and all those things. I love to cook and all my cooking is strictly practical. I'm essentially practical. I'm not a real intellectual.

Well, I don't know if that's true.

I don't understand philosophy. I mean, I have a doctor *honoris causa* in philosophy. I had one page in *Philosophie* magazine, I had one page every month. I was answering children's letters with their problems. Mostly about death and all that.

I don't know if you understand philosophy or not, but you write philosophically.

Well, I cannot understand Descartes or Kant or Hegel or all that stuff. I don't understand what the black hole is. I mean, I'm limited in my intelligence. It's practical. As I said, there's a brain at the ends of my fingers. When I work, I can feel my work. And what I just told you about culinary secrets, those are just tricks that I develop, which is inventiveness.

You do write philosophically, though.

Oh, I do. Definitely. I know that because it's what I do every day. You know, since I had my diverticulitis, I have a joint every night before I go to bed. And this is when I write. I do all my writing in the evening.

And I said to [my daughter] Aria and my wife that what I'm really leaving behind is my writing. And my wife really thinks the same. My wife – who is originally American – she really believes in my writing. She says, "Look, I'm unique." Well, whatever. I'm quaint, you see. Since I speak Old German, Old French and all, I'm bound to. Sometimes my English is nearly a bit Victorian on the side, but that's my style. I don't give a shit, I don't care. But I still need a good corrector and a good editor, that's for sure. And a good editor for me is one who knows which spelling error should be kept, which is done intentionally because I'm dyslexic, you see, and for some reason it sits right. Another editor would correct me systematically, but in *Philosophie* magazine I had a wonderful editor who knew exactly which one was misspelled because it was misspelled for that one reason.

Praising Barney Rosset

Your first children's book was published in 1957. And then in 1958 you published *Horrible*, right?

Well, before that, yes, and then with Grove Press. My marriage book is being reissued in Germany now.

you summon your friends as witnesses.

RIGHT: From *Inside Marriage,* 1960.

Yeah, *Inside Marriage.*

Yeah, right. I was already with Grove Press then in those days.

Did you work with Barney Rosset?

Yes, definitely. I would consider him the greatest, most daring American publisher. And he died last year, I was very sorry about that. How he brought Jean Genet and all those people. And he fought in every state in America, he fought for the rights to publish books. He must've spent a fortune just in lawsuits. Most courageous American publisher I can think of.

I just have to tell you a joke I played on Barney Rosset. Barney was very much into tennis and he had a tennis court in his place in Long Island. And he organized mini tournaments. A nephew of mine came from France and he was ranked like 22 on the French tennis team. And I just said, "Oh, I have this French nephew coming who's staying with me and he's pretty good at tennis. Would you mind organizing a little tournament?" So he got the best amateur tennis players around there and when they had the match nothing went beyond the first two. [*Laughter.*] And everybody was so mad at me. I didn't tell them that he was the champion, you see.

You hustled him! That's very good.

Yeah, I could fill volumes with my little jokes.

Rosset spent a fortune fighting for the First Amendment freedom of the artist. Nabokov was another author that Rosset championed.

Oh, Nabokov, that's another story altogether. Thanks to Nabokov, you know, when I was in Long Island it was always a big competition on the beach for the Sunday crossword puzzles. And it was pure luck that I just had read *Pale Fire* by Nabokov. I had learned the first line of Nabokov's *Pale Fire* [reciting it from memory]: "I was the shadow of the waxwing slain / upon the false azure of the window pane." And I remember that line, that line was going across the Sunday crossword puzzle. And I was the first one to solve it. Me, this little Frenchie that everybody was putting down for flying kites. It was certainly one of the sweetest and greatest victories in my life.

You might have been the only one.

I was the only one on the beach, because I just had happened to read Nabokov. Nabokov is a phenomenon. Like Joseph

Conrad, a foreigner who just imbibed the English language. The same way I do, actually. I can really relate to people like Nabokov because I myself write in English in my own style. I love to write in English. And in quite quaint ways sometimes, with Victorian or gothic twists. So I can really identify with writers like that.

I think your knowing three languages fluently informs your writing in English.

Yeah, and sometimes you have the other way around. Like we were talking about [Paul] Auster, who actually should be a French writer translated in English, but he writes in English in a French way. And I think we were talking about E.E. Cummings, right? My favorite poet. I haven't got many ties in poetry in the English language. It just doesn't click with me. I'm so much into German and English poetry, with the exception of E.E. Cummings. I always think of E.E. Cummings as a French writer.

How did you acquire your catholic interest in reading?

Well, I always read, read, read. And in Strasbourg when I was young there was still those American cultural centers, where they had Sears Roebuck catalogs, *Esquire* magazine and books and all that. And the thing that really triggered me were the Fulbright students in Strasbourg. They introduced me to certain authors, and I remember in those days the two big sensations were Truman Capote and Salinger. *The Catcher in the Rye* and the short stories. I was introduced to all that stuff through American students. I read what they read. And that really opened me up to American literature. I don't say English literature, I say *American* literature. It was very well said that American literature finds its roots in journalism. That's my theory.

Did you like [Tom Wolfe's] *The Painted Word*?

Did I read that one? I don't know. He did so many. I'm rereading him now. [My daughter's boyfriend] Herman is the one who put me on to him again after all those years. And he's totally brilliant, totally brilliant. And his novels, too. I mean, really, this is America. His novels are back to Steinbeck and *Elmer Gantry* and all of the great American tradition. *The Bonfire of the Vanities*. *Incroyable*! This is America! But as I said, I met a lot of famous people. I mean, some people I regret that I didn't keep in contact with, like with Tom Wolfe. I think in terms of American journalism and writing Tom Wolfe was a revolution. And Tom Wolfe could have been only American. And he could draw well! Drew very well.

Speaking of America, did you like John Dos Passos?

Very much. *U.S.A.* has been a great influence on me. A very great influence. I mean, *Manhattan Transfer*, but *U.S.A.* was really *avant-gardiste*. He was ahead of his time. I wonder if there hadn't been [John] Dos Passos, if there would be any Tom Wolfe.

How would a novel like that influence you? Take *U.S.A.* How would you incorporate that into your sensibility?

It is just like the art of the news. It's just like turning on the television and reading the news. But the way he did it, and how he injected his own things in it. And, of course, his opinions. He was leftist. But that is very wise to tie up Tom Wolfe too. I never thought about the succession thing.

Did you like the Beats? Like Kerouac?

No. I think Kerouac was a terrible writer, a terrible writer. I don't remember reading much of him. But Capote, I mean, when you think of the movie *Beat the Devil*, Truman Capote just pasted this movie together with Humphrey Bogart and Peter Lorre. And there is Truman Capote just writing things.

LEFT: From *Rigor Mortis,* 1983.

Every day he was writing the movie as they were shooting the movie.

And this is absolutely brilliant. I mean, come on. I've never read a bad sentence by Truman Capote. Now, excuse me. I'm a stickler on style. It can be far out, surrealistic or anything, but I'm a stickler on style. And one page of Kerouac, you can take this whole thing and tell me one page, show me one page that you could read aloud. Not in my opinion. It's not that I'm putting him down, but it's not my ...

Well, Truman Capote famously said that Kerouac wasn't a writer, he was a typist.

That's excellent. That's about it.

Style is all-important for you.

Yeah, for me in people's work. And the discipline, you know? If you take Dos Passos or even Tom Wolfe, an incredible discipline. When he starts adding all those adjectives and all those words, this is done nearly scientifically. I would say that Tom Wolfe is really a reporting scientist. The choice of words and the vocabulary, it's always the right word at the right place. For this, you need discipline. This is my thing, you know? The sentence and the words. It's got to be the right word at the right place.

Is style so important because it's through style that you interpret the world?

That's a difficult question. I don't know. Does the world have a style? I essentially consider myself as very un-American. I could be arrested for this in America, for being a humanist. I'm a humanist, I'm definitely a humanist.

Yeah, you would definitely go to jail for being a humanist. [*Laughter.*]

Yeah. I'm a humanist, which is open-minded.

How do you reconcile the humanism with the absolutely vicious portraits that you draw in your satirical work?

In my satire? Well, this is absolutely because I think it's humanism's duty to be accusatory. It's pointing your finger, and not only pointing with your finger, but using it to shove it up somebody's ass or touch some wound. And my God, when you look at the time of humanism, it starts with Dante Alighieri and all of them. Look at the trouble they got in because they were pointing out all the evils in society. The church and all that in nuanced ways. Humanism is somebody who perceives *la condition humaine*, the human condition. But how can it congeal and conglomerate in one piece of accusing work? I accuse, but I don't judge, and that's humanist. The humanist doesn't judge.

That's an interesting distinction.

He accuses, but doesn't judge. It just came out. You accuse, but you don't judge.

See, I'm not sure you can accuse without judging.

No, no, I think you can. Really, I'm free. And this is what I like in life, where there's this complete freedom and yet this discipline.

It amazes me that you can be as disciplined as you obviously are and have done so many things. I mean, your life must have been chaotic … I look at your work in the '60s and '70s and '80s, and you were doing a million things. You were doing advertising, you were doing various commercial work, you were doing your own personal work, you were doing satire, you were doing children's books …

A little of everything. And more afterwards, because then I got involved in European politics. Not long ago, on New Year's morning, I was all over the French news. Because I

already have the Légion d'Honneur, but usually you have to first be a knight, an officer and then commandeur. And over there Macron just made me commandeur of the Légion d'Honneur. And I'm already commandeur of the French National Merit and commandeur of the Ordre des Arts et des d'Lettres. I'm actually the most decorated person in France. Well, there might be others, but not as an artist. And that's because of the amount of work I did in the Ministry of Culture. Well, I was always well surrounded too. We don't do everything alone.

But still, you must have been a whirling dervish of activity.

Right. I made a lawsuit with the French government for us Alsatians to have the right to teach German and Alsatian in primary schools. I made it with my association for bilingualism.

You sued the French government?

Yeah. At that time, my boss, Jack Lang, was minister of education. He said, "Tomi, use your lawsuit and I'll pass your law," and he passed my law.

What year was this?

It was way back, 20 years ago.

Jocye, Flaubert, Gide, Goebbels

What writers have inspired you?

I've always had more friends in the literary field than in the artistic field. I mean, with literature I've been obsessional. You'd say of me that I'm very well read. In American or English literature, as well in French, and in German. And I can read Old French from the Middle Ages, Old English and Old German. Old German is very simple because Alsatian is like the German that was spoken in the 16th century. The thing with literature is, you'll have to ask me who were the greatest influences in English because in French you wouldn't know them and hardly in German either. I've been always very much into marginal literature too. I've been a great fan of William Burroughs, for instance. But then I'm very old fashioned.

I assume you're familiar with Flann O'Brien? He seems like a writer you would like.

Oh, yeah. Definitely, definitely. You see, the Irish, from Beckett to definitely James Joyce. For me, the most important novel in this last century was James Joyce's *Ulysses*. Oh, no doubt. And *Finnegans Wake*, since I speak French, German and English, you see. But I will not read the book all the way through. I can open it anywhere and just delight in three pages, and then I'm exhausted. So, you can ask which other books I read more than three times. Because in French, that would be *Madame Bovary*, but there is Malcolm Lowry's *Under the Volcano*. I consider this one of the greatest novels in English.

An entire novel about his being in a state of drunkenness.

But one should read his letters at the same time. It's just like *Ulysses*, you should read the James Joyce letters. My favorite reading is actually correspondence, biographies, autobiographies, history and then exchange of letters, correspondences. And then, of course, diaries. I just reread all of Gide's diaries. And I just reread all of the eight volumes of *The Goebbels's Diaries*. He was a good writer.
Huh.

Only when he talked about women did he make himself ridiculous. But all his diaries were recovered in leaden boxes. And if you want to understand hatred, you have to read that. Right from the beginning. He said, already at the beginning, "I have to go back to my demons." Unbelievable. I'm fascinated by a lot of mechanisms, like the mechanisms of hatred. Like where hatred comes from. And then the frustrations. But this is a whole other chapter. This is why I was very, very pleased when you brought up the thing of fear and anxiety.

But you actually read eight volumes of Goebbels?

Oh, yeah. I just did. And I just read all the diaries of Thomas Mann too. Ridiculous. I mean, I found only one important sentence in the six volumes of diaries of Thomas Mann [*Groth laughs.*], which I read for the second time. And I found that wonderful sentence that said, "I took my poodle for a walk. He fell in the swimming pool. He had to be saved." [*Laughter.*]

That was the most profound thing in Mann's diaries?

> "And this is what I like in life, where there's this complete freedom and yet this discipline."

Fucking profound shit. But I think I'm sometimes a pure masochist. I'm fascinated by those two guys [Gide and Mann] because they're homosexuals and Protestants. Now, I haven't got the slightest tendency for homosexuality whatsoever. And I've always been totally open-minded, I couldn't give a shit about somebody's sexuality, you can understand that. But then, to be Protestant too? These poor bastards are looking for spiritual redemption, and they can't find it and they're tortured. They're super intelligent and their language is perfect. Gide's French is perfect and Thomas Mann's German is absolutely the best German you could possibly read.

I never could take much of English poetry, for some reason. For me, poetry is French or German. But in English, there's one big exception. The one poet I like is E.E. Cummings. E.E. Cummings is totally

75

TOMI UNGERER

brilliant. But he's French. He spent so many years in a French concentration camp, as you know. He wrote a book about that. I think E.E. Cummings was a French-thinking English poet. There are other ones too. Like T.S. Eliot, of course, who I greatly admire.

You said you couldn't take much of English poetry. How about Dickinson?

Yes, Emily Dickinson. That would be all right, but it doesn't really stir me.

And Frost?

Oh, yeah. He's very admirable, very pleasant. It's easy reading. Frost is all right. I have the greatest admiration for American literature, and I know why: because some of my favorite American writers – Ambrose Bierce, even Hemingway in his beginnings – were all reporters. Most of the American writers worked for the press. From Poe to Twain, all those people had experiences in reporting. And this brought them into reality. Hemingway started writing for *The Toronto Star* before the First World War. And I'm really getting into some people which I'm very sorry are not read any more, like Sinclair Lewis. When you read *Babbitt* or Steinbeck, it's absolutely brilliant. But then you had this whole navel-picking Jewish school, New York Jewish school, that started really undermining this kind of writing. I shared a house with Philip Roth for a while.

He wrote an introduction to your sketchbook, didn't he?

Yeah, for *The Underground Sketchbook*, and they wouldn't print it because they said he's not known.

What was the occasion when you shared a house with him? How did that come about?

Because in a magazine, the Jewish literary magazine, I read one of the first stories of

Goodbye, Columbus. And I thought it was so great I wrote him a fan letter. That's how we met.

And that would've been in the late '50s. When would you have lived with him?

Just look at *The Underground Sketchbook*.

I think *The Underground Sketchbook* was '64.

Yeah, so I was with Philip Roth in '62.
Goodbye, Columbus is absolutely brilliant. Totally brilliant.

Did you like his subsequent work?

Well, while we were together, we rented a summer house in Amergansett, Long Island, and he was working on a book. He was very much taken by Tolstoy in those days and it was a bad influence on him. And he wrote a book called *Letting Go*, which was really not a good book. But then he redeemed himself with *Portnoy's Complaint*. I thought that was good. That was really up my alley. But then, he over-Jewed himself. [*Groth laughs.*] Excuse me, I'm sorry. Like Saul Bellow, Bernard Malamud, all these people. One of my great friends was Brian Moore, the Irish writer who lived in Canada. And then a lot of German ones, like Max Frisch and Friedrich Dürrenmatt, who wrote the preface for *Babylon*.

Speaking of *The Underground Sketchbook*, could you tell me how its publication came about? It's an unusual book to publish in 1964 … or perhaps any time.

Well, I was just making drawings in sketchbooks and a friend of mine, Bill Cole, who was a great friend and really the specialist on what they call American cartoonists – and I hate that word – but he became editor at Viking [Books] and he decided to do a book out of my sketches. And I was staying with Philip Roth in those days, and Philip Roth wrote a preface to *The Underground*

ABOVE: From *The Underground Sketchbook*, 1964.

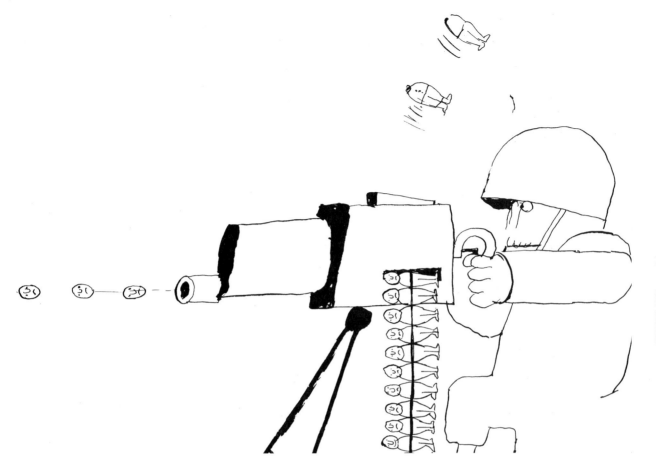

Sketchbook. And when they showed the preface to Viking they said, "Oh, this guy's unknown, we need somebody with a name." They took Jonathan Miller, not realizing who Philip was. And that was my first book of statement, in a way.

Getting back to your literary interests, how about Isaac Bashevis Singer? Did you like him?

Yeah, yeah. I'm on the European Council and one of my love affairs is Yiddish. And I organized a whole week of Yiddish in the European Council. They came from all over the world. Even the editor of *Forwarts*, a Yiddish publication in New York, came. It was Yiddish because Yiddish comes from Alsatian. Don't forget that I come from Alsace. In Alsace, you must not forget one thing: we were French. Through the French Revolution, we were French. And the French were the first ones to make statistics. And 80 percent of the Jews living in France were living in Alsace. I gave a speech once in the synagogue in Strasbourg. I said, "Listen, Alsace has been sold to the French. Alsace has been sold to the Germans. We should have been selling it to the Jews, it would have stayed in the family." In Alsatian, I would say one-fourth of the great Alsatian reporters and writers were Jewish.

Right. But you weren't fond of the Jewish-American writers of this era?

Yes! Oh, no, I love reading Saul Bellow. It's not that I'm putting them down. If you're interested in this kind of navel-picking, it's pretty good. I'm open to all that. It doesn't mean that they are out. It's not that. But America is a country that automatically

follows fashions. For a while, it was all Abstract Expressionists. Hopper was completely forgotten in all that. And then it became Pop Art. Shit, man, I don't belong to any school. As long as I can make my statements. Sometimes I wonder if I'm an artist at all. Am I just a recorder? In *Babylon* I set out to put all the evils of our modern society. Just everything. From drugs to pollution and then the German *Schwarzbuch* was on ecology. That book got the prize of the best political book of the year in Germany. But my life is completely crazy! Can you imagine in Germany once I was on the list of the hundred most popular Germans? Being one of the most popular Germans, when I'm actually a Frenchman.

> " What am I? I should have just picked up one style and developed it. "

Did you read Kurt Vonnegut?

Didn't like him, no. Look here, this is a matter of taste. I'm not condemning him. I try sometimes a lot of those writers, and I have changed my mind over a number of years, but Vonnegut never registered. At all, at all, at all. And neither did Kerouac. I think Kerouac was a bad writer. I was always heavy on style. And I like the right words. Two people who were popular in those days, Vonnegut and Kerouac, I never went for. I didn't consider them good writers at all.

How about Norman Mailer, who must've loomed large in New York at the time you lived there?

Completely went on my nerves, couldn't stand him. To this day. His first book about the War, that was a thing. But I think he tried too hard with much too much of an ego. I think his ego kept him from … he tried so hard to be a Jewish Hemingway.

Had you ever met him?

No, I wouldn't. You must understand my second wife was a party woman, that's why I met all those people. But once I was divorced, I never went to another party in my life, practically. Occasionally I would go to one but more with sabotage on my mind than anything. There are some people I wish had known better, like somebody that I admired. Someone I put absolutely on top of the journalistic thing is Tom Wolfe.

Speaking of style, there's a German author I wanted to ask you if you liked because he was such a strong stylist. His name is Ernst Jünger.

Oh, yeah, you mean about the First World War?

Yes, *Storm of Steel* and various other books.

Yeah, I think it's very good. I think it might be overrated but definitely very good. And what's interesting is that he was really a France lover during the War. For the First World War you had French people who were much better. Like Barbusse's *Le Feu* or Gabriel Chevallier's *Clochemerle*. He's part of a great tradition, but he was not major for me. I could speak with you about literature for hours. Because my passion is comparative literature. Have you read Céline?

Of course, of course.

For me, he's a major French writer of the last century.

Right. I assume you separate the writer from the work.

Oh, definitely. Because Louis-Ferdinand Céline, what he said about the Jews is … I tried to read my original edition of *Bagatelles pour un massacre*, and after three pages I felt like throwing up. And then when you read this whole correspondence that came out. In the First World War, he was a hero in the cavalry. And he had migraines all his life and I think hate came out of it. Hate became a disease.

When you were younger did you ever consider becoming a novelist?

I don't think so. I never did, because I could not have been a novelist without using things that happened to me and using other people. I'm able to write my Malparti short stories now but still – very rare is the novelist who invents his characters instead of just pulling them out of people they've met. You have the people who are traveling all of their lives just to meet people, to feed their novels. But the very few writers like Balzac really did invent their characters. I have nothing against it but I didn't want to … like Hemingway, in every novel people could find out who the characters were.

Short Stories by "Malparti"

I wish you could read French and German, because in German I have several volumes of aphorisms.

Really?

Yeah, and in French too. And some of my sentences are already used in the language in slogans or whatever. That's what I do, writing all the time. I'm preparing my book by "Malparti," my alter ego. And right now, I'm writing my short circuit stories. And my publisher started crying when he saw it.

I think you're as good a writer as you are an artist.

And I think with age now, I may be a better writer. I also have my notebooks, you see, but it's in three languages. In one of my last Malparti stories, he comes into a country where people have implants and there is a tax on orgasms. [*Groth laughs.*] So, the women pay an income tax and the men pay an outcome tax. The whole story is about all the things which are taxed. They need more and more money, so they start a tax for laughing because it's all

registered with the implant. These are my Malparti stories.

What's the word you're using?
Malparti is the name of my alter ego. *Mal*, in French, is …

Bad.

Bad, and *parti* is gone, so badly gone. And I even wrote, you won't remember when I wrote three theater plays in those days. And all these people were after me, "When are you gonna start your Malparti stories again?" And now I call them short-circuit stories. It's all written in English because I'm writing them in Ireland, you see. But some of them I wrote in French first, it's all in French and German.

Drawing is Writing

Do you prefer your writing to your drawing?

Yes. Definitely, by far. I've never been really satisfied with my drawing. It's always so scattered! I'm a jack of all trades. What am I? I should have just picked up one style and developed it. My drawing is all right. I know I'm known for that, but I would say I prefer my writing the last five or eight years.

You've talked about how there's no demarcation between your writing and your drawing.

No, there isn't. This is why I always tell to young people who are illustrating children's books, I always tell them, "Please, just write your own stories, or take a story which exists and rewrite it." All famous children's books which have remained have been written and illustrated by the same person. That's a fact.

Don't you think that when you're drawing, in a way you're also writing?

Yes, definitely. In German, *aufzeichnen* is taking notes and *zeichnen* is to draw. And so, I said, "OK, translate it in English, that's my answer." I draw what I write and I write what I draw.

That seems imperative.

When you see my sketches, I do a sketch in my sketchbook and then all the lines and the things. And when I write strange little aphorisms and stories, they're completely unrelated. I jump from one language to another, from one subject to the other. You would think, "This is impossible that this was written within the last five minutes." It's completely unrelated. I don't know where it's coming from, I've no idea. It just comes and hits me. Pop and voilà!

When you were putting together *The Party*, did you conceptualize that as a whole? Did you go into it thinking, "I'm going to make this book?"

No, I was in Long Island, in East Hampton, where I had this big villa. I was always well-advised by my Jewish friends. And in Long Island, they had a society magazine called *The Hamptons* where they relate about a party and all these rich bastards. I did some sabotage work. I'm an agent provocateur, you see. In Long Island there was this magazine, and I got hold of some of those issues and I saw those fucking things. These people at a party and so-and-so was there and so-and-so was there. So that inspired me and I said, "Fucking bastards." [*Groth laughs.*] And in those days, I was married to a woman, Miriam, who died three years ago. A fine woman, really. And she liked partying. But from the moment I divorced her, I never had another party. Never had another party ever. I hardly even went to a party again. I'm a loner, I'm a loner. I never joined a political party. No, I did politick once for Willy Brandt.

Yes, you did.

BELOW: From *The Party,* 1966.

Juge Willard goiterson from Dallas about to propose a toast to his old friend (Harvard 1915) Sen. Rockfester.

But that doesn't mean that I was a Democrat. I was always basically a socialist. But otherwise, I once joined the PEN [International] club for a while. I should have stayed, it was a good organization. But otherwise, I'm like my mother, my mother never joined anything.

Regarding *The Party*, what outraged you so much about that milieu?

Pure anger.

At what? Why were you so angry?

At those people, at their philosophy. I was at their parties. I knew how they behaved, I knew how they thought, the American way and all that stuff. Money, money, money – everything is money.

Superficiality.

And their star fucking. If they can have a famous artist or a famous something there, they love that. Oh, I took my revenge on a lot of them. One thing I did a lot of times, when I was in Long Island, I broke into these people's houses when they were not there and spent the night there. One night I went with my wife and I remember this big mansion. I'd been invited there, and there was a hose in the front of the garden, in front of the main door. It was 2 o'clock in the morning and I rang the bell and the light went on and finally the guy came down. Of course, he didn't recognize me in the dark and he opened the door and I had his own hose with the water jet directly in his face. [*Groth laughs.*] And then we scrammed. By the time the police came, everything was gone, the water was gone.

And you did things like that because you were so angry?

Yeah, it was straight out of my anger. I can tell it now. I don't care anymore. The things I would have gone to jail for, I'm not telling you. [*Groth laughs.*]

Well, you could, because the statute of limitations has run out. I think you had a huge house in the Hamptons.

A huge villa, yeah, one of those mansions. The irony was that I was in a house just like those!

Yes, right, that's what I was going to say.

And then, what did I have as a car?

A Bentley.

I got a second-hand Bentley!

You were driving your Bentley to and from this huge mansion. Now, was this a way of you saying, "Fuck you, I can afford – "

No, I would drive in the middle lane on the highway with my Bentley and a girlfriend of mine on her knees in the front seat with her behind flattened on the front window. And every car would just swerve around the line when they saw that. [*Groth laughs.*] I mean, I could have been arrested. The accidents, can you image the guy looking there who goes [*whistles*].

Right. But you're buying a Bentley, and a Bentley represents –

A second-hand Bentley, of course. Excuse me. I couldn't afford a real Bentley.

But you were doing very well, then.
I sold it for the same price to the mafia.

Is that right?

One of my neighbors in the '80s was a mafioso and had been arrested. And I was Mr. Tom, I was Mr. Tom.

And, you know, he had children. I used to go and play with his children, gave them children's books in exchange for watching my car; I could actually park my Bentley anywhere in New York. There was always somebody watching over it. I was watched

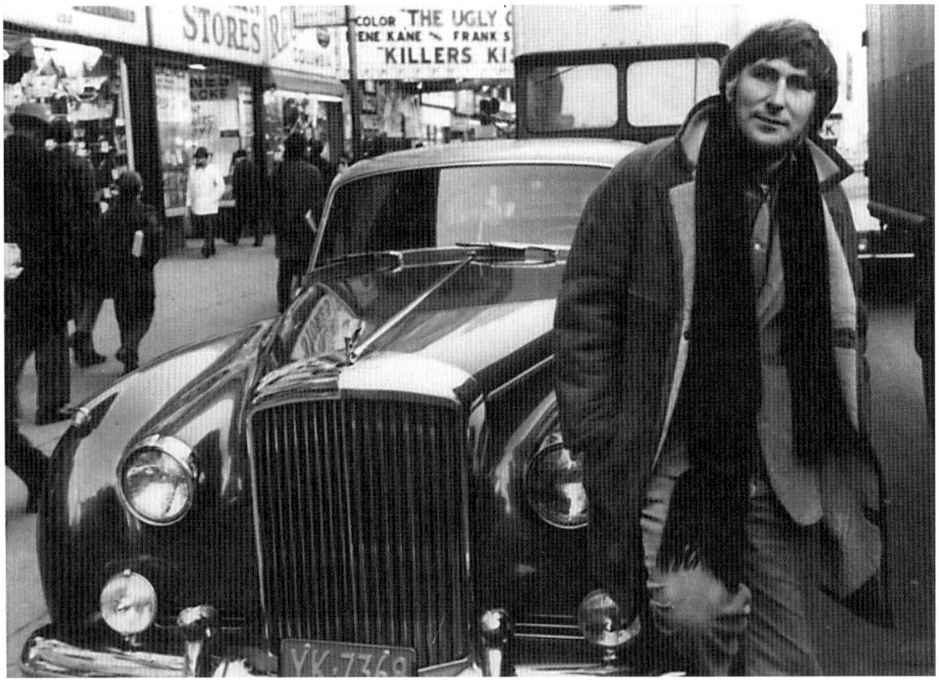
STORES
COLOR THE UGLY
KILLERS

RIGHT: Ungerer in New York City, 1969.

all over. And then one day, he says, "Hey, Mr. Tom. Everybody's got enemies, right? Everybody's got enemies. You've got enemies. We take care of everything. An arm, a leg, an eye: $250. Kill: $500."

You also had a Winchester that you would fire over the heads of partygoers.

Yeah, I took it to Canada. I had it when I came to Ireland. It had a high velocity.

That sounds a little dangerous.

Well, I mean, it was a gun. I remember, across the street, there was the son of Max Ernst, who was an artist too. But he was all chicky-nicky. And I had white columns like a southern mansion. And sometimes I had my sex slave tied on it and then when he had a party, I would be there in my rocking chair with my Winchester and just shoot a bullet over their heads. [*Laughs.*] Nobody complained! And then my neighbors up the way had a big, beautiful brass fish [statue] and I riddled it with bullets. I think I would have been the perfect anarchist. We have too much discipline. You know my triangle of life? It's very important. It took me years to do it. It's a triangle with variable angles and one is for discipline, one for enthusiasm and one for pragmatism. And if it's a rubber triangle under the pressure of goodwill, you get a pyramid. But not too much goodwill, because otherwise the rubber is gonna burst like an old condom.

Right.

I'm in another world right now. But I was sick. You see, the biggest frustration with age is the energy. Anyway, tomorrow morning I can show you my next book. My publisher cried. Not only cried, sobbed. Five people started crying.

I'm perfectly happy, for the first time in my life. I showed two Malparti stories to my son. He said, "Dad, that's a fucking best seller." I don't know.

You said that for the first time in your life, you're really happy?

With my work, yeah. No, I never was happy in my life.

You just said that you were happy for the first time in your life.

I've never been happy but I found some joy. You know, it's all relative. But in Ireland I found the place where I belong. But I felt that way in New York, too, when I arrived there. But Ireland gave me peace. I found the kind of society I can live in. I told you already it's the one society I know of where there's no arrogance and where you feel no difference between social classes. And there's a great sense of humor, this is what I like about Ireland. And in a way, with Ireland I found the place where I felt I belonged. Away from the whole Franco-German back and forth, and it's an island, too, you see.

I'm not sure I do know what you mean, because I'm not sure I found that place myself.

Well, anyways that's the way I feel. My wife and I both felt that way when we arrived in Ireland. You read my book about Canada and there was no way we would want to create a family there in such circumstances. And everybody, like my old friend Brian Moore, the novelist I was close to, was talking about Ireland. So we went here, we found this place, and we came back a few months later when Yvonne was eight months pregnant. We came with six suitcases just to be sure that our first child, Aria, would be born in Ireland. And that's been 45 years ago, so I've spent half my life in Ireland and I've never regretted it a minute.

Tomi, do you find joy in the act of creation? When you're literally drawing or writing, do you find joy?

Yes, I do find joy. It is more an elation. I'm elated when I work on a project and then the moment a book is printed I'm just overtaken with … I cannot spend my whole life correcting every drawing I've ever done. It's all relative. But my work is my refuge. As I

said, it's my sanatorium. I keep my sanity thanks to my work.

When you were in Nova Scotia, were you able to make much art? I mean, you must have been preoccupied by just surviving there.

No, no, it was not so bad. It was in a way. But I always had the discipline of working in the morning in the studio and the afternoon on the farm and cleaning woods and all that stuff. I had a lot of energy. And I did an incredible amount of work in Nova Scotia. I did my German *Liederbuch*, which was a best seller. And I did all those erotic drawings too. I did some of my best work in Canada. And I drew a lot about Canada. All the old houses and all that stuff.

Slow Agony.

Yeah.

Making Art, Loving Art: Influences and the Importance of Style

It sounds like you're culturally insatiable.

Insatiable, insatiable.

And you've always been like that.

It's a tyranny, it's a tyranny. My imagination is a tyranny. I cannot stop having ideas. Every day, all the time, I have my little cards, ideas for another book, for another story, and it's horrible because the moment I mention, let's say, *Under the Volcano* I feel like reading it again. And I feel like reading Sinclair Lewis again, I feel like reading Ambrose Bierce, all those incredible writers. I illustrated Ambrose Bierce in the German edition of the *Civil War Stories*.

You say it's a tyranny, but how else would you want to live?

Well, this is a wonderful tyranny. For me, paradise would be a library, and then at least I could remember. But now, with my age, I forget… The two last books I just read were *A History of the Inquisition* and *God's Bankers* about the Vatican finances phenomenon. I wish I could remember more.

I understand *God's Bankers* is very good.

It's unbelievable. It makes me puke.

Are you torn between experiencing culture and making it? Do you feel when you're reading something you should be drawing and when you're drawing you should be reading?

Oh, yeah, it's terrible. And still, everything you like is bound to bear influences on your work. But like Dürrenmatt said, "I'm influenced by everything but I don't copy anything."
   So, this is the whole thing. If you take *Babylon*, it was an exercise and an homage to Daumier. In the style, with the pencil.

You have no problem reading something or watching or looking at something and absorbing it and having it influencing you, but not copying it? You have no problem doing that?

BELOW: From *Babylon*, 1979.

No, no problem.

I ask because many artists will be influenced by something and you see the influence. It's obvious.

Yeah, not with me. Everybody originally compared me to George Grosz and then I finally decided I better look him up and find out.

You could be compared to George Grosz, but you're still your own …

Oh, definitely. We absolutely have the same element, and I've discovered that a lot of people I didn't know about that are exactly up the same road, we're just doing it in a different way. What would I be without influences? I'm very thankful. And my Malparti stories, I can tell you exactly who the influence is: Voltaire's short stories, *Candide* and *Zadig*. It's straight from there. You can tell that this book was influenced by this and that. So Voltaire is definitely behind that, and then of course you could add a bit of Ambrose Bierce and a bit of Oscar Wilde, too, in terms of wit. I love wit. The problem is that wit, like with Oscar Wilde, becomes automatic after a while. You can't help it, it just comes out. So what the hell? Why not?

Wilde was Irish.

Oh, yeah. Look here, you see everything that came out of Ireland from Bernard Shaw to Oscar and even nowadays, it's unbelievable. The talent's here in Ireland. I mean, when you consider it's got only four million inhabitants, you know? And culturally here, what happens in every little town in every little village, they've got some fucking festivals going on all the time. Literary, music, whatever. I've never seen anything like this. It's a craft scene, it's crafts.

I assume you love Beckett?

Yes, absolutely.

He shares your somewhat bleak view of humanity.

Yeah, well, Beckett's really a case in itself.

Even though he was influenced by Joyce, he was utterly original.

Yeah, he was his secretary.

One of the things you said was, "There's one thing I can tell you for sure: there's no such thing as a sheltering sky."

Oh, this is another great line.

Which is kind of Beckettian.

You know *The Sheltering Sky*, by Paul Bowles? Have you read his biographies?

Oh, yes.

One of the most beautiful biographies that you can possibly imagine.

It's also funny.

Oh, very funny. With his crazy wife, I mean, how did they live together? *Without Stopping* is his autobiography.

That's right, that's right. It's funny. He relates a hilarious anecdote about Gore Vidal and Truman Capote when they were all living in Morocco.

Yeah, in Morocco. Oh, my God! There's some excellent books on the subject of the time of Tangiers and Paul Bowles. Now I can't remember, especially in correspondences and all that. My mind is going. Why don't people read Capote anymore? I mean, one of his first books, *Other Voices, Other Rooms*, left tears in my eyes. This is total beauty.

Yeah, he was an exquisite writer. What did you think of Hunter Thompson?

Oh, I think he's good. He befriended my colleague that draws, Ralph Steadman.

You remind me a little of Ralph Steadman in the scope of your work.

Ralph Steadman was incredible. I kept all the originals from the first issue of *Rolling Stone*. I had them all bound for my wife.

Those images were printed nice and big in *Rolling Stone*.

I got into drinking once in Ireland with whiskey. But drugs and drinks, I don't need it with my mind. I don't know how they did it. And have you ever seen Ralph Steadman's book that he wrote about the trip?

Oh, yeah.

It's excellent! Excellent writing! Ralph Steadman is an excellent writer.

In fact, I reviewed that.

You reviewed it?

Yes, yes. I tried to review Steadman's whole career.

Oh, thank goodness.
   I'd say Ralph Steadman would be about the only artist in writing and drawing that's like me.

And he writes as well as he draws.

Oh, he does. His writing is good! Ralph Steadman, love him.

Do you know him?

Oh, yeah. I've met him several times. But now I can't travel any more.

You feel you just can't travel physically?

No, I can't any more. I can't travel without Aria, without my wife, Yvonne. The walking. I used to walk, walk, walk all over. Finished.

How irritating is that?

You have to accept it. I have my work. As long as I can work and think. In Germany I had an interview when I lost my eye there. And I said in my interview, "If I'm blind by the end of the year, or if I should be blind someday, I will still have modeling clay and masturbation." [*Laughter.*] They used it as a headline in the newspaper. There's no hypocrisy in France or Germany, and then I just say modeling clay. But the word for masturbation in German is lovely, *selbstbefriedigung*. It's self-satisfaction. It's not like when you say masturbation [in English], which sounds dirty. That's why my wife every morning asked me to wash my hands. [*Laughter.*]

Obession and Family

I'm obsessed with my work. Just so obsessed with my work.

How has your obsession with your work affected your marriage? You're able to balance the two?

It's been very hard on my wife, very hard. She complains about it.

She has to be used to it by now.

I don't think she got used to it. She had the children and the farm, you see. We had 600 sheep and 20 cows.

Being as obsessed with work as you are takes a toll on relationships.

Oh, absolutely. I was not really a good father. For me, the children were great to have some fun with, but I was not … I didn't have a father, so I didn't know how to be a father. And now I see my son holding the babies. I never held my babies in my arms and I didn't know how to do it. I was fearful of dropping them.

You were obsessed with what you did. But you seem very close to Aria.

Oh, yeah. To all my children, very much. No, it's not that I was a bad father. I was not a bad father. But I was …

The closeness came later, do you think?

I was not interested in babies, for one. So later on, it came. But no, I was always very close to the children. I was not really bad in that way. But I was away a lot for my work. You know, when you have a book, you have to do advertising. If you're not on the television, your book is not gonna sell. And you need interviews.

You've talked about how guilty you feel about a lot of things.

Oh, yeah, I feel it very heavily, this guilt. But you are what you are. I always work hard trying to change some things, because I believe in goodwill. That is the one thing. If I have two qualities, I believe in goodwill and I'm not much for grudges. So my two qualities are forgiveness and goodwill. I forgive very easily. I can just forget. Everybody makes mistakes. Everybody. Like what I said a while ago, I attack but I don't judge.

You accuse.

I accuse, but I don't condemn. Condemning is better than judging. It's the right word. I should have said, "but I don't condemn." Judging is something else, but condemning is more realistic.

Well, I can think of a few people who should be condemned. [*Laughs.*]

Well, some people. But then, other than condemning them, like Trump, you take them as entertainment. How could you bear

Trump if you didn't enjoy him as a piece of entertainment? It's abstract, it's completely beyond anything. It's like a Punch and Judy show. The level is so low. By the way, when I told Herman that Trump was gonna be elected, everybody laughed at me. But I know America, I know America. I'm talking about the bulldog American. You see, in France, in Europe, or in other countries, people will vote for somebody who's above, who's superior. But in America, they wanna vote for somebody who they can identify with. I remember when Eisenhower was against [Adlai] Stevenson. Stevenson was an egghead. He was too intelligent to be a president.

A pointy-headed intellectual.

Yeah, he was too intellectual. Now, in France, this would be a priority. The French want somebody who's more intelligent than they are, or at least with a certain degree of culture. Of course, all my friends and all the people in New England or wherever, they were all for Stevenson. But no, he was an egghead. So now, Trump was exactly what America deserved and then now they got it. And I'm sorry for the other 50 percent of Americans.

Right. We have to endure it.

But come on, only in America. [*Groth laughs.*] His English is so bad, it's unbelievable. Unbelievable!

Well, it's as bad as the Americans' English who voted for him.

Well, that is one thing, and then the other thing is I'm not that negative about America, either. I mean, I give the impression, but I tell you, if I've become successful in this life, it's thanks to what I learned in America. It's this incredible ability to just handle problems, you know? It is really the land of opportunity and there's a lot of great qualities as well. And those qualities vary with every state, of course.

I'm happy to be pretty negative about America. [*Laughs.*]

Yeah, well. [*Laughs.*]

The Consequences of Being Anti-Authoritarian

In 1969, you were in front of that American Library Association convention audience of librarians.

Was it that late? Because I met Yvonne in '70, one year later.

Yes, that's when it happened. That's when you have said you were confronted with your erotica.

It was a convention. The American Librarian Convention, which is in another town every year.

ABOVE: From *America*, 1974.

Do you remember what city the one you spoke at was in? Was that in New York?

Oh, that was in New York. I suffered a lot from that. The children's book editor from *The New York Times* refused to review my books because he said that somebody who's doing erotic books has no right to do children's books. Even when *Moon Man* came out and it was on *The New York Times* "Ten Best" from an independent jury, he refused to review the *Moon Man* in the children's book section. So it was reviewed in the adult's literature section.

I understand that you were speaking in front of an audience of librarians.

Oh yeah, hundreds and thousands maybe. All the librarians in America come for the convention. And this is very, very essential because that's where they decide what author they're gonna buy from.

Was it one librarian who attacked you, or more than one?

There was only one person. No, actually, it was not even a librarian who attacked me. It was a friend of Maurice Sendak. The guy was working for Harper, my publisher. He was a salesman, and he hated me. And I would get letters from bookshops saying, "Listen, I've been ordering your book from Diogenes and they've never been delivered." Harper wouldn't deliver them because that guy was sabotaging me. So I don't think it came from a librarian. But I cannot swear.

This guy didn't like you because of your erotic drawings or for other reasons?

I have no idea why. I don't know, because I'm basically a nice guy.

And he confronted you in front of all the librarians?

Yeah.

What I'm curious about is the mechanism by which you were blacklisted. How did that happen?

I have to tell you the whole story now. Go back to the year and find out when the goal was for the first Western state to recognize China and open an embassy in Red China.

That was about 1960.

I'm a French citizen, and I would have been one of the first reporters to go to Red China for *Newsweek* magazine. I pack my things and, like an innocent abroad, I arrived in Paris and waited – thanks be to God that it didn't arrive – for my visa for China. And then a telex came to the office of *Newsweek* magazine saying that if I went to China, I wouldn't be allowed back to the States. Then I thought, "Listen, I cannot risk my whole life. I have my belongings [in the U.S.], everything would be confiscated." So, I dropped it. And it was still the McCarthy era. It must have been in the early '60s, like '63 or '64. And so, I gave up my trip and I came back to New York. I had a while at the airport. The airport was not Kennedy yet, it was before Kennedy was [assassinated]. [New York International Airport, also called Idlewild Airport]. So I went through customs with no problems.

And in the hall of Kennedy Airport, there were three guys, all identical, like in the movies. One on my left, one on my right, and one behind me. And one says in my ear, one of my favorite sentences, "Drop your suitcases and follow us quietly." I drop my two suitcases and the guy behind took them, and then they grabbed me and whisked me off in the dark in a car and drove me to an empty room with strong lights. And I had to strip. They inspected all my clothes, they even opened up to check the soles of my shoes. And I was questioned for about an hour like I was a Communist spy, because the very idea of going to Red China meant I was a communist.

And after that, my telephone was tapped and my mail was opened. And they already knew that I was friends with Jack Gelber, who was a theater author. Him and the ambassador of Cuba. We were playing poker once a week, so that made me absolutely suspicious. And then, maybe it was my imagination, but I think I was followed a few times. But my mail was definitely opened and I could definitely tell the taps [were on the phone]. I would send myself fake coded messages. I always turned it into a joke. And then after that, when Kennedy got elected, the hassling stopped. But I remained in the black book in customs. After that, I couldn't travel with a sketchbook and an erotic drawing or anything. And if I left the United States, I had to let them know. They didn't want me, and that was really early in the '60s. I was literally blacklisted.

They put you in a car and drove you somewhere?

Yeah, but it's all very vague. I don't remember if they had me strip entirely or not.

What kind of questions did they ask you?

I forgot. With my memory, it's all gone.

But then they drove you back?

They didn't drive me back home. I guess I took a taxi after that. They just let me go, that's all.

Were you terrified?

I don't think so. I am my mother's son, you know.

Were you defiant? Did you feel defiant?

No. I got into terrible hassles with it later on, even with Yvonne and the three children. I had an A-I visa because I knew the American consul in Zurich. And because I was blacklisted still, we got stuck at customs for nearly half an hour, 40 minutes, with little children. I told them, "Come on, this is ridiculous." And then they found a can of Gerber baby food and they accused me of bringing vegetable matter into America. [*Groth laughs.*] And then they crossed out my visa and they said, "We'll let you stay three days in the States, then you get out of here."

And that would have been something like 10 years later when you lived in Nova Scotia?

Yeah, 10 years later, because Yvonne and I used to go back occasionally to New York to visit friends. Yvonne had family in Connecticut. It was a horrible day. I went to the Greyhound station. We had one day just to go to Connecticut and come back and leave from Boston. I was waiting in line, Yvonne was still waiting in line, and I came up and said, "I want to buy a Greyhound ticket for the family." And the guy said, "You're not American, are you?" And I said, "No, I'm French." He said, "I'm not selling no ticket to no Frenchman." And then somebody pushed me aside, I couldn't even buy a ticket.

Were you angry?

Yeah. But you better not, because you're gonna get into more trouble. I knew this from the olden days. I had to be like, "Howdy, stranger." Don't start something when it's already started.

When the deck is stacked against you.

Yeah. This is the story now. But I had wonderful stories about America too. Fixed up a whole brownstone. I would buy a house and fix it up. And I refused to deal with all the authorities and get a permit for building. I was just about finished when the doorbell rang.

Uh-oh.

And I knew. I said, "Are you the building inspector?" And he said, "Yes." He said, "What's going on around here?" I said, "Listen, I know you're looking for a bribe, you get out of here. I'm not paying any bribes to anyone." Within five days, I was in court. [*Groth laughs.*] I went there without a lawyer. There was the fire department, water department, electricity – they were all there. And there was a judge. And I attacked them. I said, "You see all those people? They're all crooks. That's why I didn't fight for a permit. You cannot get a building permit in New York City if you don't pay bribes, and I refuse to pay bribes."

> "When we had to go to the Gestapo, she dressed me up, took me along, and she said to me in French, "You'll see, they're all a bunch of idiots."

You said that to the judge?

Yeah. I attacked them before they even started.

How did the judge respond?

The judge said two things. She said, word for word, "This young man is just improving his neighborhood. I wish you a happy life in your new home." She said, "All you'll have to do is get an architect to draw the plans of how the building is actually now, and that's it. I wish you a happy life in your new home." And that was the last. It was done in 10 minutes.

You won that skirmish?

Yeah. With no lawyer. Had I come with a lawyer, it would have cost me money and it would have dragged. That's why I'm like my mother. My mother would have done the same. So I'm telling you that I met wonderful people in America. Unbelievable.

Well, there are wonderful people in America.

Everywhere you go, there are wonderful people. It is the systems which change.

Did you ever think of applying under the Freedom of Information Act to acquire your FBI file?

I don't know if it was the FBI. I was too foolish. I didn't ask them. I don't know. Because one of my friends tried to find out and he couldn't find anything. But I remember I was married to Miriam at the time, I was coming back from Paris. And Phoebe was born, the daughter I had from that marriage. I remember I was late and I told her the story. So it must have happened, for heaven's sake. But I don't know whether it was CIA or whatever. I don't know who they were.

Did you always feel under the gun? Do you know what I mean by that?

Yeah, I have an absolute persecution complex. How you call this … Not paranoia, but when you feel … You see, I've been arrested several times in my life, and I was not guilty. First, under the Nazis, at the Gestapo. Then the French came back and, strangely, the head of the police was the father of one of my French friends in class. And I was arrested in front of the whole classroom because I had walked by a building site and one of the workers had lost his wallet and I was accused of having stolen it. And it goes on like that.

You're saying you have a persecution complex. But if you're actually being persecuted, it's not paranoia.

No, there is a word. It's a phobia. Not claustrophobia, but I have that too.

You have claustrophobia?

Well, agoraphobia, with the crowds and people … I have a lot of phobias.

Do you think your phobias are a consequence of your anti-authoritarian inclinations and the difficulties that ensue from that stance?

Well, my mother was anti-authoritarian, so I inherited that. And I was brought up that way. When we had to go to the Gestapo, she dressed me up, took me along, and she said to me in French, "You'll see, they're all a bunch of idiots." And twinkling her eye like that. And they were. She wrapped them around [her finger] just like that. She knew exactly how to talk.

That was quite a risk.

Because to be clever is to survive. You have to be sly.

Do you consider yourself as sly as your mother?

Well, I'm clever and I can be sly when it comes to things. But I call this pragmatism. I think without pragmatism, there wouldn't be any peace.

But you also tend to attack things head on – rather unpragmatically.

Oh, absolutely. This is why I told you that story with the judge in New York. It's a big gamble. But I always played poker very carefully. I was the dullest player.

So, back to the American Library Association. Your publisher was still Harper.
Yeah, it still was, because when I was in America the last book I did with Ursula [Nordstrom] was *No Kiss for Mother*. And then I did *The Hat* with another publishing house. The one thing that Ursula Nordstrom never forgave me for is that I did *The Three Robbers*. She turned down *The Three Robbers*.

And why did she turn it down?

I never could figure out. So, *No Kiss for Mother* is the last book I did with Ursula.

That was 1975.

ABOVE: From *Symptomatics*, 1982.

Which means I did it in '72. By the time the book is printed and edited and all that. And then I did *The Hat* too. I had told Bob Weaver that a book could be written about anything. Bob then challenged me to write a book about a hat.

The Hat was 1970. Papa Snap was 1971.

That's my favorite book.

Let me get back to the ALA confrontation. What did Ursula Nordstrom make of that? Did she support you?

Oh, absolutely, 100 percent. She lived through the same anger with all those people. I remember I went once with her to a Chicago children's book convention and already there we were making jokes and said we should invite some of them to our hotel room and throw them out of the window and they would end up as jam down below. I remember that, we were laughing so hard at the idea of turning all those representatives of those children's books into a mush on the sidewalk. [*Laughter.*] She suffered maybe more than I did from all this attitude. Don't forget she was a lesbian as well, so you can understand.

Oh, I didn't know that. After that ALA confrontation, you think your publisher did support you?

Well, I was sabotaged within Harper, too, don't forget that. The general salesman there really hated my guts personally. I got letters from bookshops complaining that they ordered my books and they were never delivered by Harper. He even blocked the sales of books in shops.

Why did he hate you?

I don't know. He was an insecure guy. I remember him very well. He was a very good friend of Maurice Sendak. He was homosexual but I never had any problems with homosexuals. He just happened to have a dislike for me for no reason.

Did Nordstrom know this?

I don't know. It's quite a long time ago. I couldn't bother about this. I don't think I was a complainer, going around and complaining about so and so or whatever.

I noticed that your book *The Beast of Monsieur Racine* was published by Farrar, Straus and Giroux and not Harper.

Well, that was a horrible break with Ursula Nordstrom. One of the greatest men in my life in publishing, he spoke fluent French, he had been in the OSS in the Second World War, was Simon Michael Bessie from Harper. He had published about four Nobel Prize winners and then with a young Knopf he created [the imprint] Atheneum. And Atheneum put out *Horrible* [*An Account of the Sad Achievements of Progress*]. And then, strangely, Ursula Nordstrom turned down *The Three Robbers*.

One of your best books.

Then I went with *The Three Robbers* to Bessie and Atheneum, and he published that. And then after that I don't know what was wrong with *The Beast of Monsieur Racine*, most likely Ursula didn't like it. And she never forgave me. She never forgave me for having published with another publisher. But the last book I did with Ursula, and she was really on the ball with, was *No Kiss for Mother*.

Trusting Yourself

You moved to Ireland in 1976.

Around that time, we were in Canada and Yvonne was pregnant. And everybody was talking about Ireland for some reason, especially my friend Brian Moore, who had a house in Canada. I had close contact with him. And Yvonne and I wanted to get out. We didn't want the children to be born there, so we went to Ireland, and that's where we found the place we live in. It was pure hazard.

You said that in Ireland you needed to discover a new sense of measure. What did you mean by that?

A new sense of balance. Of orientation. I didn't have to worry about measuring my words, because in Ireland the greatest thing is to be genuine. And after the parish priest, the artist is as a gift of God.

You talk about your insecurities, your phobias, but moving from Nova Scotia to a country you'd never been to, that's a huge leap. I don't know if I could do that.

This is fate. I believe in listening to the signs. Like when we saw the property there, that was it. This place was waiting for us. I did a lot of buying and fixing houses and all that. But I never looked at a second house. I always bought the first house I found.

Because it felt right.

Because fate was sending it to me. This is superstition. I'm not a complete atheist. I don't believe in God, but I think everybody believes there are things made for them, by God or whatever. And that was absolutely that. It's drastic to just make this kind of decision. Like I said, I turn my corners and I keep them sharp.

But you did that with certainty. You just knew that was right.

Well, sure. [Before that] Yvonne and I went for a weekend to Canada, and that was the end of New York [1971]. We saw that place out there on that island, which is on the Canadian $50 bill, and we said, "That's it." We moved. With all the wood in the store, we had the mattress between the pile of wood. I sold my Bentley for what I paid for it to the mafia. And I bought a Land Rover, which is the worst car I ever had, and we moved to Canada. And that was that. We put the two cats in the car and then we just left.

To me, it's a huge act of courage to uproot yourself and move like this. Don't you think so?

I don't think it needs courage for that. It needs recklessness.

There's a fine line between courage and recklessness.

You get the message and off you go and off you do it.

What do you mean by message? It's not a higher power.

It's not a message, it's something you feel inside you. I have a lot of extra ESP, it's a big thing with me. My mother was like that. And don't forget that I lived in New York with a poltergeist. It was unbelievable. The noise and the racket and all that. In the morning, the television would be moved and things like that. So I have a lot of ESP. And remember, we're talking about instinct here. I use my instincts a lot.

And you trust them.

Well, not always. I might be wrong, but I use my instincts nearly all the time. And it's kind of a real drag. Like I can *feel* a town, this is a good town or this is a bad town. This is a good building, this is a bad building. Things like that.

Perfection vs. Soul

When you moved to Ireland you started doing some of your most incendiary satirical work.

I did already before.

Well, you just did a lot more.

I did *Babylon* in Canada.

> "Nowadays you have a lot of children's book illustrators and they're all realistic and perfect. Where's the soul, where's the clumsiness?"

Well, it was published in 1979, after you were living in Ireland.

Yeah, but I did it in Canada. I conceived the whole thing during the full moon, always on the full moon. That's how I conceived the whole book.

And then in 1982, you did *Symptomatics*.

Oh, yeah. That's when I started it. And then *Rigor Mortis*.

In 1983.

One thing you said about *Babylon* is this: "I think of this as a book of drawing writing. Technically, these drawings, which seem to have been thrown on the page, gave me a lot of trouble. Of the first drawing, for example, there exist 38 versions. In general, I prefer redoing a drawing than using an eraser to correct it."

Right, exactly. To get the right curve of the ass, you know. And all those drawings are not bad, but it was not satisfactory. I work on very cheap paper. I work on typewriter paper, on double-sheets, A3 [11.7" × 16.5"]. I just use regular type paper so I can throw it away.

So instead of correcting a drawing, you just do it over.

Yeah, I redo it. And it's very good for my practice for the line.

RIGHT: From
Symptomatics, 1982.

What is it about a drawing that you might not like? What is it you get wrong?

Like in *The Beast of Monsieur Racine*, for instance, their noses are much too big. And there are a lot of anatomical errors. I cannot stand anatomical errors, even in other painters.

And that's because you value draftsmanship.

Yeah, absolutely. But, nowadays you have a lot of children's book illustrators and they're all realistic and perfect. Where's the soul, where's the clumsiness? You look for perfection and then perfection is bland.

There's a paradox there?

Yeah, but I would say that most of the drawings in *Babylon* I wouldn't call excellent. I'm much more lenient on myself now. I try to improve my technique in drawing for all those years just to find out the first, early books, as clumsy as they were, had more charm. Since my museum opened, I can see my drawings as if they were done by somebody else, and I must say, some of them are good drawings. I think especially the drawings in *Rigor Mortis*. Oh, you haven't got the thing I did on Thomas Mann and *The Magic Mountain*, do you?

No, I don't.

Unfindable. That's my favorite book. It's called *Warteraum*.

You always had a keen sense of mortality.

Death is an obsession.

There's this drawing published in *Symptomatics*. You were relatively young when you drew this. It's especially prescient coming from someone who was young.

I don't know how young I was then. But I was, already, if you look at the drawings in *Underground Sketchbook*. That's what I learned from Steinberg: to be profound. That behind a funny drawing, there could be a whole ...

And that's absolutely what you do. Behind a funny drawing, there's something that's disturbing.

With every book, I do my own typography too. I love lettering.

The *Babylon* drawings are all in pencil, I think.

Yeah. But it's in kind of a strong pencil which is really hard to erase. It's not grease pencil, but nearly. And those are big drawings. A drawing like this is a big sheet, it's that big [*holds up arms several feet apart*].

That's huge.

Yeah, they're big drawings. And all the ideas I had in two days. All these are in a sketchbook.

There's such a sense of isolation in many of the drawings in *Babylon*.

Always isolation. My themes I always find again, there's always isolation, there's always death. This is very Germanic.

But poignant.

Absolutely.

You're able to capture such a weariness and a misery in these portraits.

Loneliness again. She's a lesbian I knew.

Another thing you said is that "The horizon line of the sea is the only sight which to me is graphically and spiritually safe."

I need the sea. And to this day, the most important moment of my life was when I saw the ocean for the first time in Normandy. And that has remained. I need the ocean. I couldn't live in Strasbourg, I have to be by the sea. This is what I really had in Canada and here again. I'm on top of the cliffs and the first point that's touched by the gulf storm.

Now when you say, "spiritually safe," what do you mean by that? Why is that spiritually safe?

Everybody is looking for some spirituality, because you are faced with death and you are faced with what is going to be afterwards, which I don't know. We've been saying that death is responsible for diseases, war and all that. No. If you believe in God, God is responsible. Death is just a customs officer that lets you get through

ABOVE: From *Babylon*, 1979.

to the other side and then for you to find out what's on the other side. So for me, the horizon line, it's just as if death were on the other side. It's like if truth were waiting for you on the other side of the horizon line. And this is why it's so spiritual. But above the horizon line, there's nothing. There's the sky. Of course, the sky is the sky, the sky is a vacuum. But what kind of vacuum? Everything is behind the horizon line.

You're an atheist.

Yeah. And I never forget one day. I was very much into kites, and I designed this huge kite that I tied up to an empty oil barrel. The oil barrel's giving enough resistance – I was in Long Island – and the wind was blowing from the land out to the sea, and this kite went off dragging the oil barrel. I let it go around 10 o'clock in the morning, and around 4:30, 5 o'clock in the evening, it went behind the horizon line. Can you imagine people in the boats just seeing a kite go by across the ocean? It was a huge thing. The kite was as big as from the end of the bed to the wall over there [approximately four feet]. It was one of my monster box kites. So, this is a way of illustrating the idea, because I am the kite, I'm dragging my oil barrel, but where will I go? You see, I would go behind the horizon line, but, in reality, there's still a horizon line in front of me. This is an important picture. This is a new idea I just had. You think you'll find this around the horizon line, but behind the horizon line there is another horizon line. I think that's a very nice picture. It is like one horizon line that actually gives way to another horizon line. It moves all the time. So even by seeing my kite going behind the horizon line, the kite still has to cross the ocean, and I don't know how long it went.

We've just witnessed how you develop an idea.

Exactly. This is how it works. It's very visual. You could make it in a comic strip.

But it's also full of meaning.

Exactly. And it is meaning, but more than meaning, interpretation.

You did four films with Percy Adlon.

They were television films.

How did that come about? Adlon is a fascinating filmmaker.

He did the first movie with me by coming to Canada. I met him in Munich and he was a radio man. He loved literature. Reading literature, talking about literature, and I was telling him about my life in Canada. And he was so fascinated, he got the finances from the Bayerischer Rundfunk – the Bavarian television [station] – and he came there with a whole team. And he made a movie, which became an ultimate classic, called *Landleben*. By the way, on television, you should look up my movie which I did on Channel 4 in England about *Fascinating Fascism*. I did that with Celia Lowenstein. It's a one-hour movie about fascism and my collection of propaganda. You can dial and get it on television. Do that, that'll fill in a lot of things for you.

Percy Adlon did a movie about my *Landleben*, then he did a movie on *Babylon*. *Babylon* was extraordinary because I had had a terrible accident and I traveled and I arrived in the Zurich airport and there was an ambulance waiting for me in Zurich. And I was taken to the hospital, where I was operated on immediately.

What kind of an accident did you have?

A farm accident. I was using a big iron bar, which started rolling and gaining momentum, and then in front of my wife it hit me and ripped the muscle behind my leg. And then I had to take my trip, and in Paris my leg started turning blue. But I said, "No, I have my appointment with Percy Adlon in Zurich for the movie." I went to the hospital, and when I woke up out of anesthesia with my ready bottle of Paddy next to my bed, there was a camera and Percy Adlon.

And it's the one program I haven't seen because I was talking out of the blue, and that was the movie about *Babylon*. And I traveled because of Percy Adlon. I traveled when I should have been in the hospital.

Can you tell me a little about working with him? What was it like?

Oh, wonderful. We're great friends, and we still see each other regularly. I just saw him in Munich when I got the [Bavarian] Book Prize last November.

I had just seen all of his movies, and then I read that you worked with him and I thought that he's exactly the kind of film-maker you'd like.

And then he went into movies. And then he started to make television movies. And he did one movie in America that's just terrible. He should have never gone to America, he should have stayed.

Did you see *Zuckerbaby*?

Oh, that's excellent. That's lovely. Percy Adlon is a very interesting case.

When you worked with Adlon, how did you collaborate? What did you do and what did he do?

He just filmed. He came with the cameras. The last movie he did just with this little camera he called his "*stylo*-camera" [*stylo* is French for writing pen].

And he filmed you?

Yeah. *Man in a Lonely Landscape* or something like that. Excellent.

You said you worked for *Ramparts* magazine.

Oh, yeah. From the beginning. And I still have all the issues of *Ramparts* magazine. It's very funny because it was raided by extremists and a lot of my drawings were torn. And now, in my museum in Strasbourg, they were glued back together.

Were they raided in California?

In California. Great magazine, that was really excellent. I wonder what happened to those people. It doesn't exist anymore, does it?

No, no it doesn't.

No, I suspect not. It was anti-Vietnam and that's it, right?

Yes, they were. They started in California. And then they moved to New York.

Oh, they did?

They did for a while, then I think they moved back. Do you remember how you hooked up with *Ramparts*?

No idea. Everything's gone.

But because you were political …

Oh, that's it! My Vietnam poster. At first, they asked me to reproduce it.

When you did your antiwar posters in the 1960s were you worried, in light of your previous run-in with the U.S. government, that you might be putting yourself in jeopardy?

Oh no, never. I never worried about anything, I just always did what I thought had to be done. And that created this peace movement with Milton Glaser and the Push Pin Studios. I came with my posters and they wouldn't want to do it because they said it was too hard. So I printed them myself with a friend of mine, Richard Kasak, who had several poster shops. And we

RIGHT: Anti-Vietnam War poster, 1967.

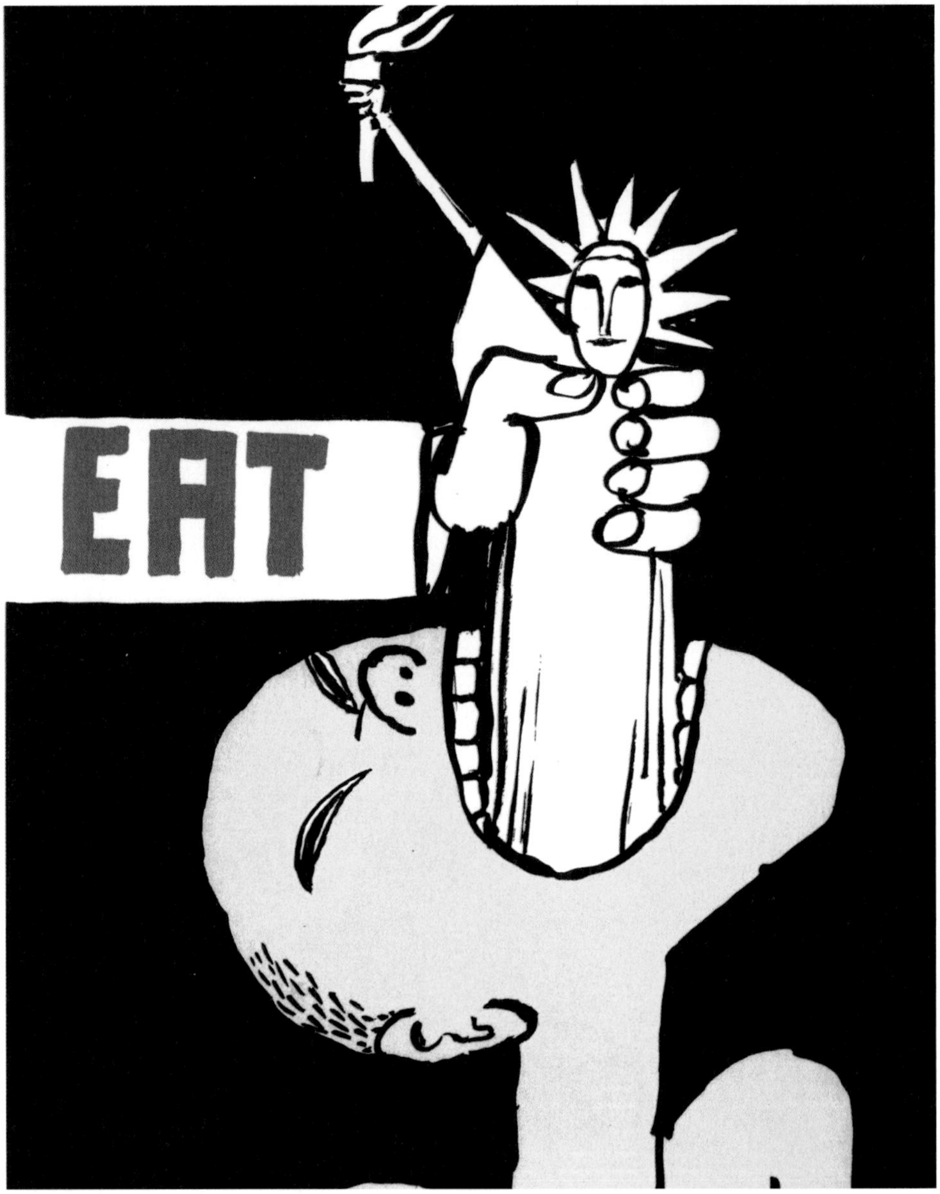
EAT

printed them ourselves. We printed them at night with only one assistant to be sure that the other workers wouldn't see them. And this is how I did the *Fornicon* too. I printed the original edition of the *Fornicon* myself and *The Party* was also done that way. I created a publishing house with a guy called Grossman and we went bankrupt and all the original editions of *The Party* disappeared. But I did two books: *Nicht Wahr?*, an anti-Nazi book, and *The Party*. Because no publisher would touch that kind of stuff. Well, there could have been Grove Press, but even Grove Press wouldn't take *The Party*.

How did you sell these books and posters?

That's how I created Paragraphic Books with Grossman. It was a collection. We did a book of Ben Shahn. And then we did *The Party* and my book *Nicht Wahr?*

You published Ben Shahn?

Yeah, among other things. I think it was *Hamlet* illustrated by Ben Shahn. Then we went bankrupt and when you go bankrupt the whole stock of books disappears. I don't know what happens to them.

Did becoming a publisher add to your anxiety?

No, I couldn't have cared less. I didn't do the publishing, I didn't run it.

OK. Because being a publisher adds to my anxiety. [*Laughs.*]

I can imagine, because you're a one-man publisher and you handle everything. But I had nothing to do with distribution or anything. And I must say when *The Party* came out it was not reviewed anywhere.

"Don't Hope, Cope": Ungerer's Existential Credo

You have said, "I don't believe in hope."

No, I'm not hopeful, absolutely not. For me, there's only one thing: it's facts and reality. No, I'm just a realist. Look here, this is an ugly world! This is an ugly world.

"I've always said hope is a four letter word."

I don't believe in taking hope from others, you see. I mean, look at the third world and all those people. If those people didn't have a bit of hope, what would they do?

You are not an optimist.

No. I'm not pessimistic either. I'm just realistic, that's all. [*Groth laughs.*] All you have to do is turn on the news and… But please don't misunderstand: I never try to take hope from other people away. I understand that humanity in its misery needs something.

Needs hope.

You have to believe in paradise after suffering when you've been in a concentration camp. I mean, my God! If you had no hope, you wouldn't make it.

But you've said, "I believe in despair. Despair is my fuel."

Oh, absolutely. I keep on writing and this is my favorite subject. If there was a muse for despair, she would put all the other muses out of work. All you need is despair. Everything, every good piece of artwork, is because of despair. Now a lot of people's pieces of artwork are judged because of the craftsmanship, like da Vinci, but real art is based on despair, especially in writing.

And that goes back to your existential beliefs, because you must believe despair is truthful.

Exactly. And from despair, you learn. From despair, you learn a lot. Through despair, you learn respect for other people. This is really essential, respect. I was gonna say, respect the unexpected. Respect the unexpected. Oh, I have to write this down. That's another good one.

A variation of your "expect the unexpected."

And this is a line that goes when we are talking about fate. Respect the unexpected!

Something else you said, though, was, "Everything I do is with a bit of joy."

Yeah. I don't believe in happiness. I've never been happy in my life, I don't believe in happiness. It can happen sometimes that one feels happy. But it's an illusion before it gets lost. But joy is something completely different. I make a big difference between joy and happiness. Happiness, you have to take seriously. And joy is more frequent.

And more transient?

Well, sure. It's a momentary uplifting. I like the word "joy." And I have my moments of joy, evidently. It was a joy meeting you.

You're the first person to tell me that.

No, no.

No, I'm just kidding.

I really feel joy, you know?

To get back to your personal beliefs – you said, "Every artist should have some cause to fight for or fight against."

> "
> Because a drawing is not gonna change somebody's mind, but awareness may change somebody's mind in the long run.
> "

Absolutely. This is where you differentiate a painter or something from a graphic artist, and especially from the guy who draws. But I would say everybody who's creative should have a cause, should have his causes to fight for. I'm talking humanitarian, you know what I mean, to make other people aware of what the problems are. Because a drawing is not gonna change somebody's mind, but awareness may change somebody's mind in the long run. Like if you expose the obscenity of waste. I cannot stand waste! I always finish emptying my plate. I'm obsessed with waste. Like a bomb is a waste of money because it's too expensive. And then the houses which are destroyed. This is all a fucking waste.

You said a drawing can't change anyone's mind, but a drawing can resonate.

We make awareness. Yeah, originate awareness. Because if I fucking make fun of something, even if I make fun of the Vietnam War, of the stupidity of it, if I make somebody laugh, that laugh is gonna remain in them.

OPPOSITE: From
Rigor Mortis, 1983.

It can make people pause and think and consider. And that's important.

Well, I've been really absolutely totally *engagé* in my children's books, all of them. All my first children's books were about animals which are discarded.

Pigs and crocodiles and octopuses.

Yeah, and bats and all that. I can't find the word! But all my children's books have been *engagé* in one way or another. The bad can be good, like the robbers in *The Three Robbers*.

There's also in your children's books a redemptive aspect.

Oh, absolutely there is. There is such a thing. Because if you believe in goodwill and forgiving, then you have to believe in some kind of … I'm talking towards oneself, not towards society.

Another thing you said was, "Drawing is the most direct and personal kind of graphic expression. Unlike painting, it doesn't forgive. You put down your black line and there it is, as inevitable as death."

Yeah, absolutely.

And is that because you feel you can't change it? It's there.

No, it's right there. As I said yesterday, you can execute somebody on the paper. You can liquidate, you can do anything with your fantasy.

Whereas with painting, you can change it.

Yeah, it's layers, and it's not minimal. Drawing is minimal, very minimal. ☀

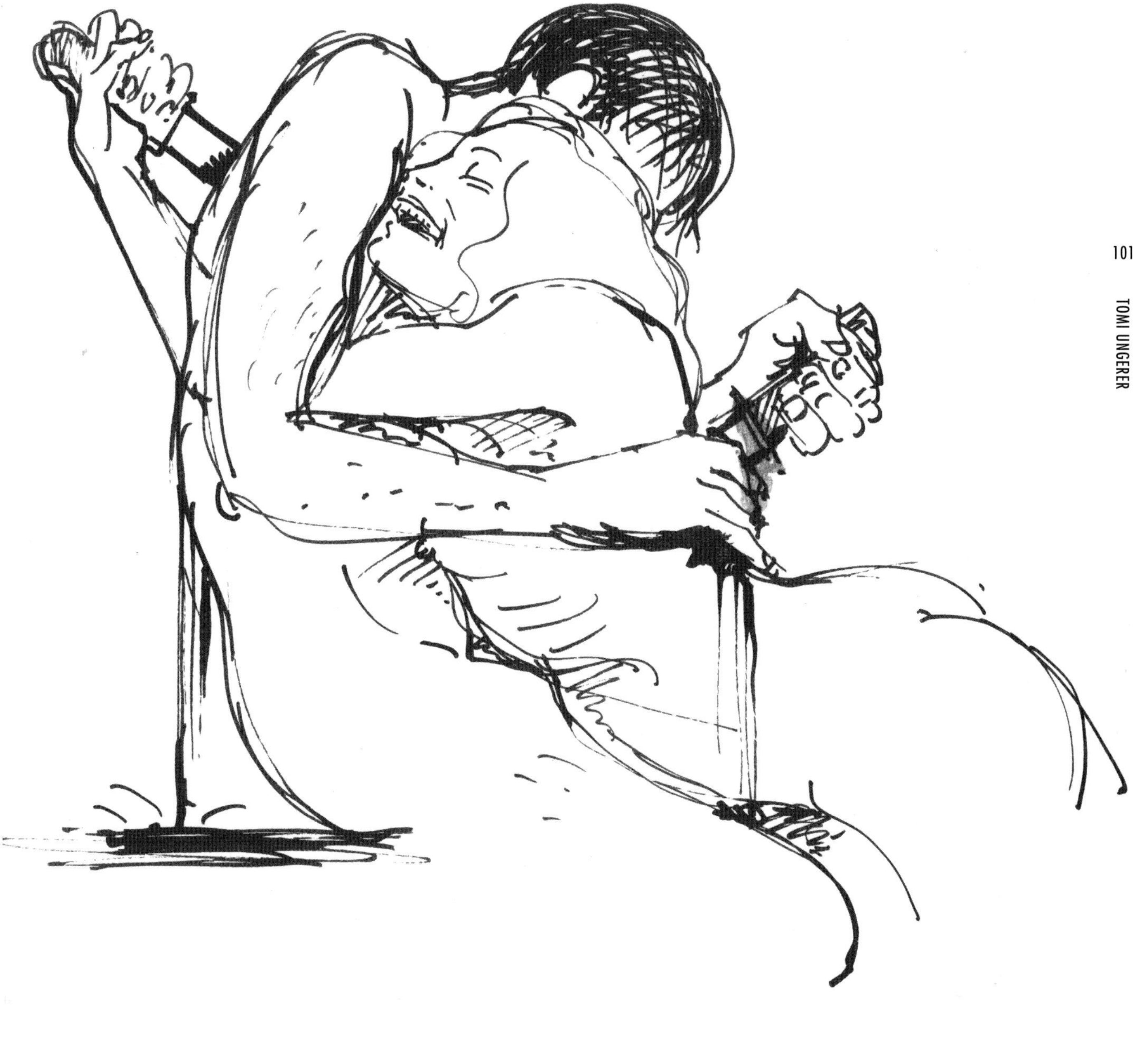

Cyberzone

Dr. Sheena C. Howard

IN 1994, AN EIGHT-ISSUE, pioneering series appeared that challenged the status quo and did something that no comic book has ever done, then or now: Jimmie Robinson's self-published *Cyberzone*. *Cyberzone* is set in Hoverton, a fictional metropolis, and focuses on a futuristic, overpopulated "ghetto" set in the 2020s – oftentimes referred to as "Section 8." *Cyberzone* presents technological advances – such as removing human consciousness and placing it into other human beings – and its city hosts an eclectic mix of people, including "organ snatchers, mecha-mutts and neuro-bots," according to the comic book review hub Beek's Books. Amanda, the main character and superheroine, can telekinetically communicate with her weapon, Gunn (which reminds me of, but predates, Gert's telekinetic ability to communicate with her dinosaur in Marvel's *The Runaways*). The book immediately launches the reader into the dynamics of Hoverton and Amanda's street-tough sensibilities as a lower-class law enforcer.

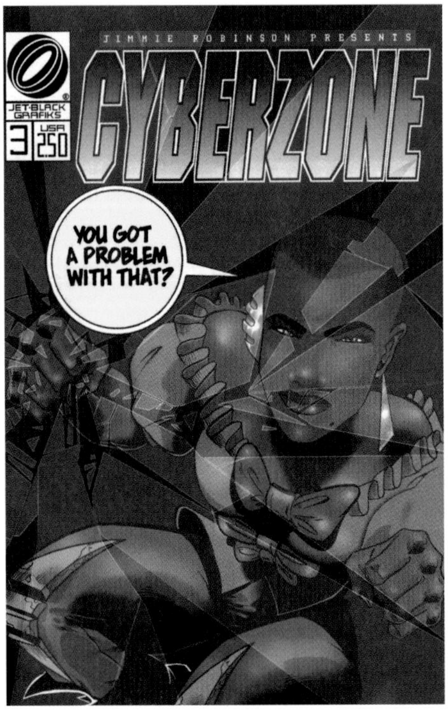
JIMMIE ROBINSON PRESENTS
JET-BLACK GRAFIKS
3
USA 2.50
CYBERZONE
YOU GOT A PROBLEM WITH THAT?

RIGHT: Cover to *Cyberzone* #3, 1994. Art by Jimmie Robinson.

Introduced early in the series are aspects of lesbian identity, such as "passing" as straight, gender presentation dynamics and the complexities of representation and coexistence as a Black lesbian female. *Cyberzone*, later published as *Amanda and Gunn* for four issues in 1997 with Image Comics, was ahead of its time. I have not seen a publishing company feature a Black, queer, female superheroine lead since Jimmie Robinson's miniseries. As a self-published work of the early 1990s, the book is not perfect – but it is a pivotal point in the history of American comics culture, and progress and cutting-edge storytelling in the medium, as well as media in general. For me, the most interesting aspects of *Cyberzone* as a comic are the setting and storyline. However, the fascinating thing about the production of *Cyberzone* – and Image's eventual pick-up of the series – is the societal context in which it was published.

One year before *Cyberzone* was released, Milestone Media, a Black-owned publishing company, signed a distribution deal with DC Comics and launched the Dakotaverse. Residents of the Dakotaverse included diverse characters such as Static, Hardware, Icon, Rocket and the Blood Syndicate team, amongst others. Outside of Milestone Media, Black writers and artists were taking initiative without the benefit of the internet as it is today. Many self-published comics during this period were published in black and white and distributed by the creators themselves. This was the case for *Cyberzone*, which was written, drawn and distributed by one man, Jimmie Robinson, through his company, Jet-Black Grafiks.

At the time, self-publishing was especially critical for Black creators who could not wait around for publishing houses to support and put out their ideas. In the early 1990s, often termed the "Dark Ages," self-published comics were popping up everywhere. People wanted to tell their stories, and to break out of the constraints of the "Big Two," Marvel and DC. Creatives wanted to create, but there were many barriers; it was extremely difficult for some of them to get their work sold in comic book stores. There were only a couple of big distributors, and comic books were pretty much exclusively sold in this "direct market." This meant that if a title was not picked up by a distributor such as Diamond – and/or didn't have brand recognition – it was unlikely that a comic book

> " As a self-published work of the early 1990s, the book is not perfect – but it is a pivotal point in the history of American comics culture, and progress and cutting-edge storytelling in the medium, as well as media in general. "

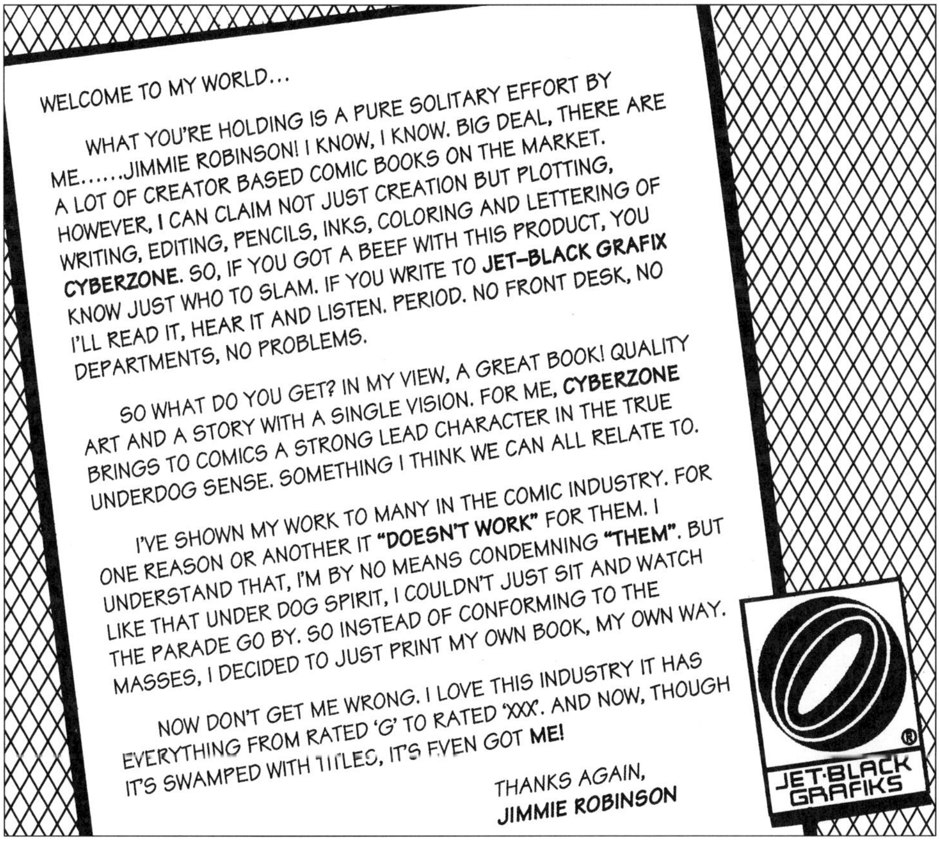

WELCOME TO MY WORLD...

WHAT YOU'RE HOLDING IS A PURE SOLITARY EFFORT BY ME......JIMMIE ROBINSON! I KNOW, I KNOW. BIG DEAL, THERE ARE A LOT OF CREATOR BASED COMIC BOOKS ON THE MARKET. HOWEVER, I CAN CLAIM NOT JUST CREATION BUT PLOTTING, WRITING, EDITING, PENCILS, INKS, COLORING AND LETTERING OF **CYBERZONE**. SO, IF YOU GOT A BEEF WITH THIS PRODUCT, YOU KNOW JUST WHO TO SLAM. IF YOU WRITE TO **JET-BLACK GRAFIX** I'LL READ IT, HEAR IT AND LISTEN. PERIOD. NO FRONT DESK, NO DEPARTMENTS, NO PROBLEMS.

SO WHAT DO YOU GET? IN MY VIEW, A GREAT BOOK! QUALITY ART AND A STORY WITH A SINGLE VISION. FOR ME, **CYBERZONE** BRINGS TO COMICS A STRONG LEAD CHARACTER IN THE TRUE UNDERDOG SENSE. SOMETHING I THINK WE CAN ALL RELATE TO.

I'VE SHOWN MY WORK TO MANY IN THE COMIC INDUSTRY. FOR ONE REASON OR ANOTHER IT **"DOESN'T WORK"** FOR THEM. I UNDERSTAND THAT, I'M BY NO MEANS CONDEMNING **"THEM"**. BUT LIKE THAT UNDER DOG SPIRIT, I COULDN'T JUST SIT AND WATCH THE PARADE GO BY. SO INSTEAD OF CONFORMING TO THE MASSES, I DECIDED TO JUST PRINT MY OWN BOOK, MY OWN WAY.

NOW DON'T GET ME WRONG. I LOVE THIS INDUSTRY IT HAS EVERYTHING FROM RATED 'G' TO RATED 'XXX'. AND NOW, THOUGH IT'S SWAMPED WITH TITLES, IT'S EVEN GOT **ME!**

THANKS AGAIN,
JIMMIE ROBINSON

JET-BLACK GRAFIKS

LEFT: Robinson's introduction to *Cyberzone* #1, 1994.

- SHHHH....
Y-YOU CANT
HELP ME...

BUT-

JUST...
...KISS ME.

ABOVE: Panel from *Cyberzone*
#5, 1995, written and drawn
by Jimmie Robinson.

store would sell it. Therefore, the only option for someone to put out something new was to self-publish via their own company. So, many comic book companies were created; and, just as fast, many of them folded.

If Jimmie Robinson had waited for a publishing house to pick up *Cyberzone*, it is unlikely it would have ever been published. In a 2009 interview with PoP!, Robinson said:

> Valentino was head publisher of Image at the time, and he was launching a sub-division called Shadowline – which focuses on non-superhero, black-and-white books. He basically invited me to continue my work there. I was beside myself. I accepted and revamped *Cyberzone* into a miniseries called *Amanda and Gunn*. And from there, I have never left Image Comics. Within six

months I went from being in the back of the [*Diamond*] *Previews* catalog to the cover, thanks to Valentino's launch and retailer interest. *Amanda and Gunn* did well, too. 12,000 orders – which would be good even today– and, unlike other books that were created by "teams," I was a lone wolf. Creator, writer, artist, letterer, colorist, etc. I think that set the mold for me. Why on earth would I be part of a chain when I can control and reap it, the whole burrito?"

For such a forward-thinking book, then and even now, the book sold exceptionally well, considering the climate for LGBTQ visibility in addition to the obstacles for Black comic creators in the industry.

Politically, both in and across the comics industry as well as the societal landscape, the visibility of LGBTQ people was still very taboo, and comics by them and representing them were relegated to alternative newspapers and bookstores. This makes the publication of *Cyberzone* significant in the history of American comics. In addition, the success of *Cyberzone*, first as a self-published comic and then as a series published by Image, speaks to the quality of what Jimmie Robinson produced, even as a one-man show.

One year before *Cyberzone*, then-President Bill Clinton made it clear that LGBTQ visibility was unwelcome in American social life. In 1993, President Clinton signed a law (consisting of statute, regulations and policy memoranda) directing that military personnel "don't ask, don't tell, don't pursue, and don't harass."[1] Under this policy, LGBTQ people serving in the United States military were not allowed to talk about their sexual orientation or engage in sexual activity, and commanding officers were not allowed to question service members about their sexual orientation. It would not be until nearly two decades later that "Don't Ask, Don't Tell" (DADT) was repealed.

The impact of DADT on Black queer women in the military should not be

---

1   *Encyclopedia of Britannica*, 2018

... I'VE DECIDED TO CHANGE THE RULES!
BLAM!

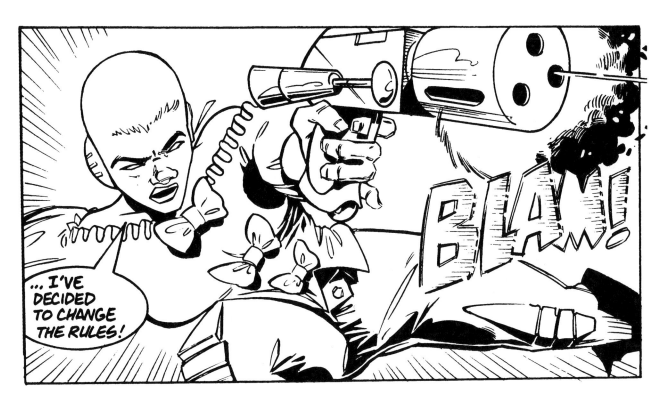

understated. According to a 2010 Service Women's Action Network report,[2] Black women in the military were disproportionately discriminated against as part of the "Don't Ask, Don't Tell" (DADT) policy. The study found that the number of military personnel discharged as a result of DADT were disproportionately women, Blacks, Latinos and Asians. In 2008, Black women totaled less than 1 percent of service members but represented 3.3 percent of "Don't Ask, Don't Tell" discharges; women totaled only 15 percent of service members but 34 percent of "Don't Ask, Don't Tell" discharges.

For Black people, art has often been inspired by injustice, but also by a lack of representation and a need to speak back to cultural norms that are rooted in oppression. Insert *Cyberzone*. During a period of blatant discrimination against LGBTQ peoples and a concerted effort to silence them, *Cyberzone* pushed back on such narrative by making Amanda visible – a Black queer superheroine who is essentially a hero for hire. The sentiment of *Cyberzone* resonates with the cultural landscape of the early 1990s but also challenges its readers to think critically about the oppressive American ideologies of the period.

ABOVE: From *Cyberzone* #2, 1994, written and drawn by Jimmie Robinson.

> "Why on earth would I be part of a chain when I can control and reap it, the whole burrito?"

Cyberzone presented a superheroine who was a law enforcer, who did not subscribe to the heterosexist notions of political policies and ideologies and created an escape from the real-world silencing of LGBTQ individuals. Though I did not read *Cyberzone* when it was first published in 1994, I can imagine the impact this comic would have had on a little girl like me, trying to find her way and looking for some representation and validation of

2 https://www.colorlines.com/articles/former-marine-evelyn-thomas-fight-end-dont-ask-dont-tell

image
Amanda
and Gunn
4
$2.95
OCT
$4.10 CANADA
AMANDA & GUNN

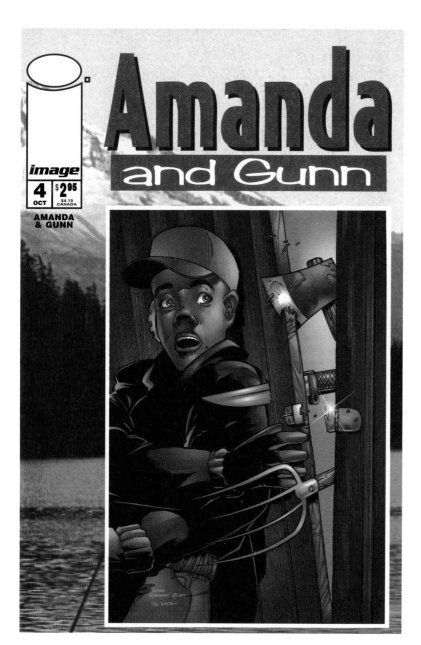

ABOVE: Cover to *Amanda and Gunn* #4, 1997. Art by Jimmie Robinson.

my identity around race, gender and sexual orientation. *Cyberzone* presents a type of cultural resistance uncommon then – and in 2019. To date, I cannot think of any comic book by a publishing company that features a Black queer female lead superheroine.

Aside from the ways in which *Cyberzone* challenged cultural norms, it also presented a multi-dimensional, non-stereotypical character that was relatable across race, gender and sexual orientation. The comic book did not try too hard to present a lesbian character: Amanda just is. *Cyberzone* positions Amanda as a hardworking member of society, trying to make ends meet like the rest of us. Amanda just happens to be in love with a woman.

The presentation of Amanda's sexual orientation is never forced or incorporated just for diversity's sake. In fact, the representation is so authentic that readers of *Cyberzone* – and, later, *Amanda and Gunn* – could not believe that a Black, straight male wrote this story. In *Cyberzone*, Amanda is fully integrated into society, yet her struggles as an LGBTQ person are not dismissed. This is important. The line between presenting a more authentic account of the character's experiences as an LGBTQ person and over-writing a character is difficult to navigate. Robinson nails it perfectly. In addition, the society in which *Cyberzone* is set, Hoverton, presents a range of complex and interesting characters which normalizes the character of Amanda, but also allows for a nuanced approach to her experience as a lesbian. For example, there are points in the series in which Amanda feels the need to hide her sexual orientation out of fear of isolation or the need to negotiate her sexual orientation strategically – this is a very real practice. However, when Amanda does share with her new partner that she is in love with another woman, it is treated as just another personal disclosure and it is not marked as an emotionally dramatic turning point in the story. This is important, especially considering the societal context. The reader is made to understand the fear of disclosing one's sexual orientation but it also teaches, through this disclosure, that it is no big deal. Essentially, Amanda is still Amanda both before and after coming out.

Amanda's gender presentation also challenges stereotypical representations of Black lesbian women in media. Amanda is not confined to a stereotypically masculine look, as you have come to expect in mainstream media representations of Black lesbians. There is nothing wrong with this presentation; it just seems to be the default

for women when they are depicted as Black lesbians. In short, the notion that lesbian women somehow seek to be "like men" is challenged.

In essence, Robinson empowers Amanda, by allowing her to negotiate her sexual orientation and by challenging gender presentation stereotypes, too often depicted in mainstream media. Amanda uses her powers to capture criminals. Thus, though many things make her different, this difference is celebrated in *Cyberzone*; it is what actually allows Amanda to survive in this futuristic dystopia.

Amanda's story is one of struggle and survival. The character and society Jimmie Robinson created challenges the typical formula of the 1990s, where the comic book ecosystem still largely focused on white-male superheroes – and continues to challenge the prevailing notion that superheroes and superheroines have to be one way. They can be different and this difference can make for a successful comic book, particularly when comic book publishers and readers are willing to accept this difference and support new ideas by talented creators.

Jimmie Robinson made a bold statement with the publication of *Cyberzone*, and, later, the miniseries *Amanda and Gunn*. If not the latter, then the former should at least be mentioned in any historical account of pivotal moments in American comic book history. ☀

Antoine Cossé

I USED TO DRAW A LOT MORE in my sketchbooks, but now I use them as a tool for stories more than anything. I do very rough drawings of full pages of characters. There are also lists for grocery shopping, notes made in museums and ideas for color combinations on pages. Very random thoughts.

There are not a lot of detailed drawings in there anymore, but I drew again in a sketchbook last summer. I did a series of sketches called *Book A.*, that Colorama Press serialized in a book afterward. But that time it was different because I drew those pages with a book in mind. ☀

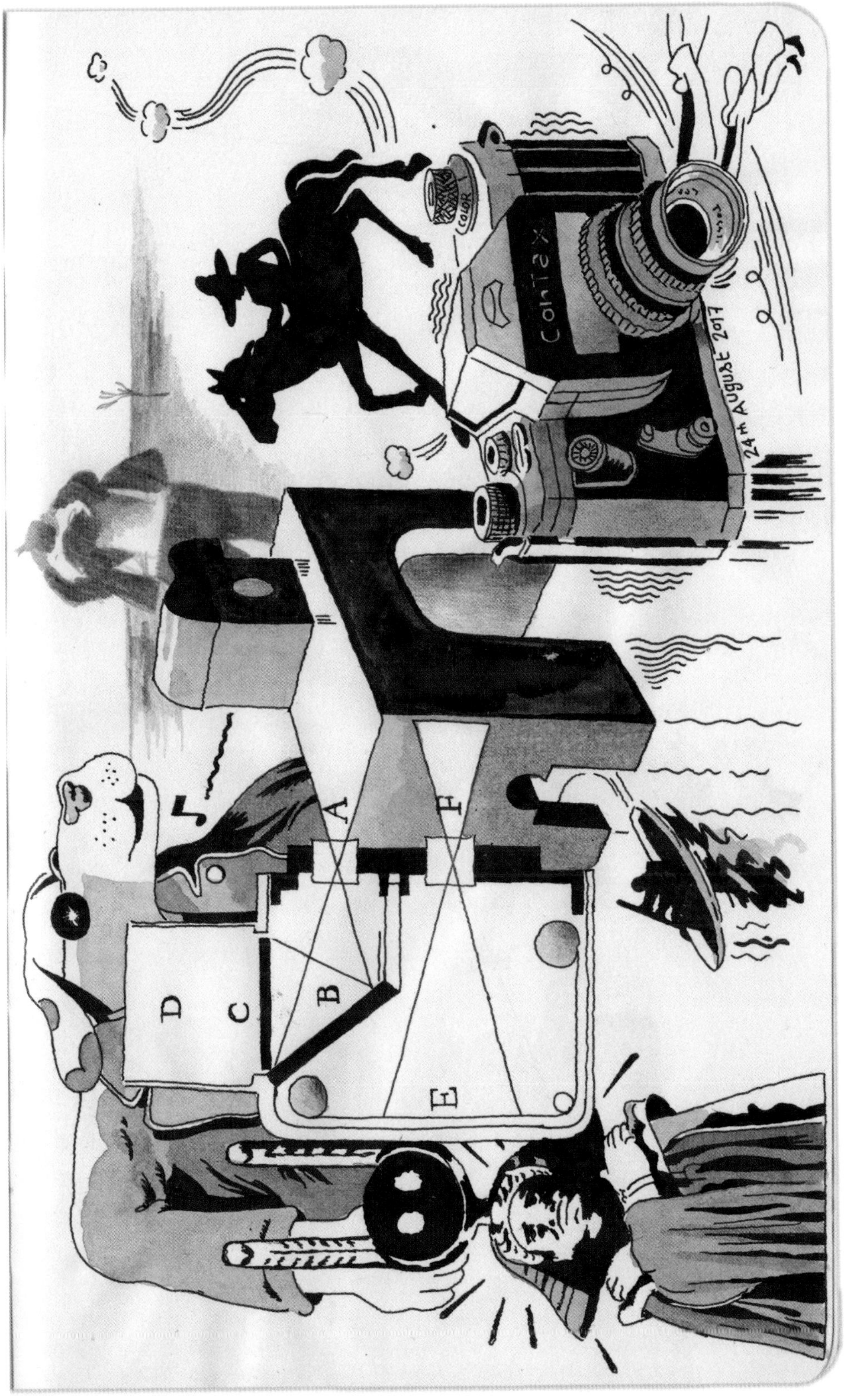
Contax
COLOR
24th August 2017
A
B
C
D
E
F

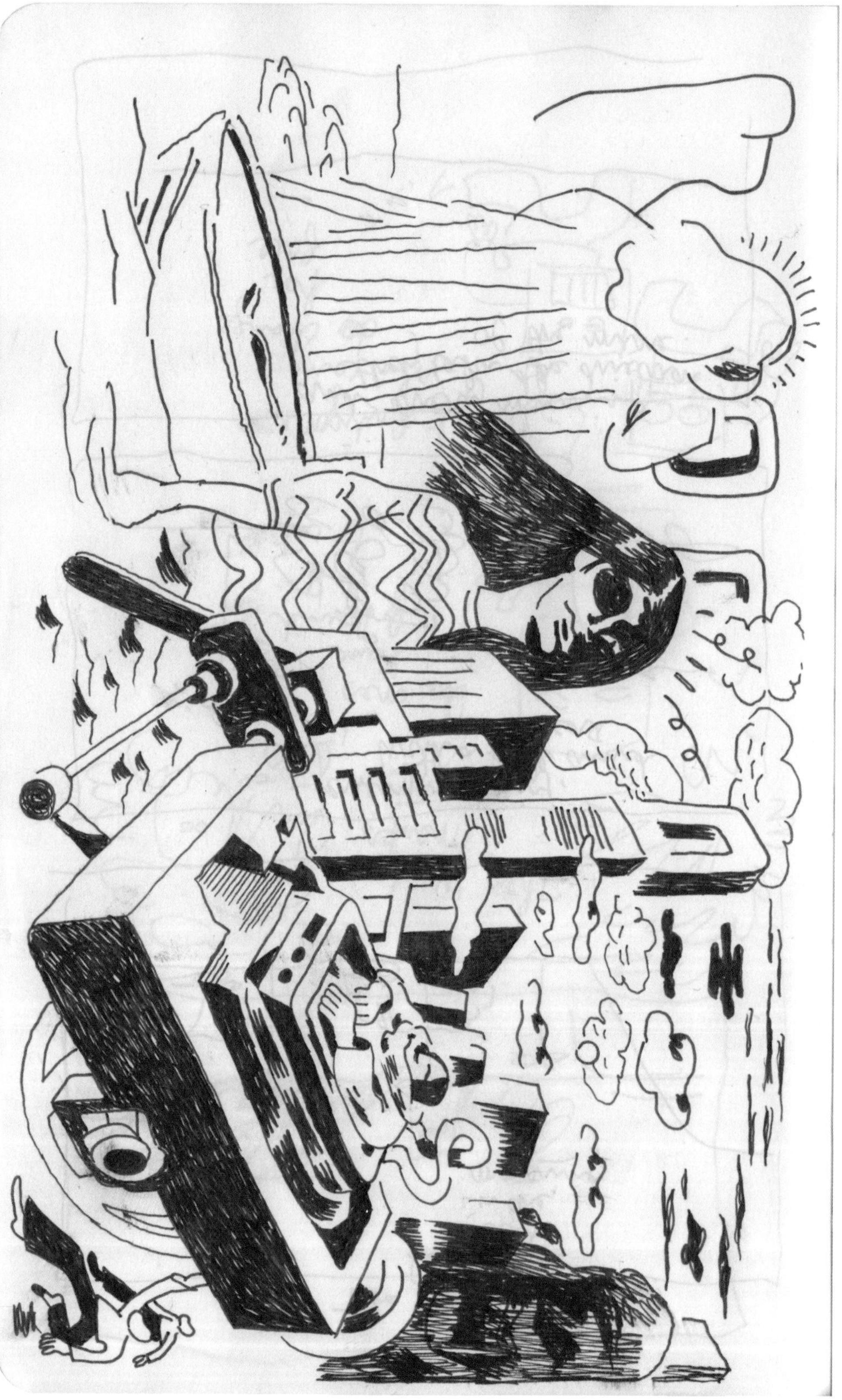

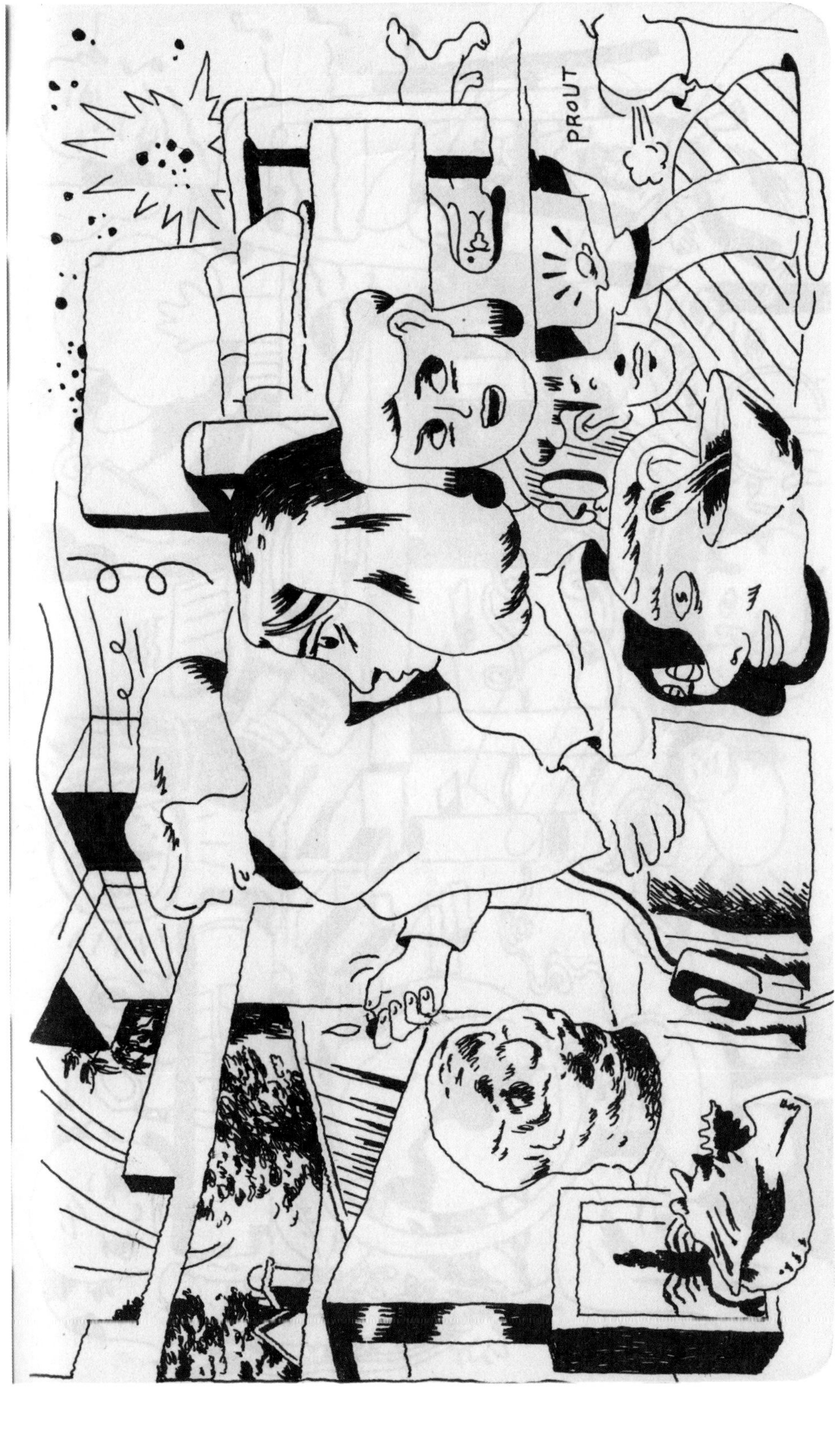
PROUT

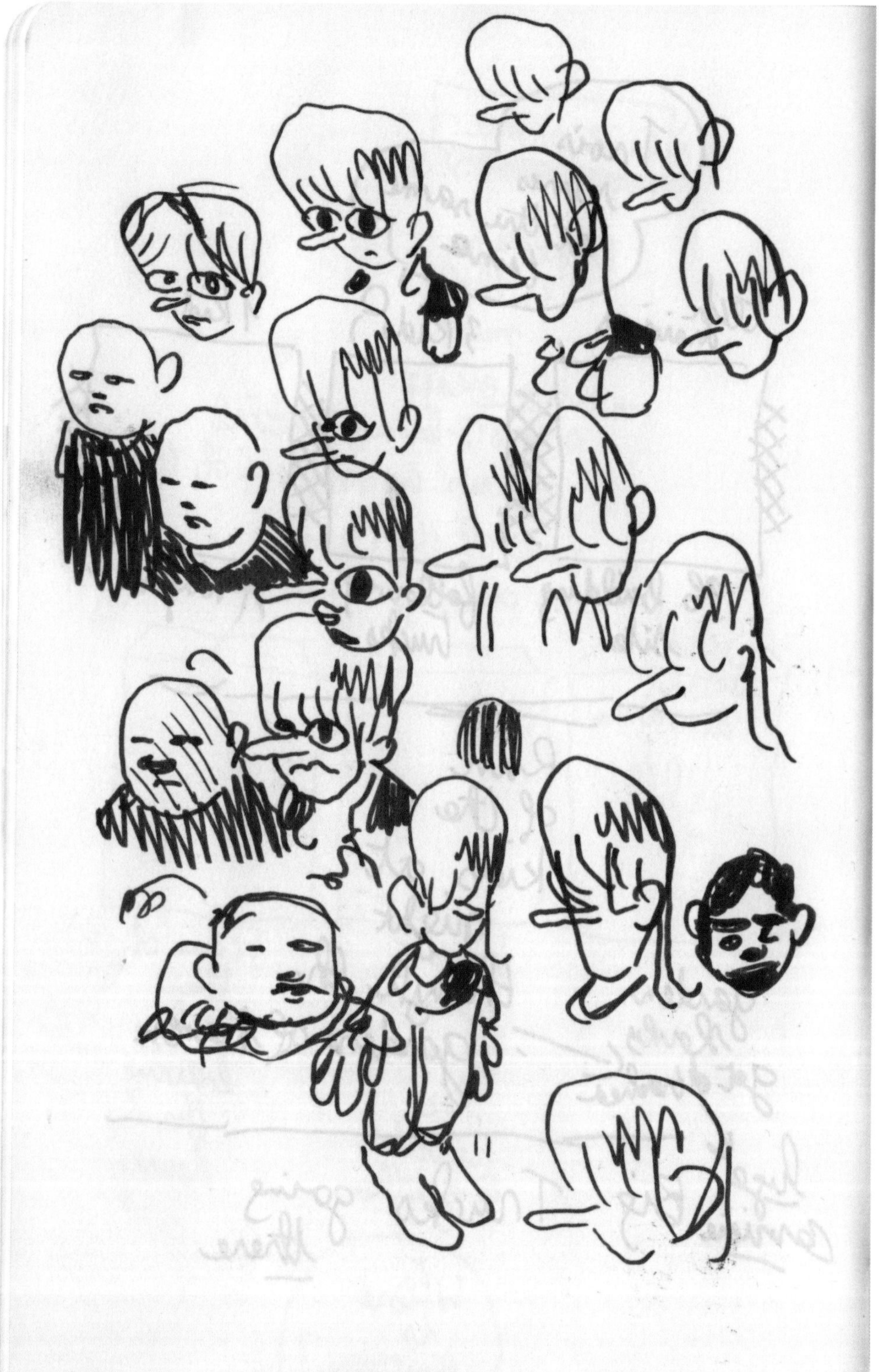

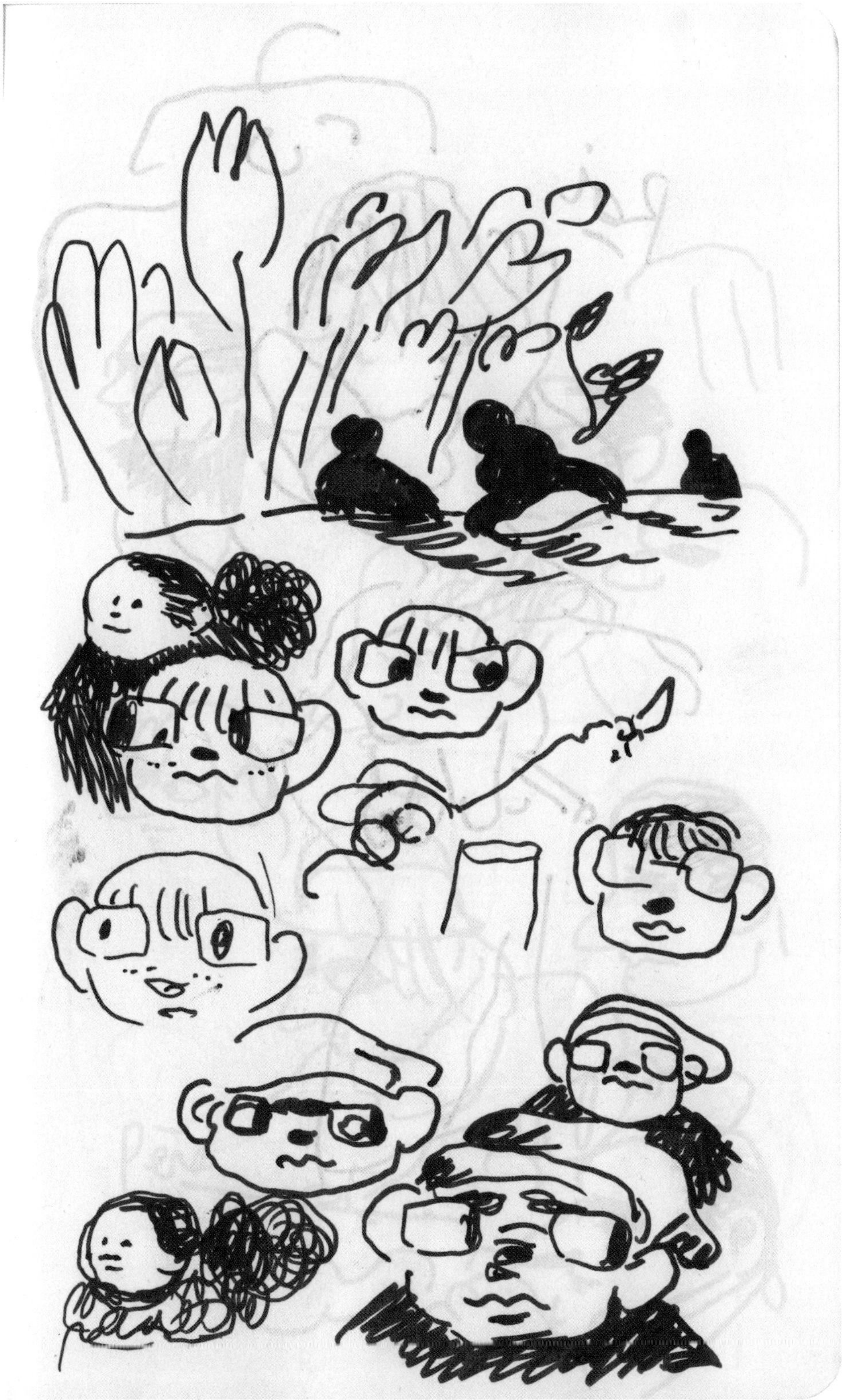

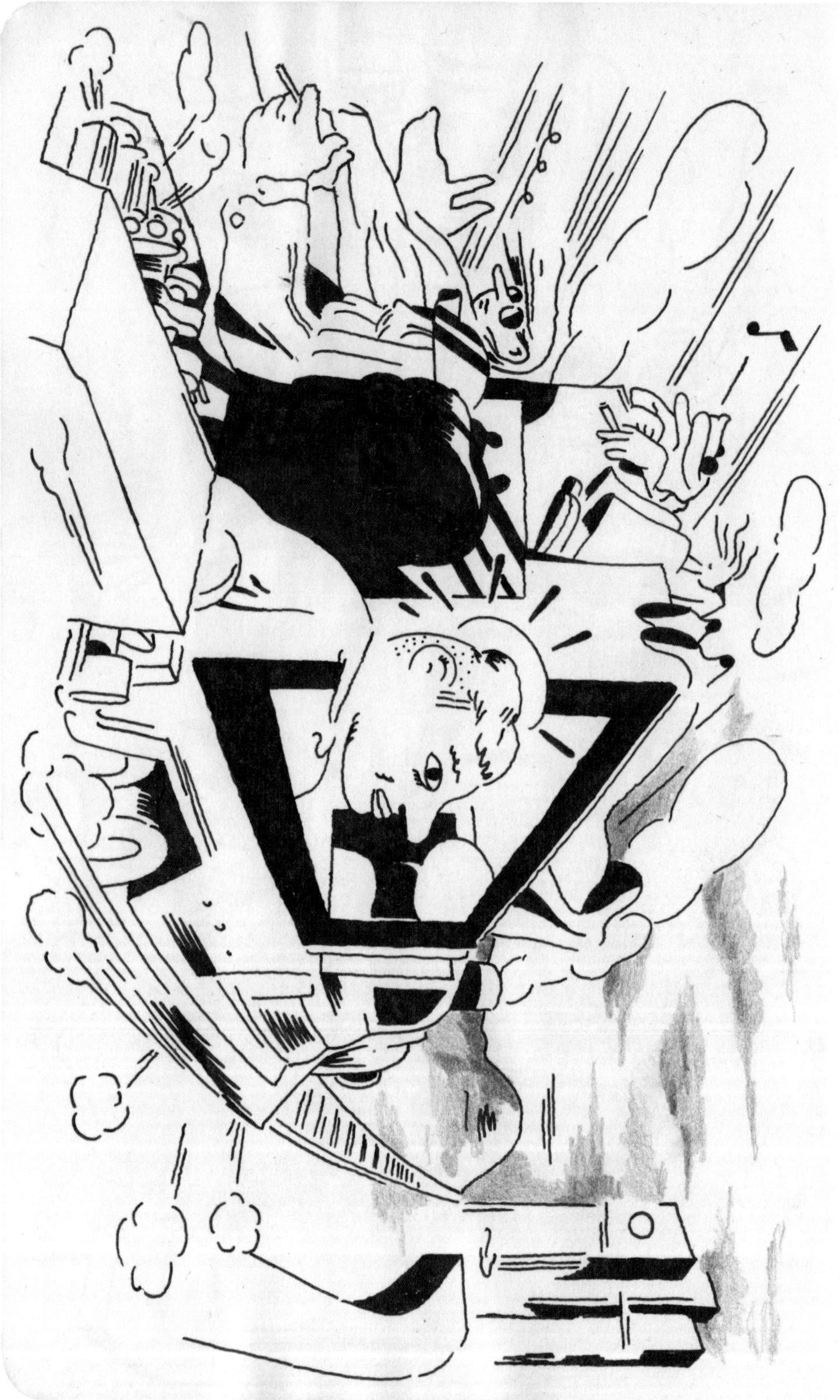

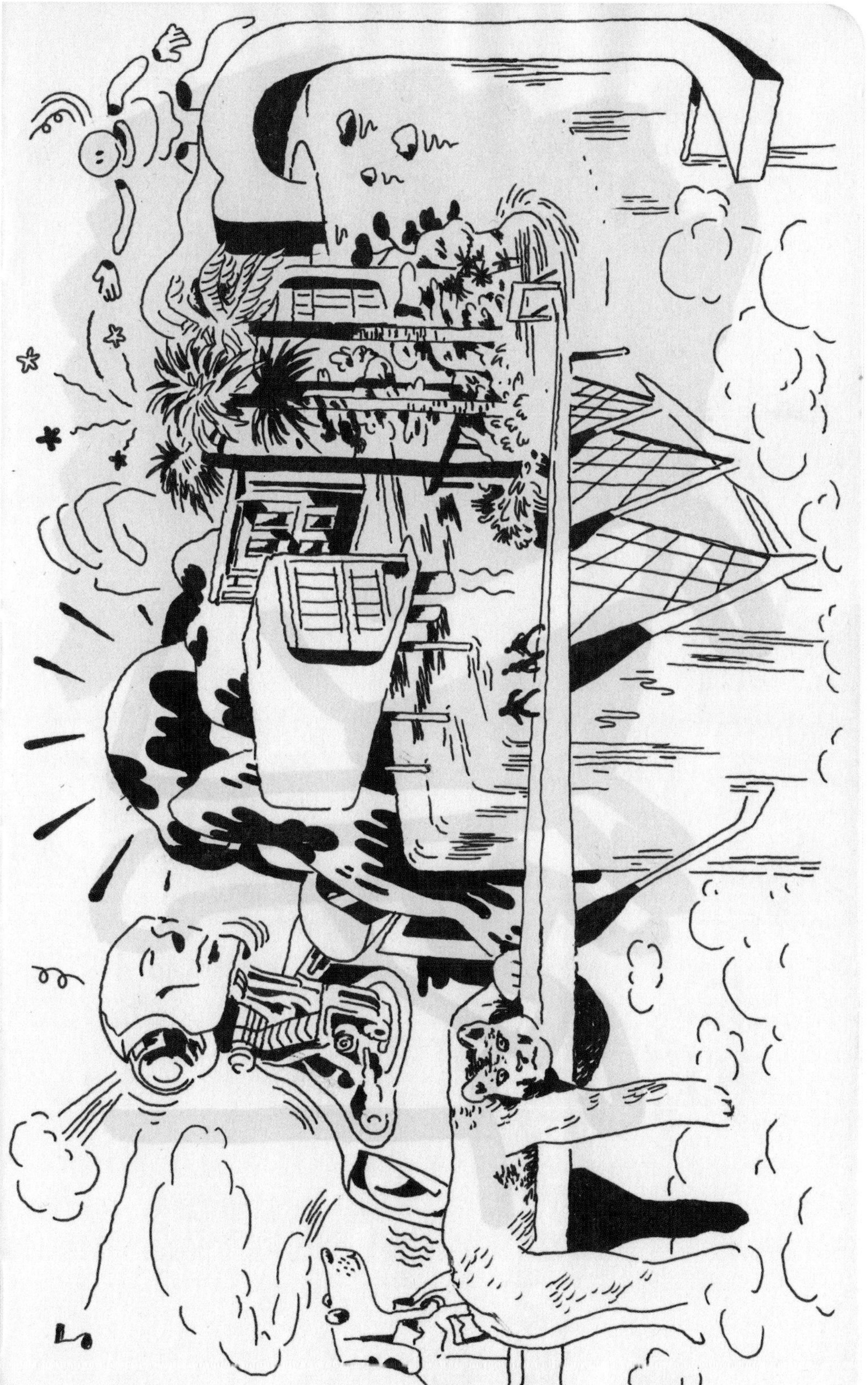

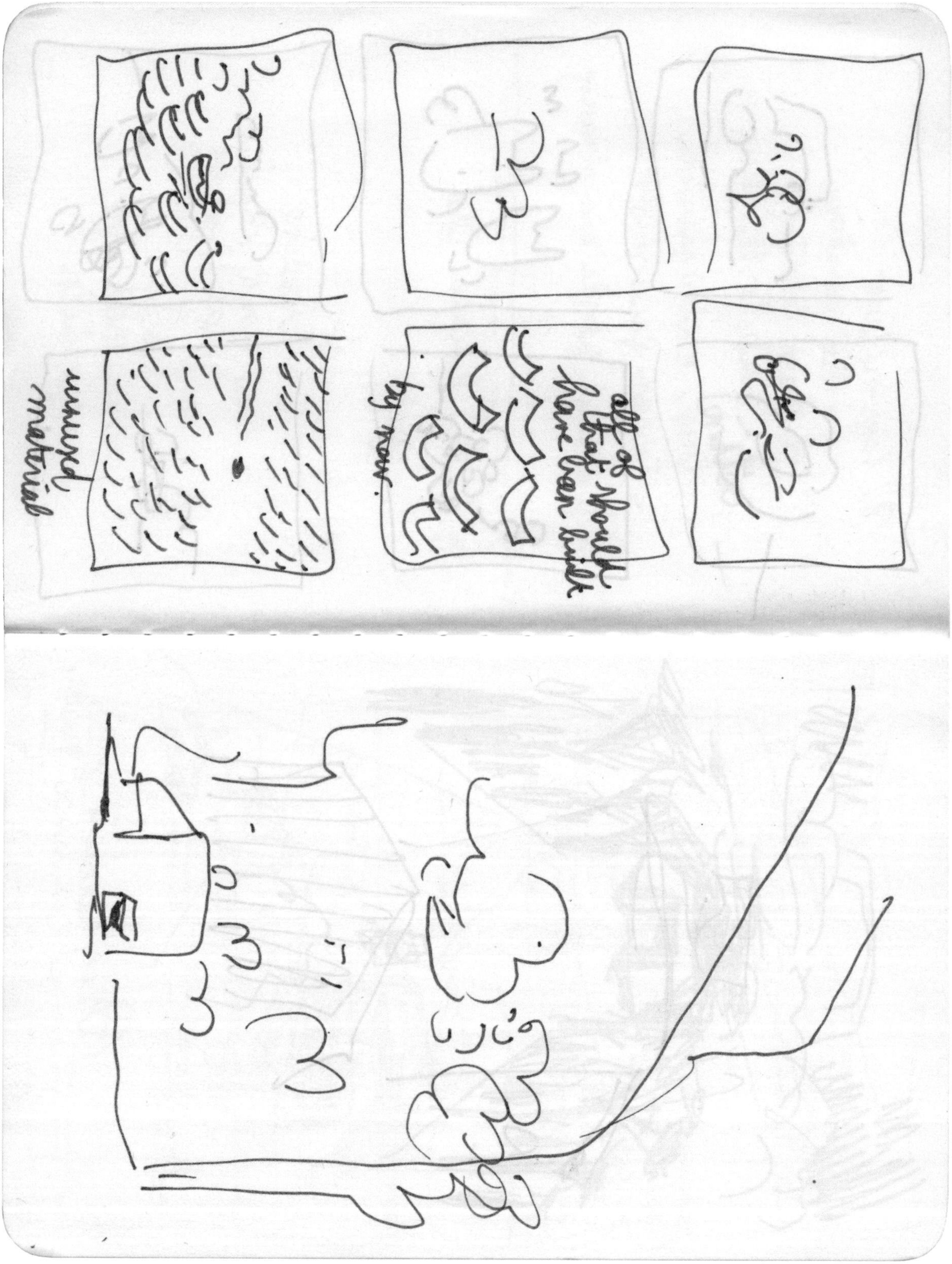
unused material
all of that should have been built by now.

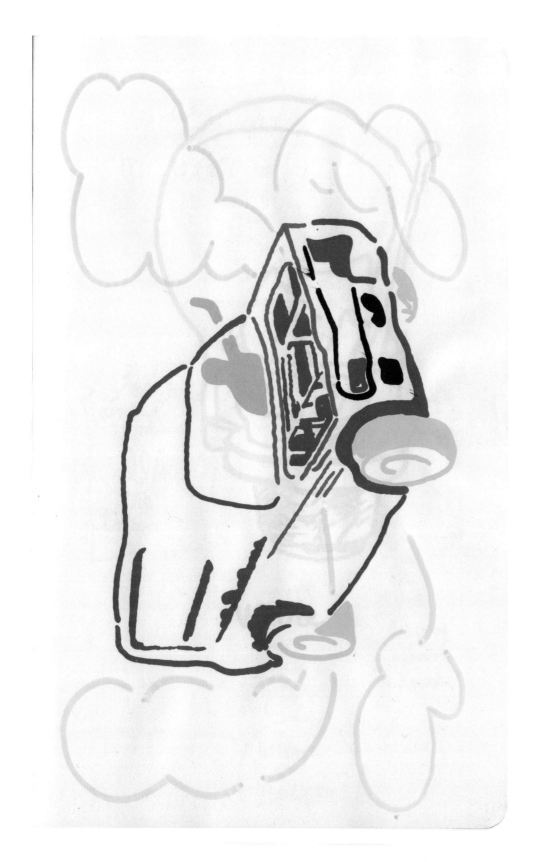

Comics as a Visual Communication System
and Erasing the Boundaries

Kim Jooha

SINCE THE DAWN OF HUMANITY, across almost every culture, there has been a need and desire to communicate by visual means, which I call Visual Communication Systems: from hieroglyphs in ancient Egypt, illuminated manuscripts in the Middle Ages, the Bayeux Tapestry, Mayan codices, ancient scrolls from East Asia, to modern communication tools like pictograms, films and picture books; from simple doodles to the "high art" of concrete poetry, to the gouache paintings of Charlotte Salomon, drawings of David Shrigley and even comics by influential fine artists like Jim Shaw.

VBI HAROLD:SACRAMENTVM:FECIT:
VVILLELMO DVCI:

ABOVE: A portion of the Bayeux Tapestry, circa 1070.

While Greenbergian modernist Abstract Expressionism often rejected such communicative or semiotic value of visual art in the early 20th century, it is not the case, at least in the last 30 years. That modernist period was the exception in human history.

I call these Visual Communication Systems "Expanded Comics" because comics is just one of many instances of Visual Communication Systems. Expanded Comics are artistic/cultural works in any medium that can be viewed as comics or comics-like objects regardless of the intention of the creator. By definition, Expanded Comics naturally include comic artists' comic-like work too, such as boundary-confusing works by Jochen Gerner or Ilan Manouach. Additionally, I call a work comics if the creators call it comics.

The concept of Expanded Comics emphasizes the universality of the Visual Communication System across human history, culture and artistic medium. It highlights how comics is just one of them, and thus underlines the potential of comics' diversity. Comics as we know and read them now consist of a tiny fraction of the comics that are possible.

This attention on universality is what differentiates Expanded Comics from previous attempts at incorporating a few fine-art works into comics canon by books like *1,001 Comics You Must Read Before You Die* or *One Thousand Years of Manga*. Selectively choosing random artworks according to an arbitrary definition of comics only emboldens the boundary of comics and "high" art, which has led the comics community to the wrong obsession for the legitimization of "comics as art" and canonization of works that only fit enormously homogenous and confined aesthetics, read: white straight male loser.

In contrast, the goal of Expanded Comics is to erase that boundary and diversify the production and discourse of comics. Creating the definitive boundary of comics is impossible. The boundary is inherently arbitrary and artificial because Visual Communication Systems are so diverse. Indeed, this heterogeneity is the feature of comics and Visual Communication Systems.

There is an exciting group of European artists currently creating Abstract Formalist comics. They study the formal qualities of comics using the clean-line, geometric, graphic, abstract style and experiment with space, time and even texture. The epitome of Abstract Formalist comics is, however, a work created in 1975–76: *Rhapsody* by Jennifer Bartlett. *Rhapsody* can teach us how to approach Expanded Comics. We can read it by analyzing the work's many details, but also appreciate all its visceral beauty. We can learn from non-comics art the infinite possibility of comics, freed from the burden of the narrative.

Aidan Koch is another artist who can help us comprehend Expanded Comics. Koch studies the idea of comics as a Visual Communication System and finds universality in her practice both in comics and gallery work. For her, those two are not at odds. Both are the continuation of the natural evolution of human expression using image-language. Many visual artists and writers like Isidore Isou, Henri Michaux, Oyvind Fahlstrom, Joe Brainard, Cy Twombly and bpNichol also explore and interrogate the same problems of universality, diversity and heterogeneity of Visual Communication Systems in their oeuvre. There is no reason not to discuss them together when they ask the same questions.

Aidan Koch or European Abstract Formalists are not exceptions among contemporary cartoonists. Due to their background in art school education and practice in gallery exhibitions, it is natural for them to work in various mediums, not only in comics. Comics publishers like PictureBox (now defunct), Koyama Press, Floating World and Fantagraphics regularly publish art books. It is not the one-way street of unrequited love as many comics fans and artists are

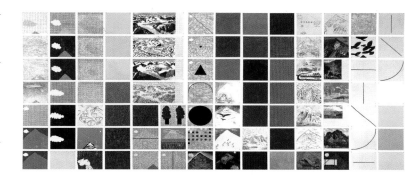

constantly worried about. The fine art world is appreciating comics more and more, and vice versa. *The Best American Comics 2015* featured a cover by Raymond Pettibon, and art publishers like Nieves and MoMA PS publish cartoonists like Aisha Franz, Son Ni and the aforementioned Aidan Koch.

When comics and "high" art are made, distributed and appreciated by the same people, it's unreasonable to consider them from different worlds. It is only natural for comics discourse to embrace Expanded Comics.

The dialogue is lagging behind the practice of erasing the boundaries. Let's catch up. ☀

ABOVE: A section of Jennifer Bartlett's *Rhapsody*, 1975–1976.

BELOW: From *Little Angels* by Aidan Koch, 2016.

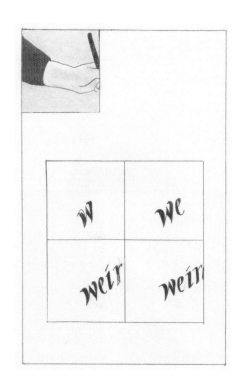

How We Got Here:
A Distribution Overview 1996 – 2019

Kristy Valenti

120 ⟶

THE TERM "MAINSTREAM COMICS" is vestigial, a holdover from the days when comic shops were the only places to find single issues and graphic novels. There were but two types of comics books: "mainstream," i.e., created work for hire and published by Marvel and DC—usually starring brand-name superheroes and other forms of licensed IP— and "independent" or "indy," i.e., more or less not that, published by anyone else. (Although newspaper strips were widely read by a general audience, they weren't considered part of comic book culture.) But, in 2019, comics in the U.S. are truly mainstream – there are book-length collections of comics for breast cancer survivors, steampunk erotica enthusiasts and people who want to learn about symbolic logic – while DC and Marvel superhero films and TV shows have supplanted the comic books themselves. Graphic YA and memoirs aimed at children spend hundreds of weeks on the *NYT* Best-Seller list, and their flagship author, Raina Telgemeier, sold more than a million copies of her books in 2017 alone, according to Brian Hibbs, a comic shop retailer who writes for Heidi McDonald's Comicsbeat.com. (Hibbs based his estimates on BookScan numbers. BookScan, which launched in 2001, is the data system that the book publishing industry uses to estimate point of sale retail purchases.) The pivot to what's being defined here as the New Mainstream – i.e., successful non-superhero genre/nonfiction,

The New Mainstream: Comics Distribution Timeline 1996–2018

1996

▶

- Diamond dominates Direct Market
- *Dragon Ball Z* debuts on Cartoon Network (CN)

1998

▶

- *Sailor Moon* on CN

1998–2001

▶

- Webcomics appear
- *Pokémon* video games, anime, manga
- Scanlations appear

> I HAD RECENTLY DISCOVERED SOME OF DAD'S OLD CLOTHES. PUTTING ON THE FORMAL SHIRT WITH ITS STUDS AND CUFFLINKS WAS A NEARLY MYSTICAL PLEASURE, LIKE FINDING MYSELF FLUENT IN A LANGUAGE I'D NEVER BEEN TAUGHT.

LEFT: From Alison Bechdel's *Fun Home: A Family Tragicomic*, 2006.

creator-driven work that is more or less a single title, is easy to access, and is not for a general audience (i.e., everyone), but a niche one (i.e. mature horror fans) – began circa 2003–2006, with the publication of Marjane Satrapi's *Persepolis* and Alison Bechdel's *Fun Home*, respectively. But the transition began a decade earlier.

1996: The Distributor Wars

FOR A WILD AND WOOLLY HISTORY of the birth of comics shops, aka the Direct Market, see *The Comics Journal* #277. Articles by Michael Dean and Gary Groth describe how comic shops where customers could reliably pick up every issue of their favorite titles (unlike newsstands), and where self-published comics creators like Jeff Smith (*Bone*) and Wendy and Richard Pini (*ElfQuest*) could survive and thrive, came to be. In that issue, Dirk Deppey's "Suicide Club: How Greed and Stupidity Disemboweled the American Comic-Book Industry in the 1990s" goes into great detail about the disastrous effects of Marvel acquiring the distributor Heroes World in 1994, and deciding to exclusively release their comics to retailers through them, which had a devastating effect on other distributors and retailers. As a countermeasure, DC signed an exclusive deal with Diamond Comic Distributors in April 1995. Meanwhile, Marvel was faltering, falling to 18.88 percent of the market, with

2000

- DeviantArt launches

2001

- Bookstore distributors: Image and Dark Horse sign with LPC, Fantagraphics signs with WW Norton
- *Ghost World* movie comes out; GN sells 30,000 copies

2002

- TokyoPop's "Authentic Manga" line, which reads right to left
- Modern Tales, etc.: subscription webcomics collectives appear
- *Shonen Jump* hits U.S. newsstands
- Diamond Book Distributors launches

DC growing to 19.4 percent. This forced the other big publishers to pick sides. On July 21, 1996, Dark Horse and Image signed exclusive distribution deals with Diamond. The ripple effect, wherein distributor Capital City tried to shore up Heroes World and failed, with both distributors becoming defunct, effectively created a comic shop monopoly, with Diamond as the last major distributor standing. Deppey concludes, "Depending upon the estimates offered at the time, somewhere between half and two-thirds of the Direct Market had been obliterated in the space of just three years." The distributor wars have literally shaped comic shop business to this day. Up until 2018, based on that 1996 business deal, Dark Horse was given pride of place in *Diamond Previews*, the catalog that comic book retailers used to preorder non-returnable single issues for their shops three months in advance. Marvel was banished to its own separate booklet. Now, Image is first, and DC and Marvel have their own booklets.

Diamond Comic Distributors sales are calculated by how many copies of a comic are sold to retailers, not how many copies of a comic are sold to customers. Any comic book a Direct Market retailer doesn't sell to a customer, they "soak," because they can't return it to the publisher. Even though they bought the comics at wholesale prices, it's still inventory they have to unload to make space for new product. Bookstore distributors like Ingram and Baker & Taylor are different. Product for these bookstore distributors is "returnable" – anything book retailers don't sell is sent back to the publisher. The perils of having a lone distributor supply non-returnable product to retailers – many of whom, if not most, were concerned with catering to speculators – have been extensively chronicled in the pages of this magazine and elsewhere. Coupled with the basic fact that most people had never (and have never) set foot in a comic shop – whether from disinterest, disgust or simply lack of opportunity – by the 1990s, the term "mainstream" in regards to Marvel and DC superhero books was becoming untethered from its original meaning, used functionally as a counterpoint to "indy," "underground" and/or "alternative."

A telling 2006 article from *ComicsBeat* again quotes Brian Hibbs. He wrote, "the next big challenge isn't coming from a Direct Market distributor (they've killed most of those), it's coming from the bookstore distributors…. I should have read the deal and figured it out two years ago (no, this isn't a new program) when my peers first started telling me about it." According to that article, "Hibbs [ran] through some numbers which shows that a retailer can order a small number of books from [bookstore distributor Baker & Taylor] at just about the

2003

- Viz publishes *Naruto* manga collections
- Image publishes *The Walking Dead* comic book
- Pirate Bay launches
- Pantheon publishes *Persepolis* Vol. 1

2004

- *One Piece* debuts in bookstores; anime begins to run on U.S. TV
- First PAX convention
- Comic shop retailers start ordering graphic novels through bookstore distributors

2005

- *Naruto* anime debuts on U.S. TV
- Scholastic launches Graphix imprint; *Bone* is flagship title

THORN?
YES, FONE BONE?
I WANT TO THANK YOU FOR STICKIN' WITH ME LAST NIGHT . . . I DON'T KNOW WHY THOSE RAT CREATURES WERE AFTER ME - - BUT THEY WOULD'VE GOT ME FOR SURE IF YOU HADN'T STOOD UP TO 'EM!

LEFT: Jeff Smith self-published the 1996 black-and-white version of *Bone: Out from Boneville* Vol. 1, via his company, Cartoon Books.

same discount as through Diamond, while the books are still returnable." The article also quoted small press comics distributor Matt High: "One recent example is a discussion on the CBIA [Comic Book Industry Alliance] board a month ago, where one retailer said 'Hey, don't forget to order the latest *Bone* trade paperback, which only appeared in the Diamond weekly update, and not in the *Diamond Previews* catalog.' Half a dozen retailers replied back immediately with, 'Yeah, we've actually had that book in stock for weeks now, ordering it from Baker & Taylor, and we've restocked it repeatedly already. Anyone who's waited to order it through Diamond missed the boat.'" Suffice it to say that, by 2019, canny comic shop owners order their (returnable) graphic novels and the like from bookstore distributors, who have reps that sell their wares to bookstore buyers. In 2018, Shannon O'Leary, in a piece about the state of the industry for *Publishers Weekly*, defined a retail comic book shop as one that relies "on the direct market for at least 20 percent of their stock."

1996: Anime and Manga

IN 1996, the *Dragon Ball Z* anime began running on the Cartoon Network, with *Sailor Moon* following suit in 1998. The *Pokémon* video games and the Saturday morning cartoon exploded then, too, in 1997–1998. Weekend marathons helped viewers binge and catch up on long-running storylines that would be much harder to put together from

2006

- Project Wonderful launches
- *Fun Home* makes the *Time* Top 10 Books of the Year
- First Second releases *American Born Chinese*
- Crunchyroll, a for-profit digital platform, starts releasing translated East Asian content, not all of it licensed

2007

- Dark Horse instantly sells out of 36,000 print run of the *Perry Bible Fellowship* webcomic collection
- Tumblr launches

2008

- *Iron Man* movie; launch of the MCU
- Last single issue of *Y: The Last Man*

RIGHT: This is the "unflipped" version of "The Decisive Battle at Last!!" in *Dragon Ball Z* #35, 2001. Note the how-to read-from-right-to-left guide on top of the page. It was written and drawn by Akira Toriyama, and adapted to English by Gerard Jones.

I SAID STOP !!!!!
EH.. ?!
I'LL... I'LL...
KILL YOU !!
YOU... WILL KILL...
...ME ?
ZMM
OH !!!
ZHOWW
HSST
TOOM

single episodes. Meanwhile, for example, while Marvel's X-Men were very popular in the 1990s due to the Saturday morning cartoon, in the comic books, the characters were mired in crossover after crossover, spanning various titles that were hard to get a hold of via newsstand distribution. It wasn't evident to a casual reader that different titles had to be read month-by-month, rather than in numerical order, to get the full story. The fans of the *X-Men* cartoon had no good entry point. With anime and manga, it was the first time in a long time that, as managing editor Dirk Deppey pointed out in *The Comics Journal* #269, there was synergy among the comics and the TV shows and the video games; one simply needed to buy a clearly numbered book or a newsstand magazine to follow the further, age-appropriate (i.e., *shōjo*, "for girls," and *shōnen*, "for boys") adventures of the same characters. (More or less. Some parents

2009

- Disney buys Marvel
- Kickstarter launches
- *NYT* Best-Seller list adds manga and graphic novel categories

2010

- Smartphones become ubiquitous; webcomics change format
- Instagram launches
- Vertigo stops publishing creator-owned titles
- *The Walking Dead* TV show begins

2011

- *Smile* on the *NYT* Graphic Books Best-Seller list for more than 220 weeks
- TokyoPop shuts down
- Bookstore chain Borders folds

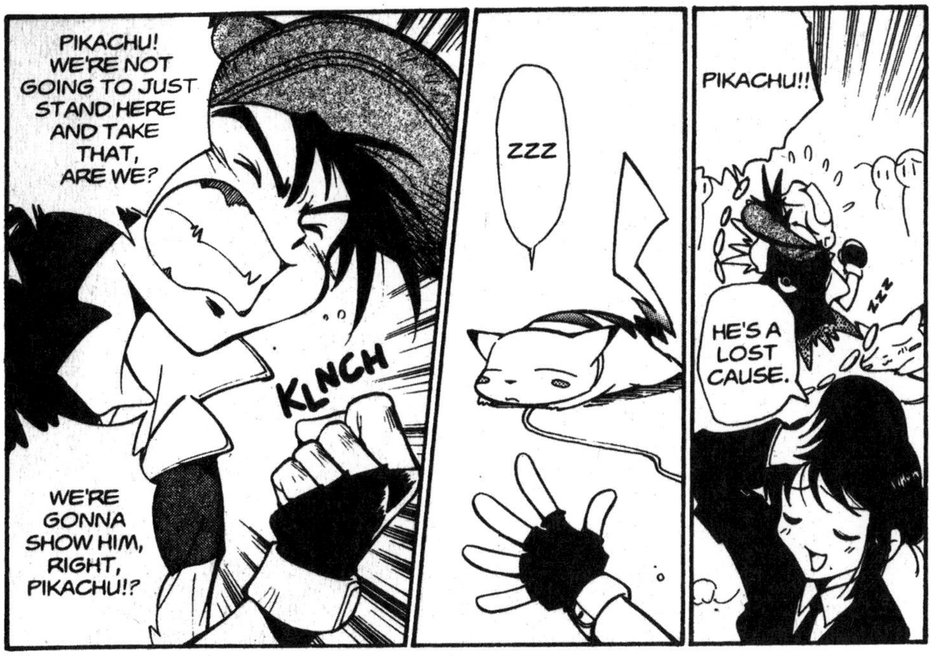
PIKACHU! WE'RE NOT GOING TO JUST STAND HERE AND TAKE THAT, ARE WE?
KLNCH
WE'RE GONNA SHOW HIM, RIGHT, PIKACHU!?
ZZZ
PIKACHU!!
HE'S A LOST CAUSE.

LEFT: "Pikachu, I See You" is from *Pokemon: The Electric Tale of Pikachu*, 1999. It was written and drawn by Toshihiro Ono, and is based on the animated series by Tsunekazu Ishihara and Satoshi Tajiri. It is an example of a "flipped" manga, as it is read from left to right.

objected to the content, which must have made it even more exciting for kids to read.) Anime, in particular, refashioned genre in a fresh and exciting way. Starring depictions of teens and children (some of whom were LGBTQA+), it reflected the audience it was aiming for.

In 2002, TokyoPop began publishing what they called "Authentic Manga," running Naoko Takeuchi's *Sailor Moon* "unflipped," teaching a generation of readers to read right to left. Previously to that, "flipping" the art, plus the cost of translation and laboriously pasting in new word balloons, had made translating manga fairly cost prohibitive. *Sailor Moon*, in particular, brought girls and women – who had largely been sustaining themselves with newsstand Archies – to the comics. The impact of manga cannot be overstated. Never, in the history of the medium in the U.S., had girls and women had access to so many comics works by and about and for

2012

- Genre mass market paperbacks essentially supplanted by eBooks
- YA domination: 55% of YA readers are adults
- The first issue of *Saga* is published

2013

- Patreon launches
- MCU expands into network and streaming TV shows
- Crunchyroll releases only licensed content. It begins digitally releasing English translations of popular manga like *Attack on Titan*

2014

- ComiXology acquired by Amazon

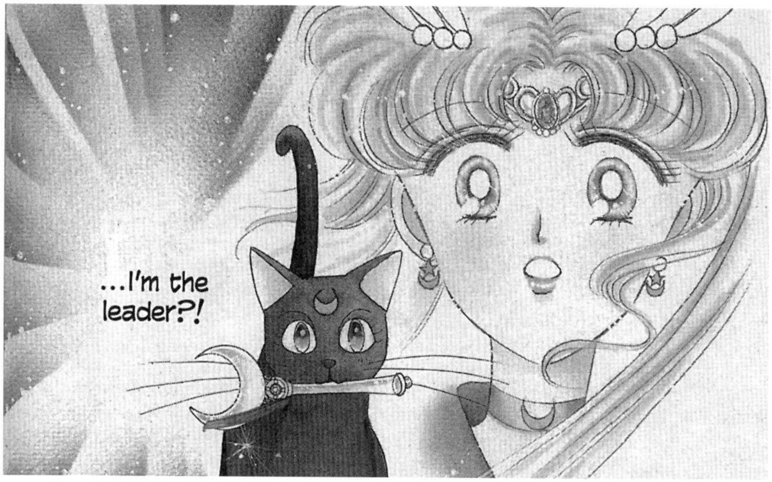
...I'm the leader?!

ABOVE: When TokyoPop released Naoko Takeuchi's *Sailor Moon* manga while the anime was running on cable, it changed both the medium and pop culture. This panel is from *Pretty Guardian Sailor Moon* Vol. 1.

women, with the creators' names right there on the cover. (The closest thing they had were newspaper strips, zero of which, circa the 1990s, chronicled the adventures of a tragic moon princess schoolgirl klutz fighting monsters with her friends.) Suddenly, writing and drawing comics seemed like something someone could grow up and do, much like writing a novel. Young women formed clubs and communities in person and online, as fans, aspiring artists or both.

The newsstands, too, were re-energized. The anthology magazine *Shonen Jump* began appearing in late 2002. It was in the same format as its Japanese forbearer; it ran chapters of different series each month, to be collected in cheap volumes. A *shōjo*-inspired *Sabrina the Teenage Witch*, capitalizing on the "magical girl" trend and rebooted by Tania Del Rio, began its run in 2003.

Scanlations – scanned art with digitally replaced text translated by fans – trained people to read comics on a computer (to the point where, in 2015, people were buying the manga the San Diego Comic-Con panelists were talking about on their phones while listening to the panelists talk about them).[1] Many people began "torrenting" anime and manga,

1 Initially, there was a code among fan translators; once a title was officially licensed in North America, the scanlations would be taken down. Crunchyroll, a platform that releases translated anime and manga more or less simultaneously with East Asia, who announced that it has 1 million paid subscribers in 2017, was criticized when it was launched in 2006, because not all of its content was licensed. This would not be rectified until 2013, when it received an infusion of capital and started releasing juggernaut properties like *Attack on Titan*.

2015

- DC moves to Burbank
- 167,000+ attend Comic-Con International: San Diego

2016

- 300,000 initial print runs of *The Walking Dead* trades

2017

- BookScan begins to include comic shop sales in their numbers
- *NYT* manga and graphic novel Best-Seller lists discontinued
- Crunchyroll announces it has 1 million paid subscribers
- 730,000 copies of 25¢ promo, *The Walking Dead* #163, preordered, breaking nearly 20-year record
- 1 million Telgemeier books sold this year
- FCC chairman Ajit Pai proposes to repeal net neutrality

among other forms of media. Torrenting, i.e., illegally downloading content peer-to-peer for free, became a common practice, with Pirate Bay launching in 2003. (It continues to be a big issue; another reason comic book retailers find it hard to compete in 2019 is that people can simply illegally download single issues for free.)[2] Anime and manga mainstays *One Piece* (2004) and *Naruto* (2005) soon followed. For the first time in decades, children and teens could get a variety of comics in a variety of genres, aimed at their age groups, from places everyone went – newsstands, libraries, online and in bookstores – bypassing the need for a specialty store. In less than 10 years, children were reading comics intended for them as a matter of course.

2000: Webcomics Supplant Newspaper Strips, Minicomics and Periodicals as the Ephemeral Form of Comics.

The turn of the millennium brought webcomics and webcartoonists such as Eric Millikin (1980s – present), *Bobbins* (1998) by John Allison, *Penny Arcade* (1998) by Jerry Holkins and Mike Krahulik, *PvP* (1998) by Scott Kurtz, *Cat and Girl* (c. 1999) by Dorothy Gambrell, *Demonology 101* (1999) by Faith Erin Hicks, *Narbonic* (2000) by Shaenon K. Garrity, *Achewood* (2001) by Chris Onstad and many others. DeviantArt, a fan-art community, began in 2000; developing talent still utilizes that platform to

"
Never, in the history of the medium in the U.S., had girls and women had access to so many comics works by and about and for women, with the creators' names right there on the cover.
"

2   In 2017, *Newsarama* linked to and quoted an academic paper by Tatsuo Tanaka, titled "The Effects of Internet Book Piracy: The Case of Japanese Comics." Tanaka drew the same conclusion that many people do: piracy hurts single unit sales, but it helps sells collections and promote series overall. "Piracy decreases sales of ongoing comics, but it increases sales of completed comics."

2018

▶

- AT&T buys Time Warner/DC
- Dav Pilkey's *Dog Man, Lord of the Fleas*, published by Scholastic, has a first printing of 3 million copies

this day. Again, it was the first time in history that anyone – especially marginalized groups – with access to a scanner and an internet connection (later, a tablet and WiFi) and an insane work ethic could put their work out in a place where people from all over the world could access it. In 1992, Ninja Turtles co-creator Peter Laird founded the Xeric Grant, which helped a group of winners each year put out a small print run of their comic. It was discontinued in 2012, replaced by the internet.

Often patterned on newspaper strips, the form seemed to hit its stride in 2003–2004. Many successful series, like *Questionable Content* (Jeph Jacques), *Girls with Slingshots* (Danielle Corsetto) and *Dinosaur Comics* (Ryan North), date from this time, and ran for a decade, if not more. Curated collectives, like Joey Manley's *Serializer.net* and *Modern Tales* (2002), sprang up, featuring the work of established and emerging cartoonists like Harvey Pekar, Raina Telgemeier, Gene Yang and Jen Sorensen.

In the early days of the form, webcomics were monetized by "tip jars," subscriptions and banner ads. Circa 2006, Ryan North and co. launched Project Wonderful, a system for bidding on ad space for a specific span of time, which was used primarily by webcartoonists; it folded in August 2018. Free webcomics were underwritten by the sale of merchandise and self-published collections, peddled online and at conventions. In 2007, Jeffrey Rowlandson founded TopatoCo, an online collective webcartoonist merch store. Some creators, like Spike Trotman (*Templar, Arizona*, 2005–2014) were able to leverage their work into a self-sustaining business. Still others transmuted their webcomics into brands. Most notably, *Penny Arcade*, a webcomic aimed at video game fans, started its own gaming – board, tabletop and video – convention in 2004. By 2007, it had moved to the Washington State Convention Center, and, by 2018, there are PAX-branded conventions worldwide. Meanwhile, titles like *Cyanide & Happiness* (2005) have crossed over into other forms of media.

In 2007, Dark Horse collected Nicholas Gurewitch's *Perry Bible Fellowship* webcomic, quickly selling out of its initial 36,000 print run due to Amazon preorders, as well as subsequent reprints. By 2018, many series

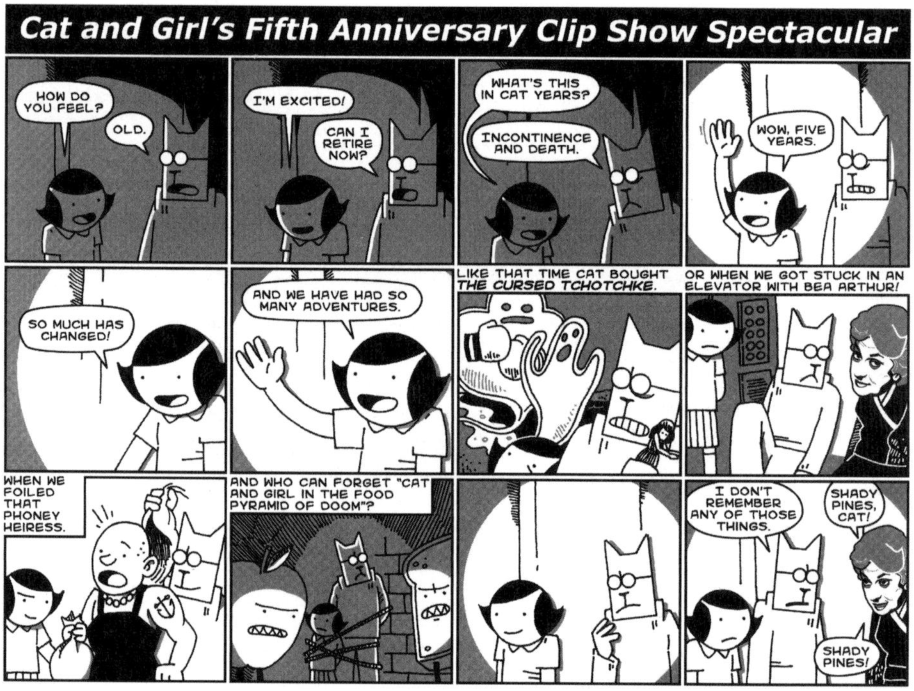
Cat and Girl's Fifth Anniversary Clip Show Spectacular
HOW DO YOU FEEL?
OLD.
I'M EXCITED!
CAN I RETIRE NOW?
WHAT'S THIS IN CAT YEARS?
INCONTINENCE AND DEATH.
WOW, FIVE YEARS.
SO MUCH HAS CHANGED!
AND WE HAVE HAD SO MANY ADVENTURES.
LIKE THAT TIME CAT BOUGHT THE CURSED TCHOTCHKE.
OR WHEN WE GOT STUCK IN AN ELEVATOR WITH BEA ARTHUR!
WHEN WE FOILED THAT PHONEY HEIRESS.
AND WHO CAN FORGET "CAT AND GIRL IN THE FOOD PYRAMID OF DOOM"?
I DON'T REMEMBER ANY OF THOSE THINGS.
SHADY PINES, CAT!
SHADY PINES!

RIGHT: "Cat and Girl's Fifth Anniversary Clip Show Spectacular" is from the 2006 collection *Cat and Girl*, by Dorothy Gambrell. It is one of the early webcomics that is optimized for viewing on a computer screen, and it is in the horizontal format.

that originated online are published by newspaper strip syndicate successor GoComics (for example, Paige Braddock's *Jane's World*), or publish/have transitioned into comic books or collections put out by Boom! (John Allison's *Bad Machinery*), Image, etc.

The next technological leap took place in 2010, when webcomics broke from a horizontal to a vertical format, thanks to the ubiquity of the smartphone (and concurrent rise in social media). Andrews McMeel, the "newspaper strip" publisher, began putting out collections of Tumblr and Facebook comics like *The Oatmeal*, by Matthew Inman, and *Zen Pencils*, by Gavin Aung Than. Instagram launched in 2010, and it has surpassed Tumblr as the platform where popular cartoonists such as Fran Krause (*Deep Dark Fears*), Simon Hanselmann (*MegaHex*) and Aminder Dhaliwal (*Woman World*) promote and/or serialize their work.

As the 21st century entered its teens, new methods of making money from webcomics emerged: most significantly, crowdfunding. Kickstarter, which started in 2009, began as a fun way to fund offbeat projects, but became a major source of seed money for self-published comics (and saved Fantagraphics's bacon in 2013; full disclosure, Fantagraphics is the author's employer and the publisher of this magazine). With Kickstarter, creators pitch their project. If the goal is met, they get the money, and Kickstarter takes a cut; if they don't, then no one who has pledged money is charged. To date, the most successful comics Kickstarter of all time occurred in 2012. Rich Burlew Kickstarted a reprint project for his webcomic *Order of the Stick*, with the goal of raising $57,750; 14,952 people pledged $1,254,120. As of 2019, Kickstarter campaigns are de rigueur, with boutique publishers like 2dcloud using it to raise money for each "season" of books.

Patreon, which launched in 2013, is a monthly subscription platform where "patreons" can pledge as little as a dollar (the platform takes a five percent cut of successfully processed transactions). Like Kickstarter, it has "levels," where the more subscribers pay, the more exclusive content or perks they receive. (In late 2017, Kickstarter soft-launched a subscription service, Drip, to compete with Patreon. As of press time, Drip has yet to gain traction.) It is notable in that it's an opportunity outside of more traditional comics distribution systems for creators to successfully get their work out there (and monetize it). The website Graphtreon estimates Patreon analytics. (Its disclaimer reads that it takes "the average earnings per patron in the same category, adding/subtracting the standard deviation from that average to get both extremes, and

BELOW: *Zen Pencils: Cartoon Quotes from Inspirational Folks* is a webcomic that is crafted vertically, ideal for scrolling on a cellphone. It is written, penciled and colored by Gavin Aung Than, and this selection contains an excerpt from "Advice for Beginners" by Ira Glass.

NOBODY TELLS PEOPLE WHO ARE BEGINNERS...
...IS THAT ALL OF US WHO DO CREATIVE WORK...
...WE GET INTO IT...
...BECAUSE WE HAVE GOOD TASTE.
BUT THERE'S A GAP.
FOR THE FIRST COUPLE OF YEARS WHAT YOU'RE MAKING ISN'T SO GOOD.
IT'S TRYING TO BE GOOD, IT HAS AMBITION TO BE GOOD...
BUGS
BUNNY
...BUT IT'S NOT QUITE THAT GOOD.
SNAP
BUT YOUR TASTE, THE THING THAT GOT YOU INTO THE GAME...
...IS STILL KILLER.
Calvin and HobbES
AKIRA

RIGHT: *Y: The Last Man* #56, 2008 was written by Brian K. Vaughan, penciled by Pia Guerra and inked by José Marzán, Jr.

130

> **"** This seems as though it was the theme going forward: comics + genre and/or nonfiction would reinvigorate both. **"**

multiplying by the number of patrons. These estimated earnings are calculated solely by Graphtreon. No actual earnings data for such creators is provided or endorsed by Patreon.") As of June 2018, the top three Patreon comics creators are Jeph Jacques (*Questionable Content*, a daily webseries), whose monthly income from the service is unlisted, but he has 6,733 patrons (so, bare minimum, he's making about $77,000 a year; Graphteon estimates he could be making between $15,000–$45,000 per month, which would push his yearly income into six figures); Abbadon (*Six Billion Demons*, a sci-fi epic with about 10 pages released a month), who is earning $6,267 per month from 1,802 subscribers; and Dave Kellett (*Drive*, a sci-fi comedy), whose monthly take is also unlisted (Graphteon estimates between $2–5,000), but he has 854 supporters.

Circa 2014, webcartoonists were experimenting with a variety of ways to subsidize their art in addition to Kickstarter and Patreon. One method, which Danielle Corsetto, Jennie Breeden (*The Devil's Panties*) and Shaenon Garrity discussed during a 2014 Emerald City Comicon webcomics panel, was Amazon "click throughs"; essentially, if webcartoonists have small links to Amazon from their sites, they get a kickback on any item a reader purchases. Also in 2014, Amazon acquired ComiXology, a company that was first an online pull list, then a comics eReader and eventually a site to buy and download digitized comic books. (In 2018, ComiXology announced that it's going to publish original comics content, as well.)

The popularity of anime, manga, webcomics and fandom in general brought the rise of conventions, including minicomics conventions. As more and more readers and creators connect online, the greater the desire is to travel and meet in person, and the higher the demand for local conventions. With the rise in social media and the ready availability of archival, collected and/or digital works, cons became less a place for publishers to announce projects and survey the landscape – and for readers to buy comics works they couldn't find anywhere else – and more of a place where fans celebrate their own communities, selling fan art, buttons, prints, etc. The term "Comic" in "Comic" cons has become vestigial, as well. Due to instantaneous internet feedback, the ubiquity of shows, a wider base of comics readers and relatively new opportunities to transition into traditional publishing, animation, film and TV, comic cons have changed tenor. While everyone hopes to turn a profit, or at least cover costs, and creators still use cons as a way to set project deadlines and to hone their business and networking skills, there is rarely that sense of one or two "buzz books" that everyone at a con – attendees, creators, publishers and exhibitors – are all talking about.

2006: Bookstores and Libraries

SOME COMICS HAD ALREADY found their way into bookstores and libraries in the 1990s, harbingers of the two strands that were to follow: genre and graphic memoir. Collections of DC's *Sandman* and *Watchmen* were there, along with Art Spiegelman's Pulitzer Prize-winning intergenerational graphic memoir *Maus* and Joe Sacco's *Palestine*. There were some alternative/literary comics flag-bearers like *Love and Rockets* by the Hernandez Brothers, *Jimmy Corrigan* by Chris Ware and nonfiction staples like Scott McCloud's *Understanding Comics*. Comics publishers experimented with bookstore distributors, but with little success.

The sea change that would crest in 2006 began in 2001, when two events occurred that would shape what a "graphic novel" was in the public's mind. The first was that independent publishers like Dark Horse, Image and Fantagraphics updated their bookstore distributors in addition to Diamond. Dark Horse and Image signed with LPC, which would quickly go under, but Fantagraphics signed with W.W. Norton, which continues to distribute their books (and this magazine)

to date. (Diamond launched its own bookstore distribution arm in 2002. As of July 2018, Image appears to be Diamond Book Distributor's only client with significant reach into bookstores.) The second thing that happened was that the *Ghost World* movie came out, and sales jumped. Suddenly, readers could go see the movie and then easily buy or check out from the library the (one!) book or series, with a clear author or authorial team, it was adapted from. According to Ken Parille, who wrote *The Daniel Clowes Reader*, by 2017, "translated into twenty-three languages, [*Ghost World*] has sold over a quarter of a million copies worldwide."

The medium always adapts to whatever genre trends are popular, but wider distribution brought non-superhero genre comics back to a wider audience. Brian K. Vaughan and Pia Guerra's *Y: The Last Man* and Bill Willingham and Mark Buckingham's *Fables* made their respective debuts in 2002. They were the last two tent pole Vertigo series, the creator-owned imprint that had been developed for a "mature audience," finite run DC titles in 1993. Fresh off his *Marvel Zombies* stint, Robert Kirkman, with artist Tony Moore, began putting out *The Walking Dead* comic book via Image in 2003. (Popular mainstream work-for-hire artists who wanted to control their own properties founded Image in 1992.) A runaway comic shop success, it was also notable in that it signaled the end of Marvel and DC as "the mainstream" qua comic books. Vertigo stopped publishing creator-owned titles in 2010, the same year *The Walking Dead* TV show premiered. In 2012, Brian K. Vaughan and Fiona Staples launched *Saga*, a sci-fi series that is incredibly popular in comic shops, digitally and in bookselling channels. It is the very definition of "the New Mainstream."

Alison Bechdel's and Marjane Satrapi's respective graphic memoirs were catalysts in the bookstore/educational/library markets. *Fun Home*, which is about lesbian cartoonist Bechdel's childhood growing up with a repressed gay father, was one of *Time*

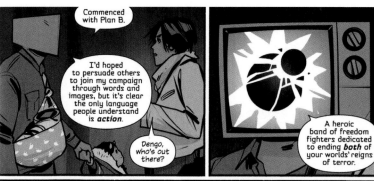

Commenced with Plan B.
I'd hoped to persuade others to join my campaign through words and images, but it's clear the only language people understand is *action*.
Dengo, who's out there?
A heroic band of freedom fighters dedicated to ending *both* of your worlds' reigns of terror.
No.
Please tell me you didn't really bring the *Rebellion* here.
"Rebellion" is for teenage girls.

ABOVE: This sequence is from 2015's *Saga* Vol. 5, which was written by Brian K. Vaughan and drawn by Fiona Staples.

BELOW: Panels from Marjane Satrapi's *Persepolis: The Story of a Childhood* Vol. 1, 2003

magazine's Top Ten Books of 2006. It was adapted into a Broadway musical, which won multiple Tony awards. Marjane Satrapi's two-volume graphic memoir, *Persepolis*, about coming of age during the Iranian Revolution was put out by Pantheon in the U.S. in 2003 and 2004. The one-volume collection was released in 2007, to synergize with the animated film adaptation. Both books are routinely assigned in high school and college non-comics classes.

Bechdel's and Satrapi's works tapped into a market for comics that had been underserved for decades. In 2007, NPR reported the results of an AP survey: women read almost twice as many books a year as men do, "in all categories except for history and biography." In 2010, according to the American Library Association, 82.8 percent of working librarians were women. Conducted in 2016 by the multicultural children's book publisher Lee & Lowe, a study of 34 publishers and review literary journals in the U.S. found that the staff was 78 percent women (and 79 percent white).

Readers consume graphic memoirs, especially when the personal is political, voraciously. (Thi Bui's *The Best We Can Do*, a generational graphic memoir about a Vietnamese refugee family, made NPR's Best Books of 2017 list.) Of *Fun Home*, Sean Wilsey wrote in *The New York Times Sunday Book Review*, "it push[ed] two genres (comics and memoir) in multiple new directions." This seems as though it was the theme going forward: comics + genre and/or nonfiction would reinvigorate both.

What made *Fun Home*, in particular, so significant was the kudos it received from a general interest publication, *Time* magazine, on a very short list of general books. Although *Maus* had received a Pulitzer Prize, it wasn't the flashpoint that *Fun Home* was. Writers such as Andrew D. Arnold (*Time*), Ken Tucker (*Entertainment Weekly*), Whitney Matheson (*USA Today*), and Douglas Wolk and Lev Grossman (chiefly, *The New York Times*, among various publications) began covering graphic novels as a matter of course, among other forms of media such as music and movies. In 2009, the *New York*

NO MORE UNIVERSITY. AND I WANTED TO STUDY CHEMISTRY. I WANTED TO BE LIKE MARIE CURIE.
I WANTED TO BE AN EDUCATED, LIBERATED WOMAN. AND IF THE PURSUIT OF KNOWLEDGE MEANT GETTING CANCER, SO BE IT.
IT'S I WHO DISCOVERED THE NEWEST RADIOACTIVE ELEMENT.
AND SO ANOTHER DREAM WENT UP IN SMOKE.
MISERY! AT THE AGE THAT MARIE CURIE FIRST WENT TO FRANCE TO STUDY, I'LL PROBABLY HAVE TEN CHILDREN...

Times Best-Seller list added manga and graphic novel categories.

After five years of throw-it-against-the-wall-and-see-what-sticks popularity, the print manga market contracted. TokyoPop had tried to develop its own line of original content by creators but lost its major licenses to Yen Press, and it folded in 2011. (It has made several thus-far-unsuccessful comeback attempts.) The Borders bookstore chain shut down in 2011.

In 2017, BookScan, which was formerly operated by Nielsen (best known as the TV ratings company), was acquired, and, for the first time, yearly numbers were released for both the comic shop and book retailer market. This is helping to address an issue for creators who questioned how accurate a picture BookScan painted of a book's sales success, and therefore the system's impact on their careers. The manga and graphic novel *NYT* Best-Seller lists were discontinued that year, too, which meant that the industry lost a valuable marketing tool. However, the popularity of young adult fiction, trending upward for the last five years, which will be covered in a future section, helped soften the blow.

2008: DC and Marvel TV Shows and Movies supplant DC and Marvel Comic Books

AS TEGAN O'NEIL OBSERVED in her essay "We Need to Talk about Thanos," "it wasn't that superheroes were holding comics back, but that comics were holding superheroes back." In 2019, the public's ability to identify which superhero characters are DC or Marvel by which "cinematic universe" they appear in can be attributed to the unexpected success of 2008's *Iron Man* film. In 2009, Disney, having lost the boys market, bought Marvel Comics for "about 4 billion," according to CNN.com. In 2015, DC moved offices from New York to Burbank. (At press time, AT&T had bought Time Warner, but the Justice Department is appealing the U.S. District Court Judge Richard Leon's approval, according to Christine Wang at CNBC.) Since there is no lack of writing about this, in media outlets such as *The New York Times*, *The Atlantic*, etc., suffice it to say Marvel and DC characters such as Batman, Spider-Man, Wonder Woman, etc. are more popular than ever.

What isn't selling very well are single-issue comic books starring the characters that are featuring in movies that take in one billion dollars. (Collections, of course, are a different story.) With line-wide reboots every year or so, old-school "mainstream" comic book publishers continue to lean heavily on

These are the people I come from.
MÁ
BỐ
LAN
Quyên
Thảo
BÍCH
It's pronounced BICK, okay?
THI
TÂM
I have figured out, more or less, how to raise my little family...
...but it's being both a parent and a child, without acting like a child, that eludes me.
We're such ASSHOLES!
Who, us?
That's a bad word.
We're the lame second generation.

ABOVE: From *The Best We Could Do*, a graphic memoir by Thi Bui.

tricks that are frankly nonsensical in 2019, like lenticular covers sales incentives (i.e., if a retailer buys double the number of copies of a non-returnable book they normally buy, they get one really collectible one with a fancy cover). Even longtime "Wednesday Warriors," shoppers who were accustomed to telling retailers some months in advance what they would like them to pre-order from *Diamond Previews* for their "pull boxes," have given up in exasperation when hyped issues simply fail to appear.

> " What isn't selling very well are single-issue comic books starring the characters that are featuring in movies that take in one billion dollars. "

The "comic book" format itself – approximately 32 stapled pages, with house ads for Sea-Monkeys, nostalgically priced 10¢ – was borne out of a need to fill up WWII surplus paper allotments, at a time when paper was rationed, with original content. In 2019, of course, paper and printing is expensive, and the average cover price of a 32-page comic book is $3.99, making it a poor bang-for-the-buck choice re: entertainment value. To put that in perspective, Netflix, a movie and TV streaming service, charges $10.99 per month, and Amazon Prime costs about $8.99 a month if a subscriber pays $99 for the year. The traditional comic book format, from an economy of scale perspective, is expensive for publishers to utilize in 2019 – and comic shop sales, in 2019, are generally not making those numbers.

And the number of comics specialty shops is in flux, according to Geoff Boucher at the *LA Times*: as of 2018, there were about 2,500 in the U.S. and Canada, a number that is in decline (as is retail, in general). In 2018, DC launched a line of 100-page superhero anthologies that only appear at Walmart stores. At press time, Todd Allen at *The Beat* said it was too early to judge the success of this venture. On July 13, 2018, ICv2's Milton Griepp, in association with

John Jackson Miller, released a newsletter in which they explained that the comic book and graphic novel market was down 6.5 percent in 2017. The sharpest decline was in comic shops. Digital sales remained flat, and graphic novels were down one percent in the bookstore market.

2010–2019: Scholastic and Young Adult Fiction

ALTHOUGH CHRIS MAUTNER will cover graphic novels and the young adult genre more extensively later in this issue, there will be just a few quick notes about distribution here. In 2005, Scholastic Books, a vertically integrated company that sells to educators, parents, institutions and kids, launched the Graphix imprint. Once the comics medium was paired with cheaply printed books directly marketed to children, there was no stopping it. (Scholastic book fairs have virtually no overhead. The stocked, wheeled shelves arrive at schools and are popped open. Parent volunteers ring up the customers.) Graphix's initial lineup included a colorized *Bone*, Jeff Smith's funny-animal-turned-young-adult-fantasy-starring-a-plucky-heroine graphic novel series. Scholastic had launched the *Harry Potter* series more than a decade earlier, so a full generation of readers was ready for it. In 2006, Raina Telgemeier rebooted Scholastic's/Ann M. Martin's *Baby-Sitter's Club* series as graphic novels. Parents who had grown up reading the series could share this new version with their children. Also in 2006, Telgemeier's webcomics compatriot, Gene Luen Yang, had his book, *American Born Chinese*, published by First Second. It was a finalist for a National Book Award.

By 2009, young adult fiction in general had taken off, buoyed by series such as *Twilight* and *Gossip Girl*. (Children and young adult fiction has traditions very similar to work-for-hire comics. For example, the book packager Alloy Entertainment, which is owned by Warner Bros., employs ghostwriters, owns the properties it publishes and keeps the rights to develop them in

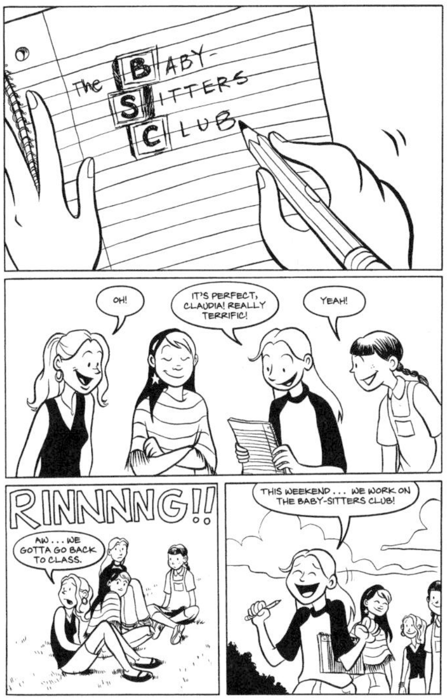
The BABY-SITTERS CLUB
OH!
IT'S PERFECT, CLAUDIA! REALLY TERRIFIC!
YEAH!
RINNNNG!!
AW... WE GOTTA GO BACK TO CLASS.
THIS WEEKEND... WE WORK ON THE BABY-SITTERS CLUB!

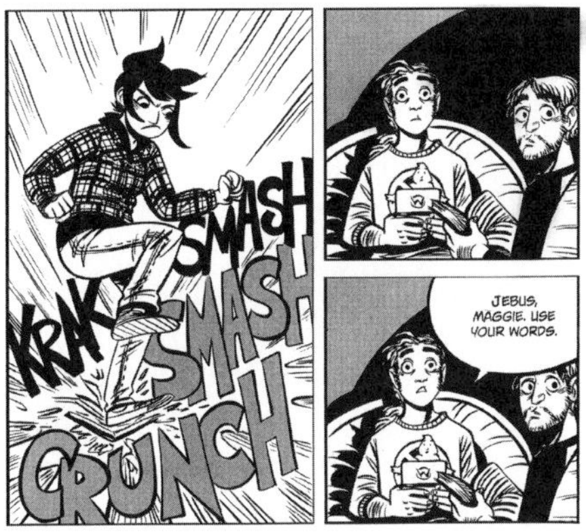
KRAK
SMASH
SMASH
CRUNCH
JEBUS, MAGGIE. USE YOUR WORDS.

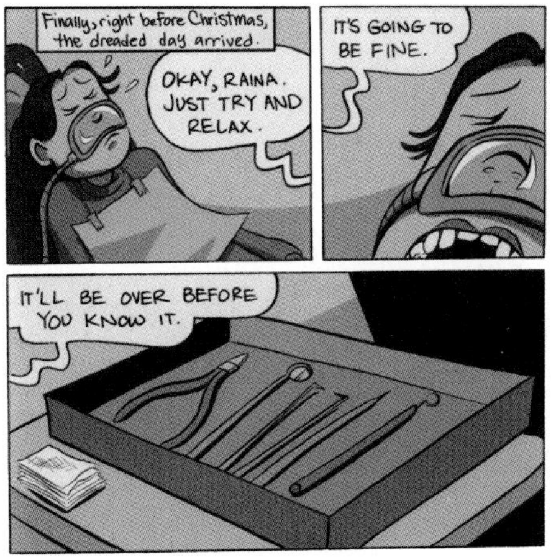
Finally, right before Christmas, the dreaded day arrived.
OKAY, RAINA. JUST TRY AND RELAX.
IT'S GOING TO BE FINE.
IT'LL BE OVER BEFORE YOU KNOW IT.

LEFT: Raina Telgemeier adapted Scholastic/Ann M. Martin's *The Baby-Sitters Club: Kristy's Great Idea* into a graphic novel.

UPPER RIGHT: From 2012's *Friends with Boys*, by Faith Erin Hicks.

LOWER RIGHT: From Raina Telgemeier's 2010 graphic memoir, *Smile*.

other media.) On Sept. 13, 2012, *Publishers Weekly* cited a contemporaneous Bowker Research survey, in which it was discovered that 55 percent of young adult fiction readers were over the age of 18. By 2012, eReaders such as Kindles had replaced the ephemeral, mass market paperback format, and the Bowker survey also noted that young adult readers, according to the *PW* article, were "early adopters: More than 40 percent read e-books, equivalent to the highest adoption rates of adult genres of mystery and romance." Accordingly, young adult fiction has subsumed genres that were traditionally associated with the mass-market book format, such as fantasy, sci-fi, horror and romance.

In 2010, Scholastic published *Smile*, Telgemeier's memoir about damaging her teeth as a child. It became a runaway success, as did her follow-up books. First Second continues to cater to the YA market, formatting their books in uniform, library-shelf-friendly dimensions and publishing books such as *Anya's Ghost* by Vera Brosgol in 2011 and *Friends with Boys* by Faith Erin Hicks in 2012. Noelle Stevenson began publishing her Tumblr webcomic about a shapeshifting sidekick, *Nimona*, in 2012; it was collected and published as a graphic novel in 2015 by HarperCollins. In 2014, YA comics series hit their stride. Boom! published *Lumberjanes*, by Noelle Stevenson, Grace Ellis, Shannon Watters and Brooklyn A. Allen. Intended to be a limited series about a group of girls having adventures at summer camp, the series proved to be popular enough that it is still ongoing. *Paper Girls*, a YA mystery series, appeared from Image in 2015, written by Brian K. Vaughan and drawn by Cliff Chiang. By 2016, creators were saying it was difficult to resist the young adult graphic novel market, since that's where the paying work is.

In Shannon O'Leary's *Publishers Weekly* article "Graphic Novels Had a Strong 2016, Though Comics Sales Slowed," she quotes Carson Moss, buyer at the Strand bookstore,

ABOVE: The *Lumberjanes* characters, illustrated by Brooke Allen.

as saying, "Marvel and DC make up 12% of sales, while 20% of sales are YA and children's comics"; and Doug Chase, graphic novel buyer at Powell's, saying, "We continue to see amazing growth in all ages and young adult graphic novels. Young adult graphic novel sales have almost doubled over the last two years." O'Leary concludes, "In fact, all the direct market retailers surveyed by *PW* are as bullish on kids' and YA comics as they are bearish on Marvel single issues. [Jeff] Ayers says that every year at Forbidden Planet, 'All-ages books keeps growing and I never really see an end in sight.' He adds, 'It's not like I'm giving it more space, I'm just having more sales and that's a good problem to have.'"

On October 6, 2017, the article "Comics and Graphic Novels Growth in the Mainstream U.S. Book Market is Being Driven by a Whole New Population of Readers, And Who They Are Might Surprise You," on NPD.com, disclosed according to "BookScan data, the comics and graphic novels category in the U.S. trade book market has experienced compound annual unit sales growth of 15 percent over the last three years, making it one of the highest growth categories in the trade book marketplace." It notes, "buyers in the 13–29 age group account for 57 percent of purchasing of comics and graphic novels overall."

2019–

IT'S DIFFICULT TO PREDICT how the FCC's 2017 repeal of net neutrality – which could profoundly affect how emerging cartoonists have been putting their comics out there for nearly two decades – the downturn in retail (and the concurrent loss of jobs, since retail was the #1 occupation the U.S., according to the Bureau of Labor Statistics), paper tariffs, the soaring cost of storefronts, etc. will affect how the medium will be distributed in the near future. There are countertrends. In that "Comics and Graphic Novels Growth …" piece, Kristen McLean, industry analyst for NPD Books, is quoted: "There is a whole new audience emerging for comics and graphic novels; these readers are younger, they are more diverse and they are getting their books from a much wider range of channels than we typically think of for comics." Carmen Noble reported on a paper written by Harvard Business School's Ryan Raffaelli. To paraphrase, the loss of big chain bookstores in the 2010s led to the resurgence of independent bookstores, which thrive on "community, curation and convening" – in other words, they're becoming the platonic ideal of a comic shop.

Disney Masters

Celebrating the great Disney comic book artists from around the world!

ROMANO SCARPA
Volume 1

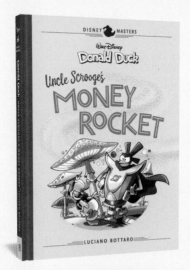

LUCIANO BOTTARO
Volume 2

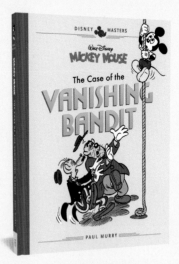

PAUL MURRY
Volume 3

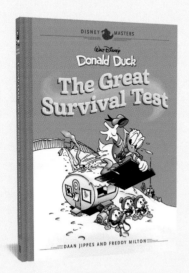

**DAAN JIPPES and
FREDDY MILTON**
Volume 4

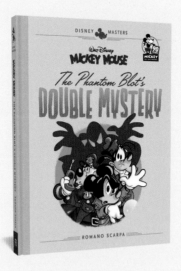

ROMANO SCARPA
Volume 5

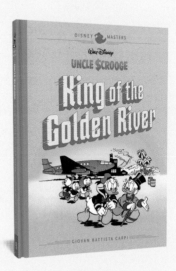

GIOVAN BATTISTA CAPRI
Volume 6

FANTAGRAPHICS BOOKS

What Do We Do with YA?

Chris Mautner

138

IT ALL BEGAN with *Bone*.

ABOVE: Scholastic's colorized *Bone: Out from Boneville* by Jeff Smith, 2005. Colors by Steve Hamaker.

OK, there were other factors in play. The manga boom of the early aughts that delivered truckloads of *Naruto* and *Fruits Basket* to Borders stores across America demonstrated once and for all that, conventional wisdom be damned, girls do read comics and it is possible to find and nurture new readers outside of the traditional Wednesday crowd market. And yes, the slow growth of the alternative/art scene in the '80s and '90s, fueled by publishers like Drawn and Quarterly and Fantagraphics, helped comics gain a critical and cultural cachet that made all the fancy folk pop their monocles out of their collective eye and exclaim, "Oh ho, what have we here?"

But if the "new mainstream" is largely referring to the glut of young adult and teen graphic novels that dominate the sales charts, then that moment in 2005 when children's publishing behemoth Scholastic decided to publish Jeff Smith's epic – in full color, no less – must also be regarded as a milestone.[1] The fact that it was published by Scholastic and not, say, Random House or Simon and Schuster, is significant. As one of the top dogs in the world of children's publishing, Scholastic has an extra advantage in the form of its book fairs[2], which brings their extensive back list to just about every elementary school in the United States on a regular basis.

And this is the key point: Those fairs (and Scholastic's aura of respectability in general) gave *Bone* and similar family-friendly comics access to an important demographic:

---

1 According to Jeff Smith's website, *Bone* is one of the most requested graphic novels in libraries across the country.

2 The official Scholastic website notes that book fairs sell "more than 100 million books to 35 million children and their families visiting more than 130,000 fairs in preschool, elementary and middle schools around the world." That's a lot of copies of *Bone*.

Educators[3]. Teachers and librarians saw how popular *Bone* is and then quickly turned on their heels to their book dealers and said, "You got any more of these?"[4]

So goes the armchair theorizing, at any rate. I could go on and list other influential all-ages material like the Studio Ghibli films, but I remain steadfast in my assertion that Smith's little fantasy-epic-that-could was a huge factor in ushering in the proliferation of Young Adult graphic novels that line bookstore shelves.

Of course, *Bone* has both feet fully planted in the fantasy genre, and genre[5] fiction – fantasy and otherwise – is something that children's and adolescent's literature has in abundance. Here, for point of reference, is a quick, thrown-together list of what I regard as some of the more prominent genre templates on display in most young adult graphic novels:

- **Fantasy.** One of the seemingly more prominent genres out there. Examples include *Amulet*, *Nimona*, *Nameless City*, *Cleopatra in Space*. You could probably lump sci-fi and superheroes in here if you're so inclined.

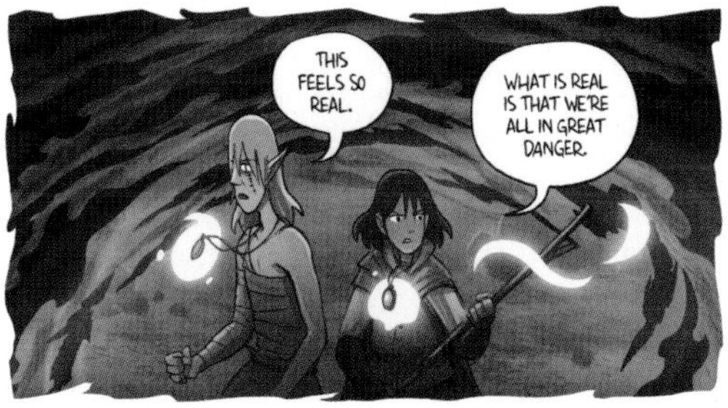
THIS FEELS SO REAL.
WHAT IS REAL IS THAT WE'RE ALL IN GREAT DANGER.

- **Historical Fiction.** Stories set within a noteworthy or turbulent time period, e.g. World War II. These stories usually have a child or teen as the protagonist, to provide a relatable viewpoint. Examples: *Resistance*, *Boxers and Saints*, *The Silence of Our Friends*.

- **Biography/Memoir.** Profiles of notable historical figures, or stories of the author's childhood struggles, usually designed to uplift and inspire, or at least let readers know they're not alone. The popular *March* series easily falls into this category, as do more personal works like *Stitches* and *Spinning*.

- **Plucky Kids.** Not perhaps an official genre *per se*, but there certainly are a wealth of comics about headstrong children/teenagers who learn that something is terribly amiss in their community and try to set things right against seemingly insurmountable odds. Kid's adventures stories like the *Boxcar Children* series, *Nancy Drew*, *The Secret Garden*, etc. could also fall under this rubric.

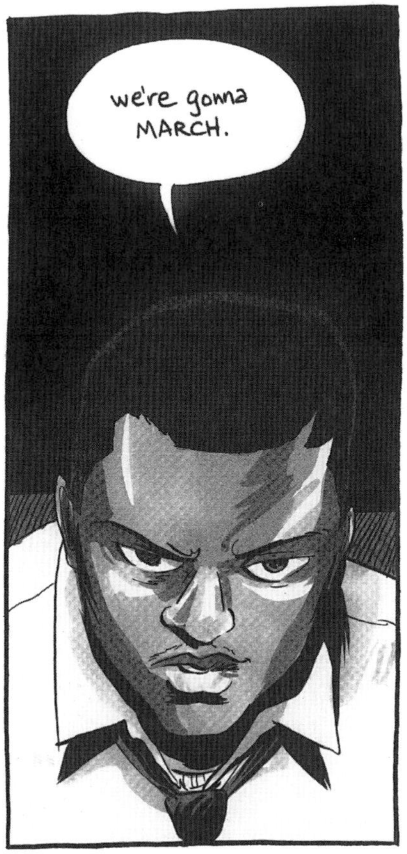
we're gonna MARCH.

LEFT: Panel from *Amulet: Prince of the Elves* by Kazu Kibuishi, 2012.

ABOVE: From *March: Book One*, written by John Lewis and Andrew Aydin and drawn by Nate Powell, 2013.

3 Mention should also be made of the American Library Association's 2002 convention, where the "Get Graphic @ Your Library" event was held, featuring folks like Neil Gaiman explaining why comix were kewl.

4 David Filipi, in his essay in the *Handbook of Research on Children's and Young Adult Literature*, writes that the various Scholastic editions have sold more than 4.6 million copies by 2010, compared to the 1 million copies of the original Cartoon Books (i.e. black and white) editions. The first Scholastic volume of *Bone* sold almost 16,000 copies in 2017 alone, according to Brian Hibbs.

5 Though I think it's worth noting that it's a fantasy epic with some decidedly non-traditional aspects: None of the *Bone* cousins fit the classic fantasy hero template, leaving Thorn to (reluctantly) fill that role, while Grandma Ben serves as the Ben Kenobi mentor (look, she even shares the name!).

I WANT MY NAME TO BE UP THERE IN THE BRIGHT LIGHTS! I WANT PEOPLE TO REMEMBER ME **FOREVER**!

RIGHT: Panel from *Big Nate: Great Minds Think Alike* by Lincoln Peirce, 2014.

LOWER RIGHT: An image from Jeff Kinney's *Diary of a Wimpy Kid: Do-It-Yourself Book*, 2008.

- **Slice of Life.** Could also be dubbed "coming of age." Stories about kids – just like you! – attempting to get through the daily grind of school and juggle problematic parents, teachers and siblings. *The Diary of a Wimpy Kid* and *Dork Diaries* series are the primary examples of these, but also consider *Amelia Rules*, *Be Prepared*, *Big Nate*, *Smile*, etc.

- **Mile in Their Shoes.** A subset of the slice-of-life books, with the perspective being attuned to that of a LGBTQA+ or ethnic minority figure. My experience was just like yours, except different! Ex: *American Born Chinese*, *El Deafo*.

- **Educational**. Comics that delve into the whys and wherefores of a particular K–12 (and perhaps beyond) topic (history, math, etc.), for the benefit of your edification. The bulk of Larry Gonick's bibliography falls under this category, as does Jay Hosler's.

- **Humor.** Silly stuff played strictly for laughs and generally designed for a younger audience. Think of Dav Pilkey's incredibly successful run of books.[6]

There are other categories, of course, and many of these books and graphic novels overlap various genres to form some sort of multi-pattern Venn diagram, but, generally, many of the "new mainstream" graphic novels that have captivated young readers fall neatly into one or more established themes.

And it's that notion of "established" that I want to emphasize. An important thing to keep in mind is that these types of genres have been in plentiful supply in prose form decades before this graphic novel boom took place. It's not as though children's literature lacked in fantasy stories, even prior to *Harry Potter*'s world domination. The Newbery Award list is full of stories of spirited kids from various time periods and backgrounds who struggle against family, friends or society (*Number the Stars*, *Bud not Buddy*, *A Single Shard*). And Barbara Park was detailing the humorous stories about the highs and lows of school life in her *Junie B. Jones* series years before Jeff Kinney.

BONK
HEY!

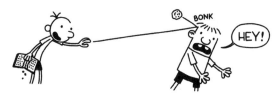

In other words, in producing comics for kids, publishers and authors didn't reinvent the wheel; they merely took the existing formulas and genres they were familiar with and laid that framework on their comics. It's tempting for those of us familiar with comics history and culture to see books like *Smile* as an extension of the sort of autobiographical tales that the indy comics scene abounds in, or the plethora of fantasy stories littering shelves as a direct result of *Bone*'s success,

---

6 A 2018 Scholastic press release proudly touts a first printing of 3 million copies of Pilkey's latest book *Dog Man: Lord of the Fleas*.

LEFT: *The Baby-Sitters Club* as drawn by Raina Telgemeier in 2006.

141

WHAT DO WE DO WITH YA?

but a lot of that groundwork was already established.[7] There's a reason, for example, that Raina Telgemeier's first books for Scholastic were adaptations of the popular *Baby-Sitters Club* series.

But even if you're aware of all of this, navigating these YA waters can still seem like a tricky or perhaps even unenviable proposition for the discerning comics critic/reader. For one thing, in North America we, as a general rule, have a distrust of genre literature, a suspicion that books that indulge in certain fantastic situations or adhere to a well-established list of rules and tropes are less worthy of the moniker of "Art" than those that attempt to grapple with serious topics in a more overt and self-conscious manner. It's a prejudice that's particularly pronounced in the world of comics, where fantasy, specifically superheroes, has dominated the landscape for so long and so thoroughly that many critics (myself included) have a tendency to chafe at any well-established genre comic that earns a plethora of plaudits (e.g. Tom King and Mitch Gerads's *Mister Miracle*).

And then there's the somewhat separate issue on how to best critically evaluate a book that's expressly written for children. As with genre fiction, many critics outside the YA market might view graphic novels expressly created for teens and children in a

---

7   Note, for instance, that the Book Industry Study Group (or BISG) lists far more subject headings under their Young Adult Fiction list than their Comics and Graphic Novels list.

RIGHT: From *Smile* by Raina Telgemeier, 2010.

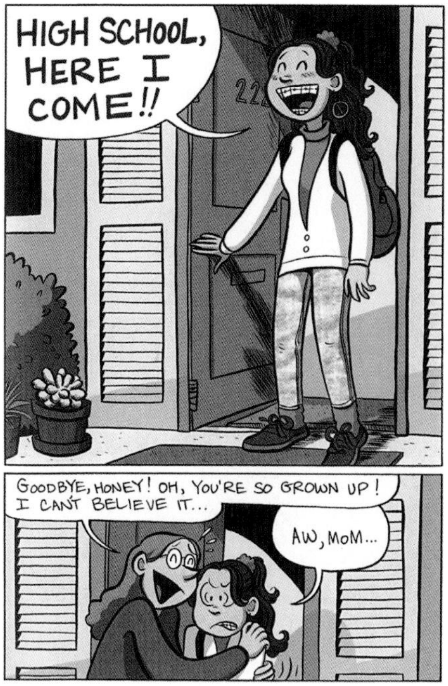
HIGH SCHOOL, HERE I COME!!
GOODBYE, HONEY! OH, YOU'RE SO GROWN UP! I CAN'T BELIEVE IT...
AW, MOM...

lesser light since they're made for a younger audience, one that perhaps has yet to appreciate the narrative subtleties of *Patience* or *Doomsday Clock*. What is the seemingly never-ending grim-and-gritty era of superheroes after all but an attempt to prove that they are NOT FOR KIDS?

But beyond that, I suspect there's a certain hesitation among critics about how to properly critique a book that's very pointedly not written for them. Children's literature, after all, often has goals that go beyond mere entertainment. Picture books for the very young, for example, are usually designed to teach reading or explain concepts like time or colors. Dr. Seuss's books are delightful, to be sure, but *The Cat in the Hat* was also expressly written to get children to recognize certain words.

So, does that mean that you need an educational background and five years of child psychology and library science in order to properly write about these books? Should you be grading on a curve if you don't? Well, yes and no. In general, it can be important to understand who the audience for a particular book is and what their particular concerns and interests might be. The plot of Raina Telgemeier's *Smile*, for example – young girl breaks front teeth, has to get fake ones and deal with embarrassing headgear – might seem shallow to adult readers. But, of course, if you're anywhere between grades four and eight, you know what a big deal that experience is.

More to the point, librarians and teachers (and those ensconced in the world of academia) often have a different–or perhaps to be more precise, an additional–set of criteria when evaluating a book than your average *Comics Journal* critic. Yes, they might be concerned about depictions of sex, violence or other "adult" topics, but you'll also often find concerns about visual literacy, sentence comprehension and other educational issues in these discussions of YA books.

Then there's the question of what exactly is a YA book anyway. If you had asked me before penning this article I would have given the term a wide berth, say, anything involving chapter books and beyond. Sarah Hunter, senior editor of books for youth and graphic novels at *Booklist*, however, notes a definitive demarcation point between middle grade (fourth–sixth) books and young adult (grades seven through 12). "Middle grade is about discovering the world," she said. "Young Adult is about discovering yourself."

In her book *Disturbing the Universe: Power and Repression in Adolescent Literature*, Roberta Seelinger Trites notes juvenile or middle school books tend to deal with an innocent world, one where evil is externalized and endings are happy. Teen or YA books, on the other hand, feature protagonists living in a flawed and corrupt world in which traditional institutions are untrustworthy or downright abusive.

"The trope of having fantasy heroes who are young adults literally trying to save the world ... and set things right ... is not accidental," said *Journal* critic and author Charles Hatfield. "It's kind of wired into the fact that young adult literature deals with power differentials and young people setting themselves against the powerful forces, which may include their teachers and other institutions that seek to control them. That's highly appealing to many comics readers."

To put it another way, there are reasons why these types of genre fiction are so popular for middle schoolers and teens, beyond the simple fact that kids like to read about people similar to themselves. Kids and teens have struggles that are different from adult ones, and being attuned or at least aware of those struggles can be useful when evaluating comics designed for that audience. But the guidelines for judging quality work applies to YA graphic novels just as much as it does to other kinds of comics. Basic questions such as: are the characters compelling, is the art engaging, does the work manage to do something interesting with familiar tropes, still apply.

There are going to be conversations we have about Raina Telgemeier and Jeff Smith that we wouldn't necessarily have about, say Tim Hensley or Aidan Koch. But that doesn't mean those conversations shouldn't be happening. There are children's books out there that are sophisticated in how they approach their subject or look back to past children's books in ways that might not immediately be visible to us. "What we expect from a tough-minded young adult book might not be what we expect from a tough-minded example of literary fiction that's written for adults, but that doesn't mean they're not complex and tough-minded," Hatfield said.

At the same time, we shouldn't allow our unfamiliarity with the YA market to prevent us from saying when a book fails to live up to its promise. Sometimes things are just flat-out awful, even if you're grading on a curve. Comics for young readers are a great thing, but we shouldn't allow boosterism to blind us to a book's faults. "There is still a perception that comics aren't real books. There are still a lot of librarians that are still pushing back against that mentality or are themselves feeling unfamiliar with the world of graphic novels," Hunter said. "I think librarians are just hungry for guidance."

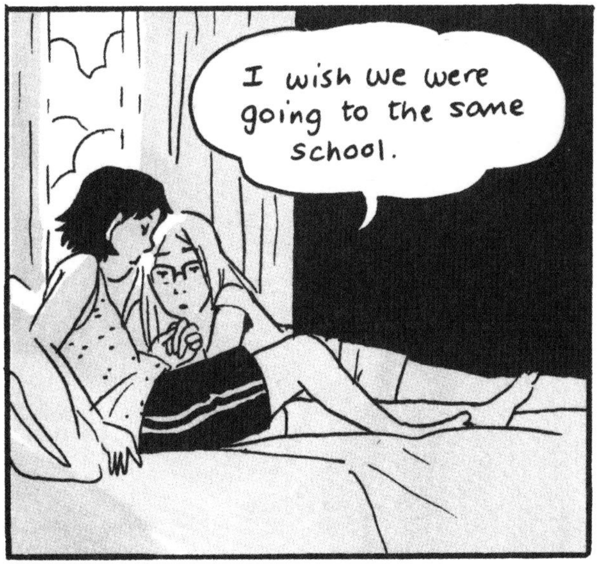
I wish we were going to the same school.

ABOVE: Panel from Tillie Walden's *Spinning*, 2017.

In her essay "Reading Literature in Elementary Classrooms" (found in the *Handbook of Research on Children's and Young Adult Literature*), Kathy G. Short writes that by reading literature, "children gain a sense of possibility for their lives and that of the society in which they live along with the ability to consider others' perspectives and needs. Engagement with literature thus allows them to develop their own voices and, at the same time, go beyond self-interest to an awareness of broader human consequences."

What goes for prose certainly goes for graphic novels as well. And if that's so, then it is fundamentally important that critics be willing and able to engage with these "new mainstream" books to evaluate and demand some semblance of quality, not in some false "wholesome" or didactic manner, but in creating work that rise above the substandard dreck that's prevalent, well, everywhere.

"Comics for young readers will have standards that arise historically from their own discourse. But on the other hand, [you should] still demand a lot from them," Hatfield said. "Ask a lot from them. Don't ask less. Just ask different questions."

Fifi Martinez

RJ Casey

FIFI MARTINEZ HAS the unique ability to make readers feel sheepish. Should someone be putting this much vulnerability and heartbreak into the world? Should we be spying through these murky peepholes that are Martinez's frantically paced pages? Is this allowed? The answer to all of these questions is, of course, an emphatic yes. And the sooner you embrace this brazen and beguiling art, found in her minicomics and on social media posts, the sooner you can witness an artist that will surely be one of the next steps in the evolution of autobio comics.

TOP RIGHT: Fifi Martinez, 2018. Photo by Tomás Perez.

FIFI MARTINEZ: I just got out of work.

RJ CASEY: Where do you work?

At a coffee shop. That's my "not die" job.

Do you make those fancy milk leaves on the top of lattes or whatever?

Yeah, I do the fancy milk leaves. I do that. [*Laughs.*]

Those are pretty impressive.

Thank you. It's the only creative thing I get to do during the day.

I read all of the comics again today. It oftentimes makes me feel like I'm reading something too intimate, or viewing something that's really private. Do you think that there's a voyeurism element to your work? While reading some of your pages, I feel like, "I don't know if I should be peeking in on this."

One of the comics I sent you actually was about voyeurism, so it's kind of funny that you say that.

Which one?

The pink one – *I Hope You Have a Nice Day.*

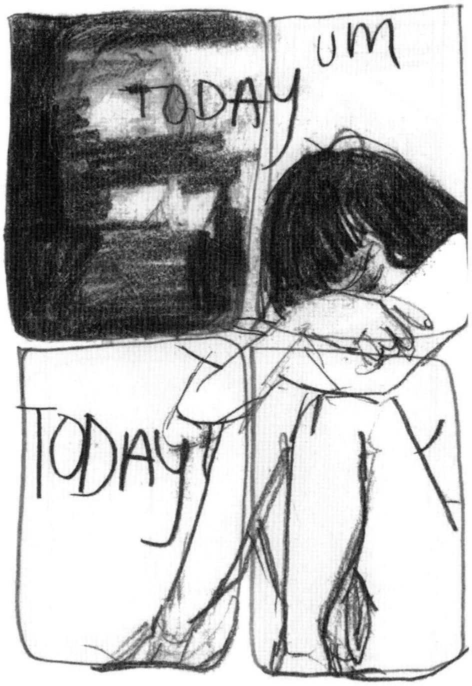
TODAY
UM
TODAY

TOP LEFT: From *I Hope You Have a Nice Day*, 2018

But you're aware of that and play around with that?

Yeah. That usually is a conscious effort. I think you might feel that way because you've caught the very, very beginning of my work. My first real comic *It Felt Like Nothing* was my intro back into drawing again. All of it is diary pages and sketchbook pages, sometimes even collaged together. They aren't really even comics. It is some really personal, heavy stuff. I shared it though. When I think about it, it can be really embarrassing.

Your intro back into drawing?

Yeah. I've been drawing since I was a kid, but I stopped drawing when I was in my early 20s. I didn't draw again up until last year when I started making comics.

Was there a reason for the absence?

I got married when I was 21. I was married to another artist and was just really focused on him. I didn't ever feel good enough to draw when I was with him. He was so good and eventually became sort of known in the art world. I was focused on him and that relationship, so I gave up doing stuff for myself.

Then what changed? What was the catalyst to start drawing again?

Losing him.

That relationship ended?

Yeah. It ended a few years ago. When it was over, I didn't know what to do with myself, so I impulsively volunteered at SPX. It was crazy, especially considering that I live all the way in Southern California. I flew there just to volunteer and be around cartoonists. I ended up being introduced to Raighne Hogan, the associate publisher of 2dcloud. We became friends and he encouraged me to start drawing again.

So, you were following comics already if you knew about SPX.

I've been reading comics since I was a kid, then started getting into weirder comics and art comics when I was around 23 or 24. I used to know a guy who reviewed comics who worked at the museum across the street from my old coffee shop. He would bring me boxes of comics that people would send him. I found some of the artists that I love today through that. I got really into it.

I'm projecting here, but after reading your body of work, you seem like an anxious person. Is that a correct assumption?

[*Laughs.*] Yes. I'm pretty anxious. Not as much these days, but that might not be true. It's manifested itself in a less obvious way. But, yeah, I have a ton of anxieties.

Does making these deeply personal comics help release that anxiety? Or the opposite? Is it triggering to relive some of these unpleasant recent memories?

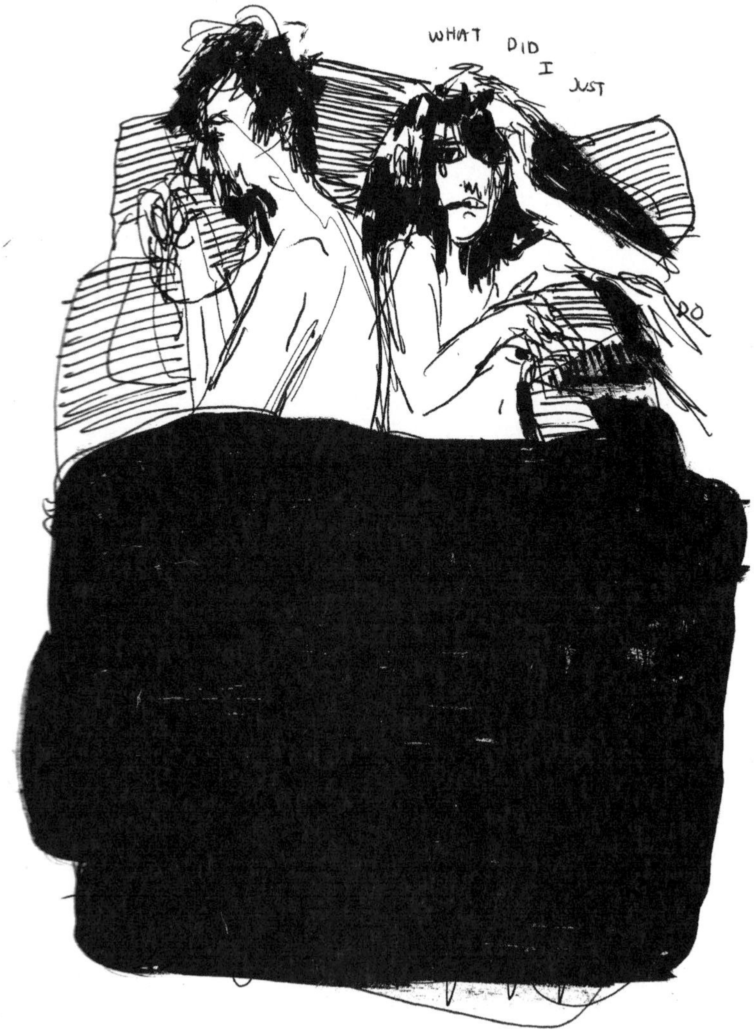
WHAT DID I JUST DO

ABOVE: From *It's You, Beautiful and Sad*, 2018.

Both. I draw as a coping mechanism and it helps me practice mindfulness. To draw helps me be in the moment.

Even when you're drawing pretty painful things you're still mindful?

It depends on the quality of work. If I'm really in a lot of pain, I'll draw the emotion out of me until I'm tuckered out. If I'm calm and I really want to try hard to make my pages more formal and technically attractive, then it becomes a practice in mindfulness. That's when I'm more focused on the quality of the drawing.

What do you mean by "draw the emotion out?"

I'm a very emotional person, which you might be aware of after reading my comics. [*Laughs.*] Recently I started drawing daily diary comics. Through that, it helps me cope and process with what happened that particular day. It helps me process how I feel about certain moments or exchanges or feelings. I force myself to see things this way, no matter what happens, and recreate them and deal with them. It's kind of like exposure therapy. I'm not only getting that catharsis of just getting it out, but I'm also healing because I'm forcing myself to face things.

Do you create comics to validate your emotions and feelings?

MARTINEZ: I don't think about that too much while I'm doing it, but there is something validating about making work that is so emotional and so personal. I have a lot of people who reach out and connect with me after reading my work even though I'm just starting out and I don't have that big of an audience. I do have people messaging me quite often because I portray certain feelings in my comics that resonate with them or that they connect to. In a way, that's pretty validating. I took the time to make the work and for someone to relate, that just makes me feel like my emotions aren't stupid.

What do you think causes people to reach out?

I've had people reach out to me for different reasons and different intentions. I mean, some people have no intention other than just to talk to me. It ranges from a "thank you" to they want to get to know me and have a conversation or be my friend in real life. They are mostly young women. I tabled at the Womxn of Color Zine Fest in Los Angeles and afterwards I had a good amount of young Chicana- and Chicanx-identified people message me. They were telling me they could relate to my work and wanted to have conversations about things like what inspired my work. Then they tell me what they've gone through. But I also have weird dudes who have come forward and ... uhhh ...

Yep.

I make a lot of comics about sex and pain. I have these pure interactions with these sweet people, then I have weird interactions with dudes who are like, "Oh, I've felt this way before too. I'm in pain, also. Want to meet up?"

How do you navigate that grossness?

I'm not really sure yet. I've already had a handful of experiences where men have come forward and attempted to prey on me based off the sensitive nature and sexuality of my work. I don't know. I'm learning how to look out for red flags in life. Making very personal work like this, it kind of makes you open to people thinking that they know you or feeling like they have a right to talk to you in a certain way. I'm becoming aware of that. Before, I just thought I should be nice to everyone that likes my art. [*Laughter.*]

You mentioned that you are attempting to do daily diary comics.

Yeah, I've been trying to do diary comics. Sometimes they are about my day and sometimes they are about certain situations that really fuck me up.

When you're making those types of comics, do you let those intense types of situations breathe a little bit and reflect on them? Or do you try to get them on paper immediately? Your work has a frantic feeling a lot of times.

The more frantic stuff I am doing as I'm freaking out about that situation.

You're making those in real time?

Yeah, sometimes. My comic *It's You, Beautiful and Sad*—every single page of that comic was made as I was freaking out about the situation I was in. It's funny because it goes back and forth between me feeling good about it and not feeling good about it. If something hurts me a lot, I have to wait until I feel OK about it before I can make a comic describing it. It just depends on how much it affects me.

Have you thought about what your comics would look like if you got into a happier relationship?

I don't think that will ever happen. [*Laughter.*] I don't know. I feel like I've

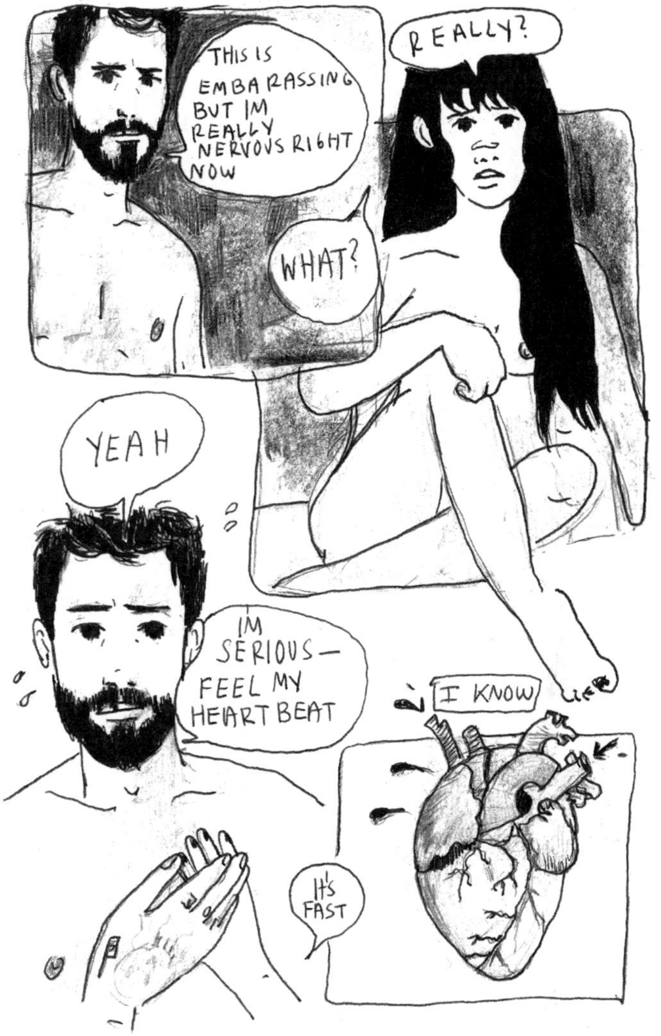

THIS IS EMBARASSING BUT IM REALLY NERVOUS RIGHT NOW
REALLY?
WHAT?
YEAH
IM SERIOUS— FEEL MY HEART BEAT
I KNOW
IT'S FAST

ABOVE: A page from *It's You, Beautiful and Sad*, 2018.

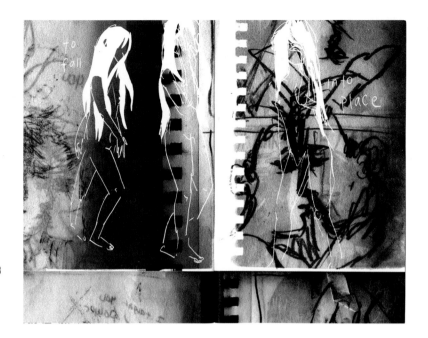

ABOVE: From *It Felt Like Nothing,* 2017.

always been a naturally sad person. The happiest I was in the past was when I was in my marriage and I wasn't even making art. Here's what I think: by the time I'm healthy enough to be in a happy relationship, I will be a better artist technically. There will be other stories outside my own that I will be able to tell.

Like veering toward fiction?

Maybe. Or other people's stories. There are more topics other than myself that I eventually want to explore in my work. I'm still just starting out and it's been easier to focus inward. Like I mentioned earlier, it is a coping mechanism for me. I've been through a lot and making art like I am now is working for me. But when I get into a better place, I'd like to do some historical comics. I want to do comics about other people's stories. I have a lot of friends and family members who have gone through crazy stuff. When they tell me these things, I think, "God, that would make such a good comic." It would be work that would be less about me and more about other people. I'd like to eventually draw different-looking characters and more complexly drawn things.

You said that you were the happiest when you weren't working on art at all. Is there a correlation there?

I don't think there was a correlation. Since I've started making art, I've grown as an individual and feel like I'm in this weird period that most people go through in their early 20s. But I've been delayed in my growth because I was so dormant in my marriage. I'm happier now … no, I'm not. Hold on. Let me really think about this. When I was in my marriage, I had that relationship to make me feel good. I didn't know how to make myself feel good. I didn't have to do anything for myself. There was no need to be an individual. There was no need to travel, to meet other artists, to make work, to push myself. I didn't need that. I just had this person who could give me endless compliments and validation and affection. It really stopped me from growing as a person. Now I don't have that at all. I'm left to my own defenses. Drawing is the only thing that makes me feel like I want to keep going. That sounds so bleak, but it's true.

When you draw, you're using mostly ink and paper?

I was into graphite for a little bit, but it was too smudgy. I mostly just use ballpoint pens and ink. I'll fill in larger spaces with a paintbrush dipped in ink. I use a little bit of paint and recently I've started to work with color. I'd like to incorporate more markers into my work. I'm not really into doing anything digitally. I don't know how to make things not look corny that way. That's why I do everything on paper.

Do you just burn through sketchbooks?

Yeah. I go through a sketchbook every two weeks at this point. I probably draw two to three hours a day. I guess for a lot of people that's not a lot, but for me it is. I work two jobs and go to school. I definitely prioritize making comics and drawing over everything else, though.

What do you do with the full sketchbooks after every two weeks?

I tuck them under my bed and pretend they don't exist. [*Laughter.*] I make a new minicomic almost every month. I usually scan the images from the sketchbooks that I like the best and figure out what makes the story I want to tell. Most of the time it's easy to decide because I make work about the same types of things. Then I go to Fedex and print it out. I'll assemble it and there it is – a new comic.

Recently you posted some videos on social media where you were drawing on these huge canvas-sized pieces of paper.

Uh-huh.

Then ripping them up when you were finished with the drawing.

[*Laughs.*] Oh God, yeah. That was a moment. I was going through a weird time. Sometimes I work in other mediums that I don't do anything with except stupid shit like that. I was feeling really manic at the time. I used to have a lot of unhealthy coping mechanisms and didn't know how to self-soothe at all. I'm still not very good at either of those things now, but sometimes when I'm feeling really bad I just want to destroy something. In that moment, I thought if I drew these things out then destroyed them, maybe it would be good enough. It was the perfect amount of destruction to just make me feel OK.

Better to destroy paper than …

Right. That was a very specific thing … I was going through some relationship issues that had to do with another person. Then it was really funny because he logged in and was actually watching after I started filming. I started writing messages to him and drawing pictures of him. Then I started drawing pictures of myself in a way that … I wanted to show him the way he made me

feel. Eventually, I couldn't deal with him watching me anymore and it made me feel really insane. That's when I started ripping all the drawings up and punching them and throwing them around. [*Laughs.*] Felt great.

Have you seen him or talked to him since then?

Yeah, just saw him two days ago. He thinks I'm insane. [*Laughter.*] His attitude toward me seems to be like he thinks I have an endearing type of insanity. "Oh, you're so crazy."

How'd that conversation start? "Hey, I saw you shred pictures of me live on my computer?"

I mean, he's gone through it with me. I think he's getting used to it. I post a lot of my work just temporarily on social media. I'm too afraid to leave some of it up permanently. That way I know who sees it and I know exactly what to show. He's seen me draw very intimate moments between us. Naked drawings of him. Drawings of us having sex. He's seen me make a lot of art that has to do with him. He's an artist too, so I think he gets it. He also just might be a little bit terrified of me. [*Laughs.*] That's fine.

Touching upon this same topic, you once wrote, "Making comics has alienated people in my life by making them mad or uncomfortable."

[*Laughs.*] Yeah.

There are more instances than just this one guy you were talking about?

I've made comics about every man that I've had in my life. It feels kind of shitty sometimes to do that, but I am deeply inspired by … You know, I didn't always think this is what I was going to do with my artwork. I met Laura Lannes at SPX last year and I read her comics. After I read those, I thought, "Wow! I could do this too." You know? "I could be this open in my work about my relationships with these people." I started making work afterwards that was a little bit more straightforward. It's become the work I do now and it helps me. I'm pretty stable in my life, but the one thing that throws me off and causes me to lose balance is men. Usually when I'm seeing someone, my work is just about them: how I feel, little interactions, what they put me through.

How has it gone for these men?

There's been a whole spectrum of reactions, from, "Fuck, no!" to "Fuck, yeah!" [*Laughter.*] Depending on the person, it's been different. Recently, I was seeing someone who's not an artist and not into comics. I notice that when I date men who aren't into art, they find what I do to be really creepy and really weird. I get it, I get it. The only reason it makes sense to me is because I've been reading diary comics since I was really young. I remember first reading Jeffrey Brown comics, then David Heatley comics, then Noah Van Sciver comics. I'm used to people sharing embarrassing and horrible things about their lives and exposing their relationships. It seems normal to me. But I forget, that to other people, it's not. I'll make comics about first dates, having arguments, having sex, things I've done to them, and things that they've done to me. Some men just don't want to see that. I've had guys specifically say, "Do not make a comic about me." That person who I've been seeing recently, I put him in a quick four-panel diary comic just about the day. I didn't write his name or say anything about him. I only used his likeness. We got into this argument about it and he stopped talking to me. Just because of a stupid four-panel diary comic on Instagram, you know? I have other people who are super stoked to be included. The guy who watched the live video of me losing my fucking mind laughs about my comics. He thinks they're funny. He's a good sport about it. Some people think it's cool and other people think I'm a freak of nature.

They think I'm a creepy, silly girl making these comics out of spite.

Overall, what do you want to get out of comics?

Out of making comics? Like, where do I want to go?

Sure. What's the future of comics look like for you?

I just want to keep making work and want to continue to grow and progress. I haven't really thought about it. One of the cool things about doing comics is meeting so many people while traveling to different comic shows in different cities. Meeting other cartoonists has been one of the greatest things for me because I feel like we have this kinship where we can deeply relate to one another. We're all these weird, anxious artistfolk who just want to draw it all out. I want to keep making friends, traveling and getting my work out there. In terms of the emotional stuff, I want to help people in some way. I hope the more emotional and raw stuff helps people process things. That feels really cool. I want to become a better artist. I want to keep making comics and get better at drawing. Eventually, I want to tackle bigger and longer projects. Do more refined, nice-looking things. Making books that aren't just little manic, self-published zines. ☀

OPPOSITE: Colored page posted on Martinez's social media account, 2018.

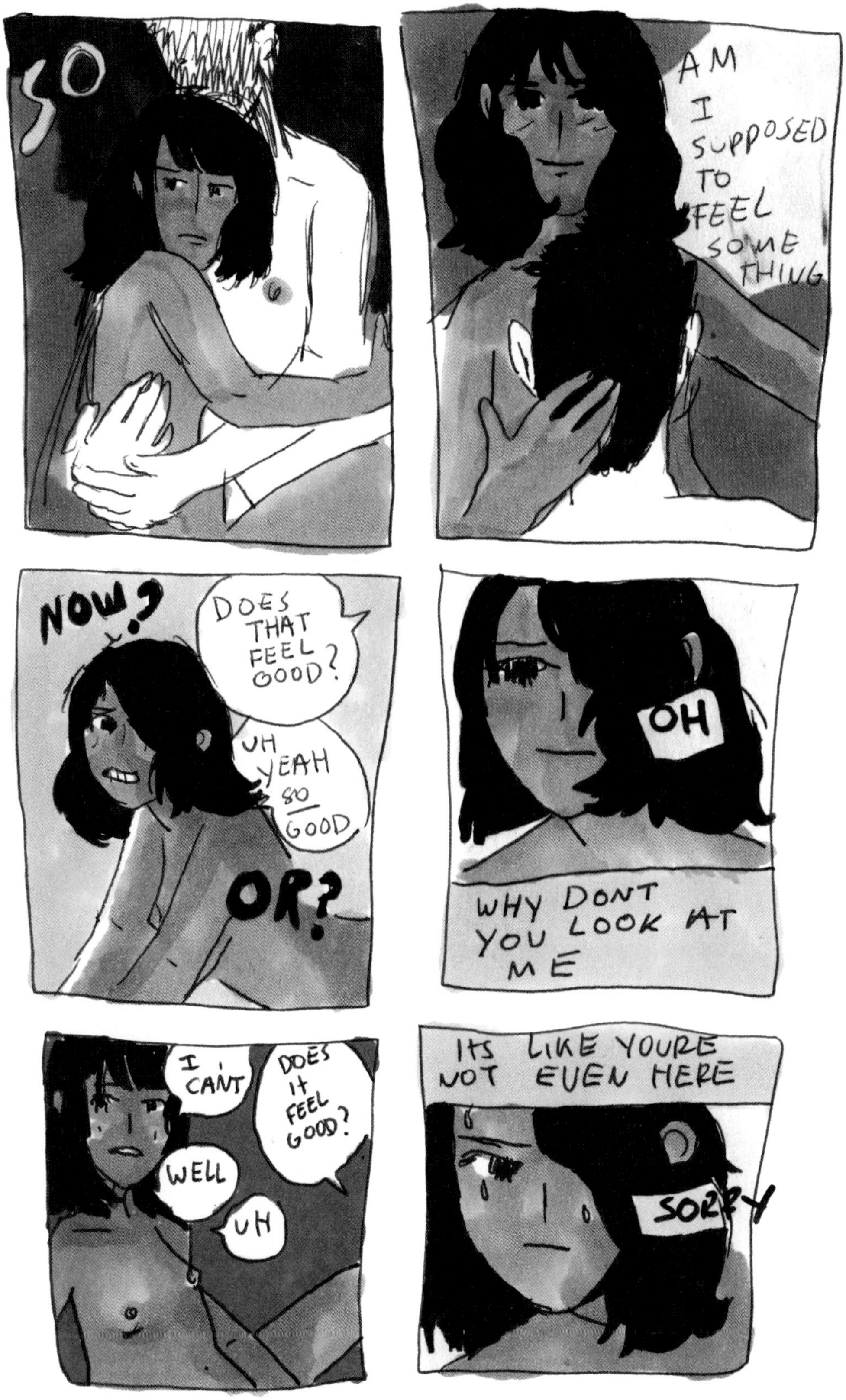
SO
AM I SUPPOSED TO FEEL SOME THING
NOW?
DOES THAT FEEL GOOD?
UH YEAH SO GOOD
OR?
OH
WHY DONT YOU LOOK AT ME
I CANT
DOES IT FEEL GOOD?
WELL
UH
ITS LIKE YOURE NOT EVEN HERE
SORRY

Steve Perry
A Comics Tragedy

Ally Russell

I FIRST BECAME AWARE of Steve Perry during a "Legends of Indie Comics" panel at the 2017 Vancouver Fan Expo. Each of the panelists, all born in the 1950s, had enjoyed a long career in the field they aspired to since childhood. Had life taken a different path for Steve Perry, he might have pulled up a seat at the same table. *Concrete* creator Paul Chadwick told the audience, "I got my first job drawing Salimba the Jungle Girl, which was a short-lived series Blackthorne published in 1986. She was like Tarzan, only black and female. It was written by a strange guy with a tragic life, Steve Perry. He later got cancer and was murdered and cut up in pieces by his roommate." There was a shocked pause and nervous laughter from the audience before the conversation moved on. It was only when I tracked down a copy of *Salimba* that I began to understand the true extent of Perry's tragedy.

A collection of *Salimba* was published in the last year of Perry's life; he sold the rights for $500 in a desperate bid for cash. It also contains his final work, "Baby," about a child born into violence and addiction. Abandoned by its mother, the baby, by some good fortune, falls into the loving arms of Salimba. But Salimba is heartbroken to discover that she cannot provide the necessary milk to sustain the child. Vivid, dark and devastating, that story shook the earth for me. I soon learned that it was autobiographical.

The second of three children, Stephen James Perry was born in Maine on December 12, 1954. He evinced an early interest in literature, devouring the works of Edgar Rice Burroughs and Robert E. Howard from age 5, before acquiring his first comic, a copy of *Fantastic Four* #4, in 1962. When his salesman father abandoned the family, Steve's mother fell into depression, attempting suicide. Steve fled his home with his younger brother, became a ward of the state, and what followed was an unsettled upbringing that set the course for the rest of his life. Longtime friend and collaborator Stephen Bissette, who is best known for his work on *Swamp Thing* and the self-published comics anthology *Taboo*, believes Perry's childhood neglect and betrayal imbued him with an expedient survival instinct and an opportunism that warped his moral compass. "Short-term immediate gain trumped long-term relationships," Bissette said. "One time I was visiting his apartment, showing him some artwork I was doing on a current job, and accidentally left a piece of art," he recalled. "When I got home and realized – I lived about 40 minutes away – I drove back to Steve's apartment, and he had already sold it to someone! That that would even occur to him as a thing to do was maddening."

Bissette met Perry in 1974, at Johnson State College in Vermont. A sophomore majoring in English, Perry had already written, staged and produced two original

...THEATAR-RRRGH!
OHHH... NOOO... NOOO... L...LOO...
UGH... M-MY...
...LOSING IT...
...MY... FEET...
KA
THE END

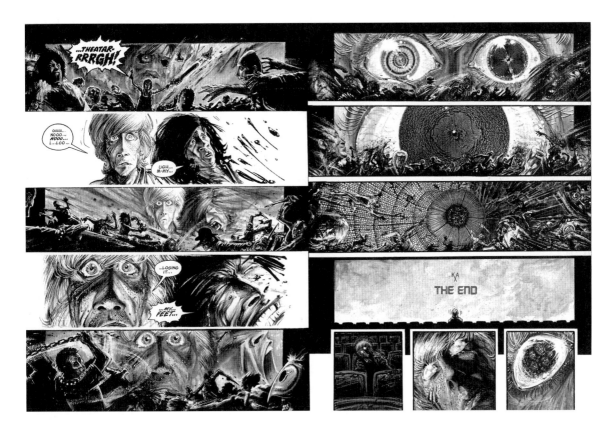

science fiction plays that enraptured student audiences. He was also, at this time, writing hundreds of missives to Marvel Comics, desperate to see his name printed in their letters pages, and succeeding on a number of occasions. Faculty members encouraged Bissette to meet the 6'3" brooding loner – whom Al Williamson would later describe as resembling a young Nick Nolte – and the two formed a lifelong bond over their shared obsessions with horror, fantasy and bad Steven Seagal action movies. While many people couldn't get past Perry's brusque, intense persona, he revealed to Bissette his acerbic wit; he was also a prodigious guitarist and an unrivaled chain-smoker. Perry didn't do anything by halves. He was also a voracious reader, repeatedly revisiting books to study their writers' craft, and able to recite vast passages verbatim decades after reading them. Perry and Bissette collaborated on their first comics work in 1976; the black-and-white one-shot *Abyss*, which Bissette used to successfully apply to the Joe Kubert School of Cartoon and Graphic Art. There, he met fellow artists Rick Veitch, Tom Yeates and John Totleben, whom he introduced to Perry. "We shared gigs, contacts, subsidized each other's rent when needed … Around 1980, we were all getting established somewhat in the biz and Steve Perry was looking to follow suit," Veitch recounted. "He moved close to Bissette and I, and became part of our local creative and social group.

ABOVE: "Kultz" from *Epic Illustrated* #6, 1981. Written by Steve Bissette and Steve Perry with art by Bissette.

LOWER LEFT: Steve Perry, circa early 1980s. Photo taken by Debra Rausch.

Dear Rich, Roy, and Joe,

I think you are doing everything that could be done correctly with the Fantastic Four. Rich's art is not really Rich Buckler, it's Rich Buckler's tribute to Jack Kirby and to the style and excellence of the F.F. in their former day of greatness. FANTASTIC FOUR is still worthy of its logo, and for the past five issues has lived up to that logo.

Roy, you treat the F.F. as if they were your own, as if you live with them. In the F.F. is the writing and grasp of everything that was in the first 25 issues of CONAN. It's really the Roy Thomas of a year ago, of two years ago, and it's fierce. Keep it up.

Rich and Joe are not copying just another, possibly more sellable style. They are *heralding* that style, but also innovating on it dramatically, something that cannot be helped, considering Rich's brilliant concepts of paneling.

I, for one, am itching to again see the F.F. involved in an intergalactic adventure, possibly relating in some way to the current and future dealings of Adam Warlock. Just a hint; that's all it could be. Thanks.

Stephen Perry
P.O. 933
Johnson State College
Johnson, VT 05656

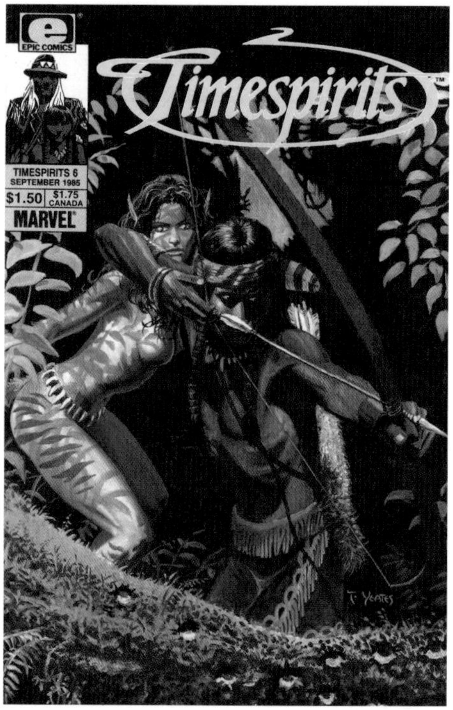
EPIC COMICS
Timespirits
TIMESPIRITS 6
SEPTEMBER 1985
$1.50
$1.75 CANADA
MARVEL

LEFT: A Perry-penned letter published in an issue of Marvel's *Fantastic Four*, circa mid-1970s.

RIGHT: The cover to *Timespirits* #6, 1985. Art by Tom Yeates and colors by Steve Oliff.

I really liked him as a person. He was smart as a whip and fun to talk to. Well-grounded in the nitty-gritty of New England life and a complete pop culture geek."

Tobe Hooper, Stephen King and Guy N. Smith were among his idols; Perry specialized in the dark side of humanity, and his collaborators tell me many of his stories were simply "too fucked up" to ever see print. Nevertheless, fueled by innumerable hits of a bong he'd fashioned from tubing and the thimble from a Monopoly board game, the years 1981–1986 saw him scripting an impressive body of work that appeared in *Heavy Metal*, *Epic Illustrated*, *Bizarre Adventures*, *T.H.U.N.D.E.R. Agents* and the newly revived *Creepy*, to name a few. The strength of this portfolio was bolstered by the valuable industry connections Perry forged through his employment at Moondance Comics in Brattleboro, Vermont, where he handled mail orders and often tabled at national conventions on behalf of the retailer. It was also during this period that Perry wrote *Timespirits*, an eight-issue limited series edited by Archie Goodwin for Marvel's creator-owned Epic Comics imprint. Following the exploits of two Native American time travelers, *Timespirits* was unlike anything Marvel had ever produced. "It was one of the only ongoing series they did where the heroes weren't superheroes in the classic sense," series artist Tom Yeates said. "They weren't big muscle-bound guys going into ten-page fistfights." Though lighthearted and fantastical on the surface, Perry's signature darkness seeps through characters driven by greed, jealousy and familial hatred. There are disturbing creatures such as the "Bloodless Ghebe," an eyeball-on-a-stalk who enters hosts and sets them on murderous sprees. *Timespirits*' blue-skinned cat-girl character, Thornypaws, also bears an undeniable likeness to the Na'vi of James Cameron's *Avatar*, released a quarter century later, though Perry and Yeates are uncredited for this inspiration. Perry soon fell out with Yeates and Veitch over monetary issues. "He was the kind of guy who always demanded a larger financial cut at the expense of his collaborators," says Veitch. "We didn't prey on each other in business deals; instead, we looked out for each other.

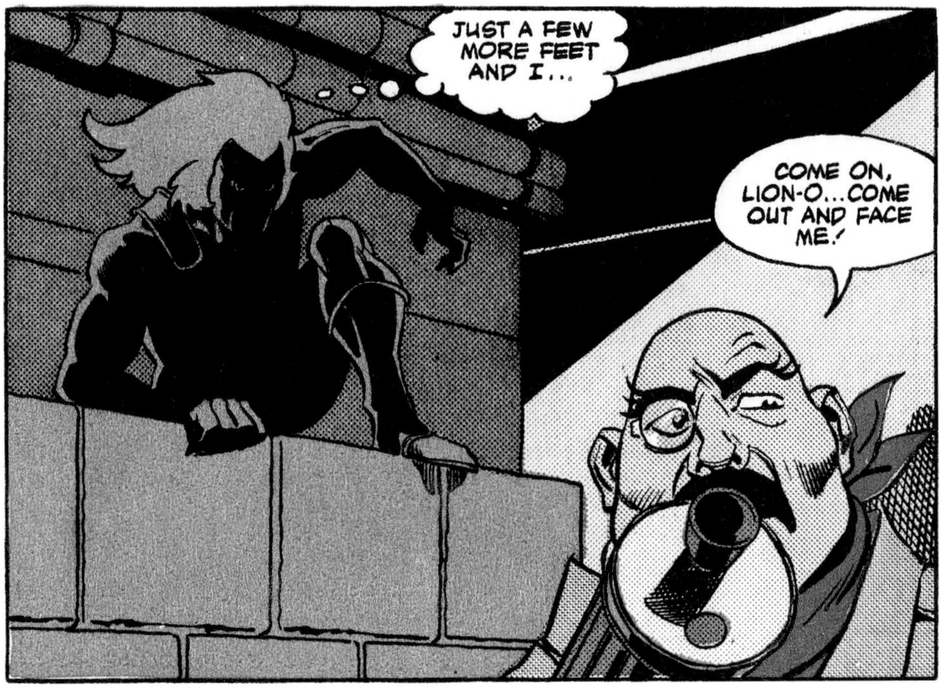
JUST A FEW MORE FEET AND I...
COME ON, LION-O...COME OUT AND FACE ME!

LEFT: Perry creation Safari Joe in *ThunderCats* #14, 1987. Written by Steve Perry, penciled by Ernie Colón, inked by Al Williamson, lettered by Ed King and colored by Marie Severin.

But Perry didn't get that at all. He had a predator mentality when it came to business."

That mentality saw Perry use Veitch's connections at Rankin/Bass Productions to score a writing gig on TV's *ThunderCats* in 1985 (where he scripted at least six episodes), plus its space-bound spinoff *SilverHawks* (where he scripted at least four episodes) the following year. Perry's limitless imagination and curiosity to explore other worlds enabled him to invent storylines and characters that delighted audiences, spawning merchandise lines and amassing significant profits for his employers. Writing under aggressive work-for-hire terms, Perry was paid a flat rate of $3,500 per script. He received no royalties for his creations – including iconic villains "Safari Joe" and 'Ratar-O', diminutive alien "Snarfer" and the ThunderCats' mode of transport, the "Feliner" – which would all go on to feature throughout the show's 130-episode run. When *ThunderCats* toys based on his characters hit the shelves, Perry had to borrow money from friends to purchase them for his sons. The fatal blow, however, was delivered when Marvel imprint Star Comics launched *ThunderCats* and *SilverHawks* comic series companions. Seeing an opportunity for more work, Perry used his standing at Rankin/Bass to spearhead an unprecedented process of pre-clearance for TV script adaptation, allowing Marvel to quickly turn around their comics issues and correspond them to what was happening in the cartoon series. The move misfired spectacularly when the Marvel series editor promptly assigned the comics adaptations to other writers, cutting Perry out of the picture entirely even though he was the one who had originally conceived of the idea. According to one Marvel staffer at the time, when Perry went to confront that editor, he had locked his office door, turned the lights out and hidden under his desk to avoid confrontation. Other editors stopped returning Perry's calls, and his comics work rapidly dried up as a result.

Perry never recovered from this betrayal at Marvel, and soon gave up his dream of writing altogether. He embarked on an itinerant lifestyle, moving from state to state and working a variety of odd jobs; delivering milk to low-income mothers on the WIC assistance program, buying and selling "antiques"

RELEASE!
TOP OF THE SHOULDER JETS-- FIRE!!
DESTROY THEM! DESTROY THEM!
WE'RE TRYING MON*STAR WE'RE TRYING!
THE TEST OF STRENGTH BEGINS...WITH THE FATE OF THE LIMBO GALAXY GOING TO THE WINNER!

ABOVE: Panels from the *ThunderCats* spin-off *Silver Hawks* #1 (August 1987). Written by Steve Perry, penciled by Mike Witherby, inked by Jim Sanders III, lettered by Jack Morelli and colored by John Wellington.

at flea markets, working the traveling carnival circuit… Described by friends as a scoundrel and a rake, he also went through a great many relationships, frequently with much younger women, entering into at least three marriages and fathering five sons. Perry embroiled himself in schemes and situations so unbelievable that friends urged him to return to writing, using his own experiences as inspiration; but he lacked the self-esteem to do so. He nevertheless managed to scrape together a hand-to-mouth existence, until March 2009, when a medical crisis sent his life into a tailspin.

By this time, he was based in Zephyrhills, Florida, a community outside of Tampa known for its 55-and-over RV parks. He was facing bladder cancer without insurance, and had lost his most recent job managing a 42-unit apartment complex, along with the free accommodation it provided, when cancer took his ability to meet the physical requirements of changing toilets and fixing sinks. Sent packing on $1,000 severance, Perry found himself living in his broken-down vehicle with his 4-year-old son. He was also fighting a custody battle with the boy's mother who was thirty years his junior, and already pregnant by her twin sister's ex-boyfriend, a fellow carnival worker. Every day became a scramble to summon funds from any means conceivable (mowing lawns door-to-door, selling secondhand DVDs, hawking flea-market bedsheets on eBay) to afford food, utilities, repairs on his ever-unreliable van and, of course, his medical bills. The details of Perry's dire financial straits are measured in dollar amounts, and numbers of miles walked to welfare offices in the Florida heat, explained in emails sent to friends from an employment center computer. They reveal just how desperately Americans in Perry's situation – without insurance, a phone, a car, a fixed address and/or internet access – must struggle to survive, especially when libraries, phone booths and other not-for-profit public services fall prey to lack of government policy and privatization.

On borrowed time and at Bissette's behest, Perry settled the rights to any shared properties with his collaborators, the comics community rallied to send online donations and vital funds were raised by the Hero Initiative; a charity supporting comics creators in need. That organization helped Perry and his son into a house and set them up with Medicaid – a joint federal and state program that assists patients with limited income. He was surviving on free church meals and the kindness of strangers. But the money only stretched so far. One rent payment, one utility bill, one prescription or the drive to an unsuccessful job interview would set him back to zero and onto a new scheme for quick cash. The outlook of his correspondences grew bleaker as the obstacles to unemployment and disability benefits became increasingly insurmountable. Perry wrote on November 2, 2009:

> Unemployment DENIED me BECAUSE ... they say in their letter ... I am too SICK to seek employment. This is interesting ... CASH ASSISTANCE DENIED ME, TOO ... BECAUSE I did not go and seek employment ... It seems to me THEY CANNOT HAVE IT BOTH WAYS ... I believe a welfare caseworker has the authority to make a special dispensation and not require me to conduct their 40-hour-a-week job search if they accept that unemployment has deemed me too sick to look for work ... This desperation is such a physical and emotional drag on whatever minor energy I can summon in between the days of debilitating pain from the fucking cancer. I feel so hopeless and helpless.

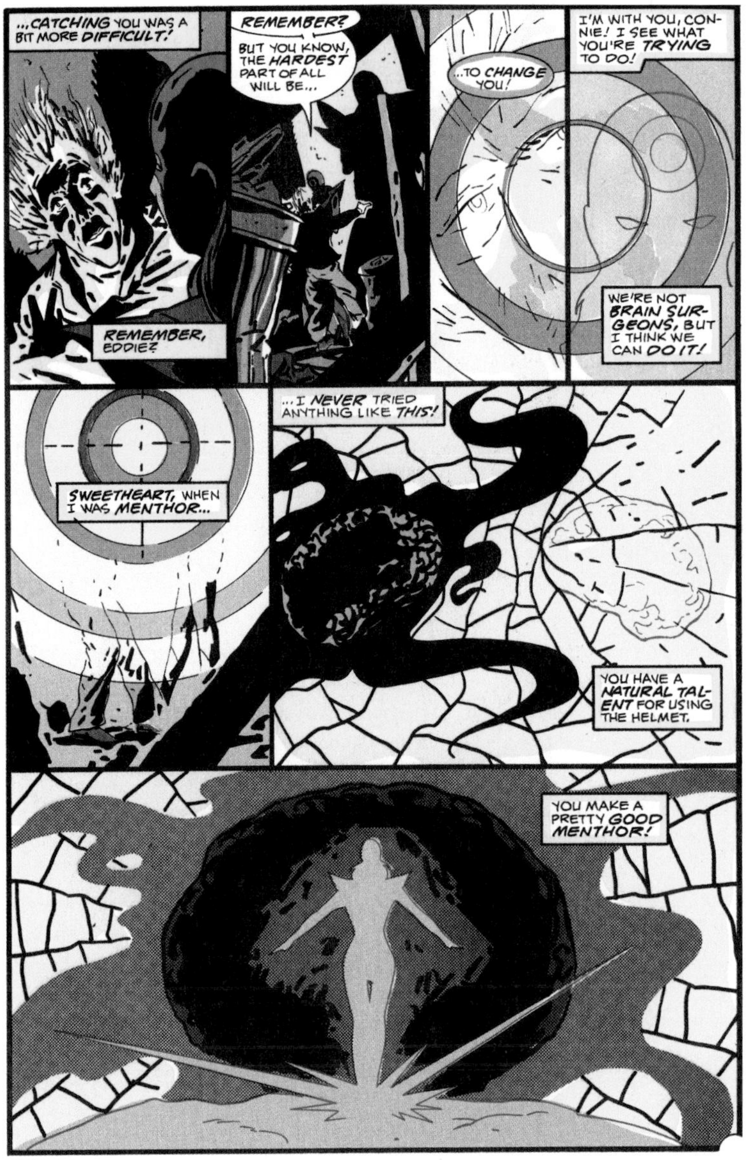
...CATCHING YOU WAS A BIT MORE DIFFICULT!
REMEMBER, EDDIE?
REMEMBER?
BUT YOU KNOW, THE HARDEST PART OF ALL WILL BE...
...TO CHANGE YOU!
I'M WITH YOU, CONNIE! I SEE WHAT YOU'RE TRYING TO DO!
WE'RE NOT BRAIN SURGEONS, BUT I THINK WE CAN DO IT!
SWEETHEART, WHEN I WAS MENTHOR...
...I NEVER TRIED ANYTHING LIKE THIS!
YOU HAVE A NATURAL TALENT FOR USING THE HELMET.
YOU MAKE A PRETTY GOOD MENTHOR!

ABOVE: This page, written by Steve Perry, penciled by Keith Giffen, inked by Rick Bryant, lettered by John Workman and colored by Paty appeared in *T.H.U.N.D.E.R. Agents* #1,1984.

Encouraged by the Hero Initiative and the comics community, Perry returned to writing in the final months of his life, providing some refuge from his pain. In addition to "Baby," he scripted two emotionally flooring one-pagers, "Breakfast of Chumpions" (which was commissioned as a promotion for the Hero Initiative, but dismissed for being too oblique) and "Worlds Fall Apart," (never paired with an artist and hence, never published) documenting the struggles he and his son faced. He completed his final extensive composition, "Death's Long Scalpel Scars Deep and Sacred," in April 2010. A feverish 3,827-word tract emailed to friends, it evokes the EC comics and Cronenbergian body horror that Perry loved. He graphically details his suffering, his revelations upon inching ever closer to death and his belief that, had he not been dismissed by doctors for his lack of insurance, his health would not have declined in the way it had. "Unable to pee and able only to shoot out clots (they looked like chunks of steak the size of one's thumb) I urinated blood for months until I clogged," he wrote. "It is a horrendous story, and I am afraid my piteous emails to some of you, so couched in misery and desperation as they were, could not come close to the coherent and straightforward matter-of-fact account I would like you all to be aware of." He recounts having phoned 67 urologists before finding one who accepted Medicaid, yet who required a five-week pre-authorization period ahead of each consultation. He recalls waking from a six-hour operation to be told his doctor had already left for the day. He was discharged with four prescriptions, and later informed at the pharmacy that only one of those medications was covered by his insurance: "I had $24. $69 on a debit card. My 'ride' wanted $20 for gas. This is the true nature of the horror tale."

Come May 2010, aged 56, Perry had been killed; not by the seven cancerous tumors for which doctors had set his life expectancy at two more years, but by his roommates: James William Davis and his wife, Roxanne, who both had extensive criminal histories. Perry had reluctantly taken the couple into his rundown home in January to relieve his rent, although they never did pay their share. All three of them residing at the 38046 Eighth Avenue property in Zephyrhills were reported missing when Perry's friends suddenly stopped receiving calls and emails from him. A former girlfriend, Gail Flatow, had been speaking with him regularly from Indianapolis, where she practiced law and was advising him on legal matters. He had been awaiting the custody hearing about his son, which was going to take place on May 13. "If he lost custody, he was going to come here," Flatow said. "I had promised him he would not die alone and in the street." On May 10, her repeated calls went straight to voicemail. She alerted the police five days later.

Perry's dismembered body parts were gradually discovered in locations between Tampa and Wesley Chapel, Florida, after his right arm was found on May 16 in his temperamental blue van. Friends suspect the vehicle, which caused Perry much aggravation in his final days, had broken down on the assailant(s), forcing them to abandon it in the Quality Inn parking lot where it was found. News reportage speculated whether the murder may have been connected to an unclaimed $10,000,000 winning lottery ticket that had been bought at a nearby store just prior to Perry's disappearance, but was inconclusive. Before Perry's remains had been identified, James and Roxanne Davis were picked up for drug trafficking charges and violating probation, respectively. James was subsequently recognized on surveillance footage purchasing a saw blade and cleaning materials, driving Perry's van and using Perry's ATM card at two Zephyrhills banks in the days leading to the grim discovery. When his DNA was found on incriminating evidence at the trio's ransacked address, Davis was charged for the murder, his motive put down to money and Perry's prescription medications. At the time of this writing, there has been no record of a trial for James Davis. One can only surmise that the murder of a destitute, dying man is not prioritized in the courts. In the absence of a body, there was no funeral.

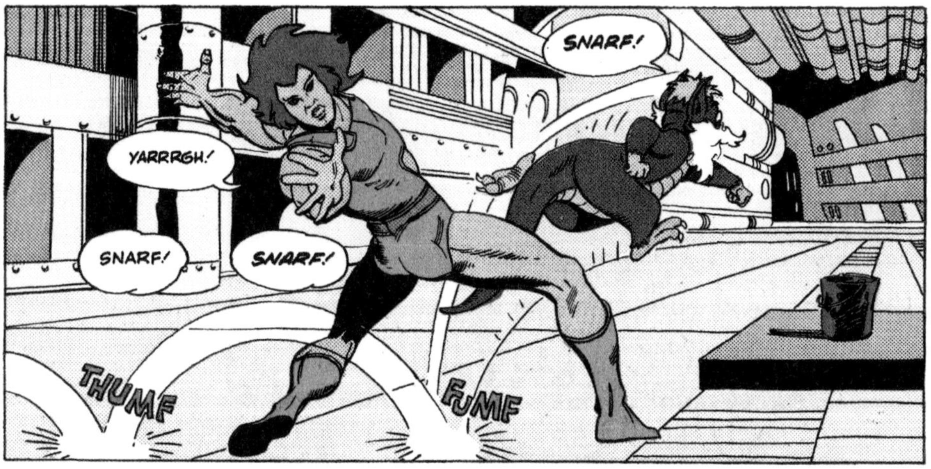
SNARF!
YARRRGH!
SNARF!
SNARF!
THUMF
FUMF

RIGHT: From *ThunderCats* #14, 1987. Written by Steve Perry, penciled by Ernie Colón, inked by Al Williamson, lettered by Ed King and colored by Marie Severin.

It would be a great injustice for the sensational murder of Stephen Perry, who suffered such wrongs during his life, to overshadow his legacy. Friends make no illusions that he was a self-destructive, complex, at times infuriating man, who had many vices and was in many ways his own worst enemy. Yet he was also a creator whose characters inspired a generation, a writer who desperately aspired to the comics industry and a father who clung onto survival. The tragedy of Steve Perry is not a matter of his work being unappreciated in his lifetime. Safari Joe and Ratar-O action figures are selling on eBay for upwards of $350. A new *ThunderCats* series will air in 2019, and a second installment of *Avatar* creeps closer on the horizon. Yet the uncompensated and unacknowledged talent of Steve Perry – a man callously cut out of the industry and forced to live an existence that paved the way to his ruin – continues to evade the public's attention. "He loved the comics, but as is true for so many creators, the love was not returned in full," said Nat Gertler, from About Comics, who published the *Salimba* collection. The comics industry has long relied on the sacrifices of freelancers working on meager page rates out of passion for the medium. Steve Perry is one of the countless creators who have found themselves without a financial safety net as they approach their own "golden age."

We all knew this was my destiny … So much undone, so little lived, such a tiny ripple to mark my existence. I suppose it's all the sons that will shout I have been here … The glass is not half empty, it's half full … but it's half full of fucking poison.

Steve Perry
December 1954–May 2010 ☼

Queer Eye
For the Straight Comic Book Guy
An Alex Gard Gallery

Mannie Murphy

"What's so gay about the Navy?" Gary Groth earnestly posed this question to me as we strolled together through the Short Run Comix and Arts Festival in Seattle, Washington. Agape, I struggled to find words for what I thought was common knowledge. I thought of old photographs of sailors in drag, crossing the Equator for the first time; secret tattoo codes fluttered behind my eyes as I struggled to contextualize what I took as common queer knowledge to a straight man. I thought of the Village People, of Tom of Finland, of "don't ask, don't tell." I thought of the gay naval inquisition that was the "Newport sex scandal" of 1919. Cowboys, nuns, sailors, nurses: these iconic same-sex cominglers are sacred to the gay sect, and yet, are still considered sacrilegious to the straight and narrow because they interrogated the accepted sexual norms of their times – and our times. And that is what I see Alex Gard's work doing: interrogating the rules of masculinity the WWII Navy enforced around him in in a funny, creative and frankly beautiful way.

SAILORS
IN
BOOTS
by
ALEX GARD
Q. M. 2c. U. S. Navy

TOP RIGHT: *Sailors in Boots*, 1943.

A couple years before my confounding convo with Gary, I made a find at a favorite junk store in Portland, Oregon, that would lead me on a very queer journey indeed. All cartoonists seem to have an obsession with comics' past, and everyone knows the curious joy of "discovering" a brilliant artist, heretofore unknown. I opened the book and saw names and numbers scrawled horizontally across the inside covers. I saw a black-and-white photograph in the back; ambered scotch tape preserving this odd scrapbook. When I leafed through Alex Gard's work for the first time, I slapped the book shut. Holding it in my hands, I felt my heartbeat increase and actual chills go down my spine. You know the feeling, right? Yeah. I broke out in a cold sweat. I bought the book for $4. I didn't just fall in love with the artist, I fell into an obsessive research wormhole that led me through an era I was absent from. How to convey the well-earned queer reputation of the Navy? Which led, finally, to this *Journal* article resurrecting one of the

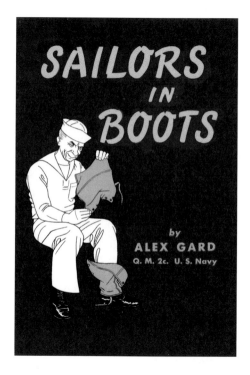

SICK BAY
by
ALEX GARD
U.S.NAVY

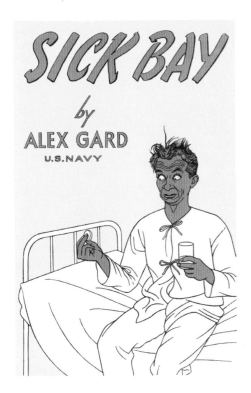

greatest caricaturists of the 20th century – with a 21st century twist. A *Bill and Ted's Excellent Adventure* from the perspective of gay Ted and his lover, Bill.

Alex Gard was born Alexei Mikhailovich Kremkov in 1898 in Kazan, which was then part of the Russian Empire. It's known that he served in the Russian navy during World War I. It's not known how influenced he was by the Bolshevik Revolution's treatment of artists or their massacre of thousands of sailors in the Kronstadt Uprising, but his decision to leave his homeland was likely affected by both. It's evident, in his flippant treatment of life in the U.S. navy, that he was used to far worse. Gard left after the Russian Revolution, and he traveled throughout Asia and Europe before settling in Nice, France. He drew cartoons for several European magazines, including *Le Matin* in Paris. When Gard immigrated to the United States in 1924, he landed in New York City, where (along with fellow port city San Francisco) large communities of sailors and gay men were harbored. During WWII, gay men were outed and dishonorably discharged. They returned to an inhospitable family and social life – there really wasn't anywhere else to go. This is how and why San Francisco gained its reputation as a gay city. Gard fell in with the Broadway crowd, became a ballet aficionado and developed a fan base at Sardi's restaurant. Gard drew caricatures of the stars who came to patronize the establishment, and Vincent Sardi wrote him up a contract ensuring daily free meals in exchange for a steady supply of drawings. The contract lasted until Gard's death after his collapse on Seventh Avenue and 41st Street. He was buried in Arlington National Cemetery.

I admit: A love of ballet and a lifetime in the Navy does not a gay man make. Straight people might wonder why it even matters to me so much. Most gay people know why; representation matters and sometimes it is important to re-envision history through a more holistic lens. Plus, there's no proof Gard wasn't gay. Gard's work covers queer and hetero content alike. He never married, never had children. As far as I can tell, nobody has yet attempted to contact his family in Russia and most of the people who knew him in the U.S. are dead. The only view we have into his mind is what he left behind in his work, the most telling of all being the gag strips collected in *Sailors in Boots*, *Getting Salty* and *Sick Bay*.

The strips in these three books are arguably autobiographical, apparently self-referential and daringly critical of the U.S. Navy. From what we know about Gard's ballet work and his caricatures at Sardi's, we can deduce that at least some of the characters in *Boots*, *Salty* and *Sick Bay* were in fact caricatures of real people; these are likely very close to a visual diary of his time spent in the U.S. Navy. That makes the three books a crucial document to anyone interested in what naval life was like during World War II. What makes them fascinating is that they were written from the perspective of an immigrant, someone who – decades prior – had experienced firsthand the cruelty and conditions of the Russian navy. Gard offered the perspective of an artist caught in the machinations of war

TOP LEFT: *Sick Bay*, 1945.

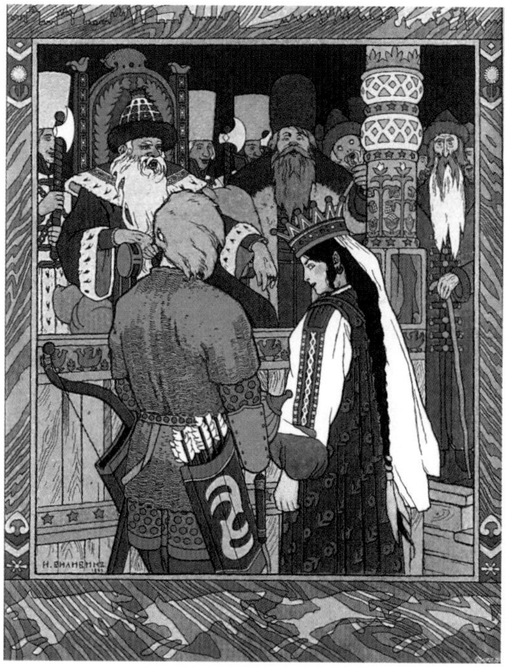

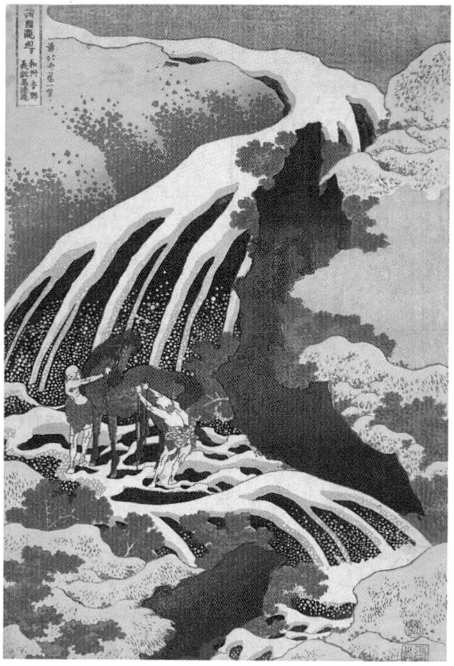

LEFT: By Ivan Biliban, 1899.

RIGHT: By Katsushika Hokusai, circa 1832.

who wasn't afraid to voice a certain defiance toward that machine, albeit humorously.

There was what I see to be an openness and a queer fluidity throughout his work, an attitude that an older salt might achieve after decades at sea, decades of (chosen) forced intimacy with other men, and the opportunity for cultural shiftiness that can come from a life of world travel. One can certainly see in Gard's work the influence of both near – Ivan Bilibin's Russian folklore illustrations (see Gard's compositions in "Show Your Present Physical Condition" and "About Size 36") – and far, such as the iconic work of Hokusai and other ukiyo-e artists (see Gard's use of background and movement in "The Sky, the Trees and the Water" and "In and Out of the Gas Chamber"). He would have had the opportunity to visit a lot of the world's original classics in person in museums while at port, as well as during his own travels. His work employs extreme one-point perspective for effect; his understanding of the male anatomy and his appreciation of the male physical form in gesture are beyond compare and constitute a basis for this work.

A notable gay historic milestone is mentioned in Gard's *Sailors in Boots*. Back before the word "gay" was used to describe our kind, the military was getting an earful from the new set of clinical professionals under their employ – psychiatrists. World War II was the first time the military utilized the help of this new wave of practitioners. One of the goals of these new doctors was to weed out homosexuals, who were seen as individual threats to the masculinity and strength of the U.S. military forces. What they didn't realize was that, by asking these men in the initial stages of their military careers whether they were queer or not, they gave many of them their very first experience of questioning their sexuality – specifically in a clinical and military context. Gard's "Do You Like to Go with Girls Once in a While?" could be the earliest version of the psychiatrist gag comic. We see a very effeminate, young manboy squirming under the sexualized scrutiny of an elder in military garb, behind a door labeled "PSYCHOANALYSIS." On the opposite page, we see more doctors (and one astonished young medic) ogling the assets of a naked beefcake with the caption, "Perfect Specimen." If that's not gay, then I don't know what is. But don't take my word for it.

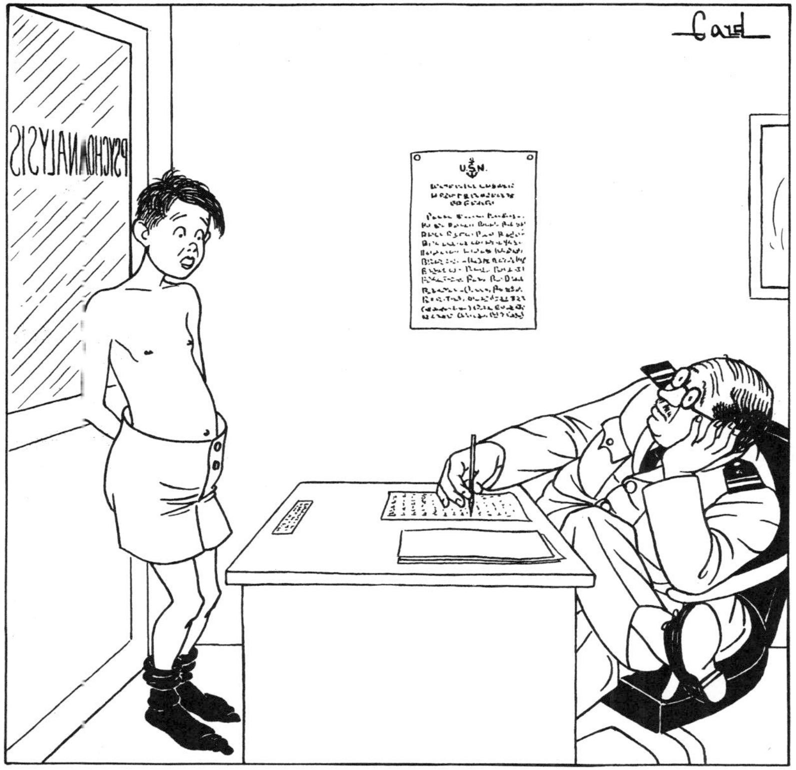
PSYCHOANALYSIS
U.S.N.
Card

"Do you like to go with girls once in a while?"

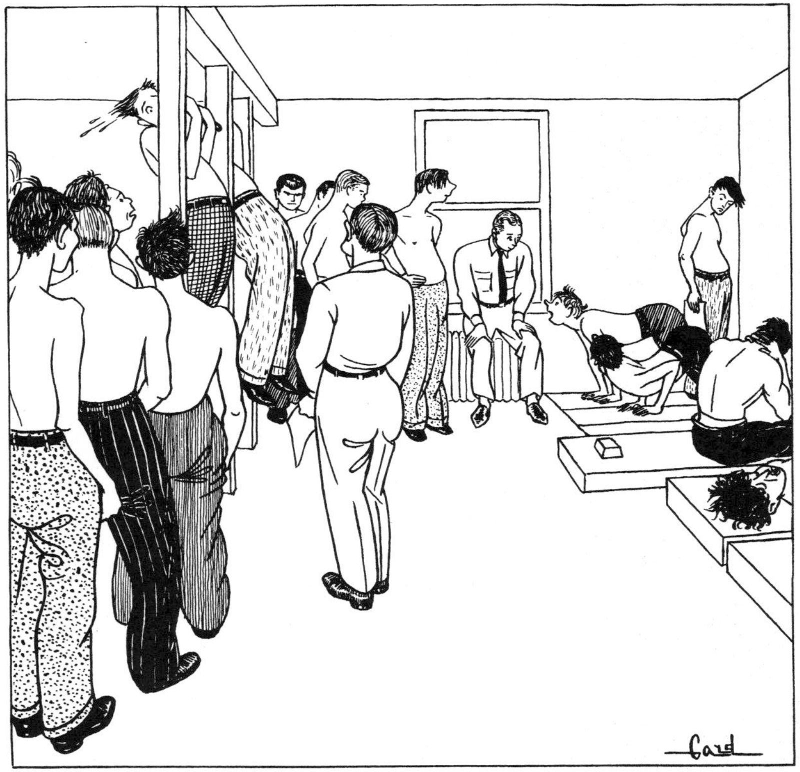
Card

"....Show your present physical condition"

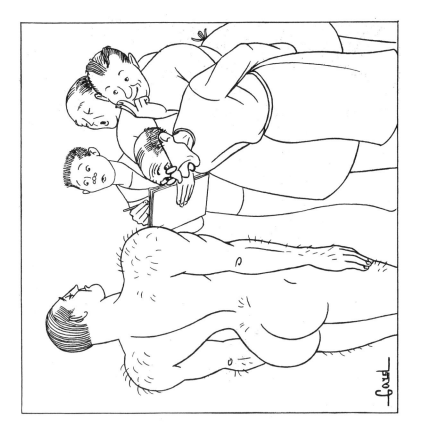

PERFECT SPECIMEN

4:45 A. M.
"HIT THE DECK!"

"About Size 36"

Hair today, gone tomorrow

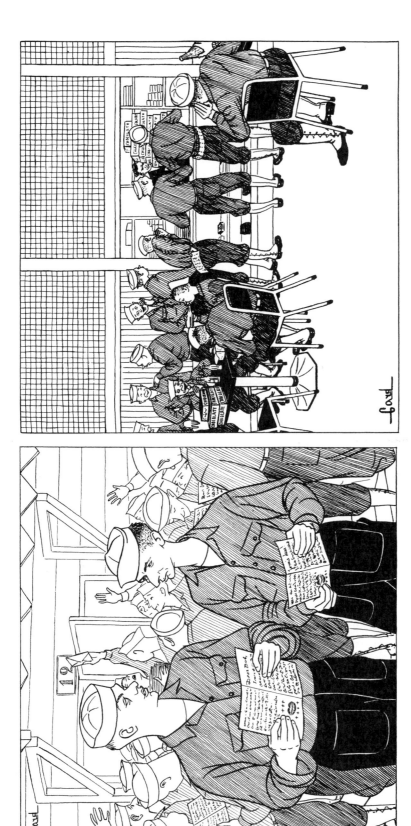

Gard
12
Dear Bob,

My girl writes better letters then yours!

CHOCOLATE
Gard

Hour of Leisure

"Cleanliness in the Navy is next to Godliness"

The Morning Exercise
(Double Time)

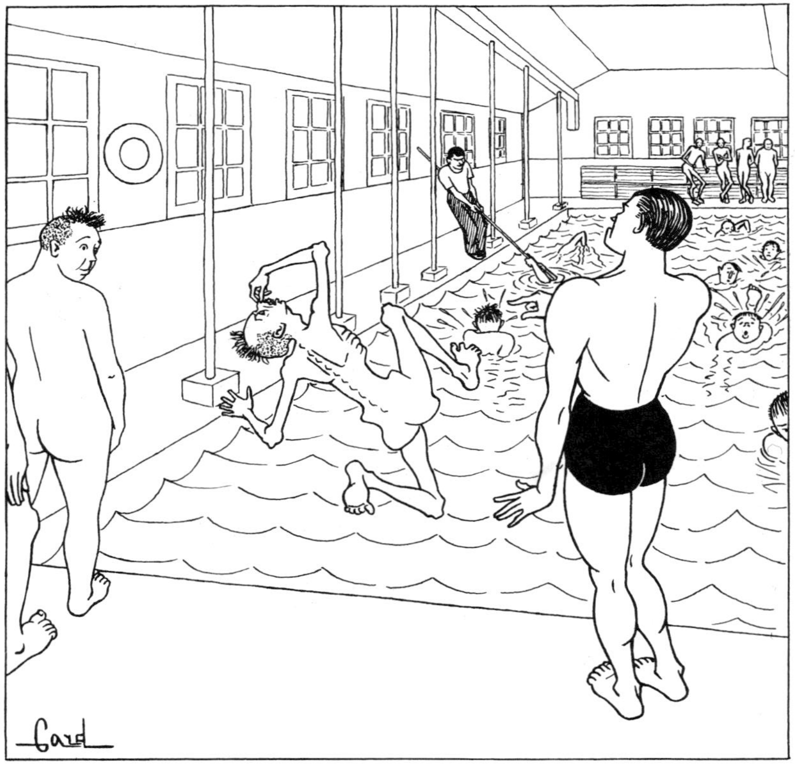
Gard

SWIMMING TEST
("JUMP IN YOUR MOST CONVENIENT MANNER...")

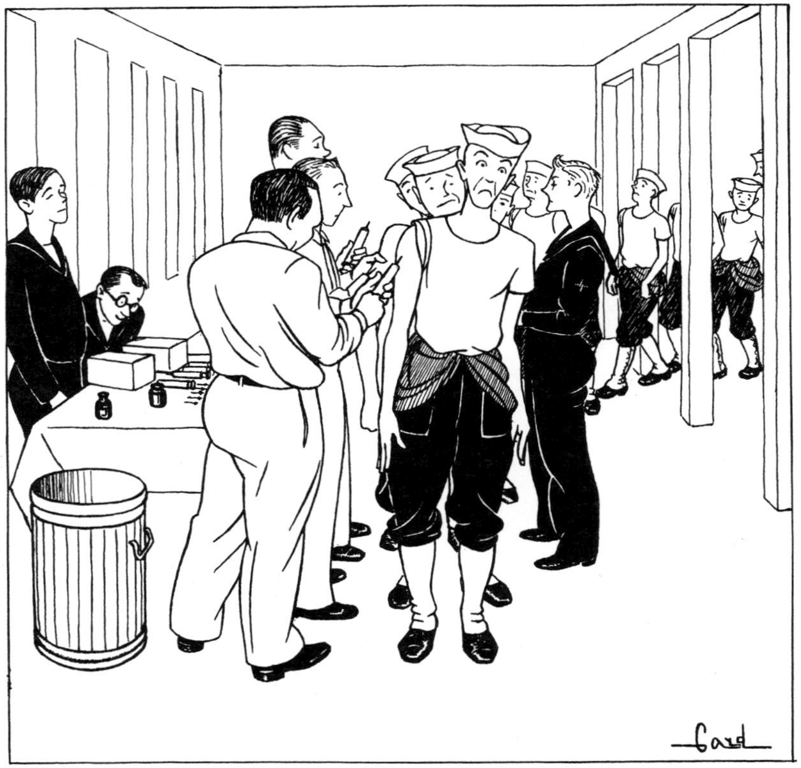
Gard

SECOND INJECTION

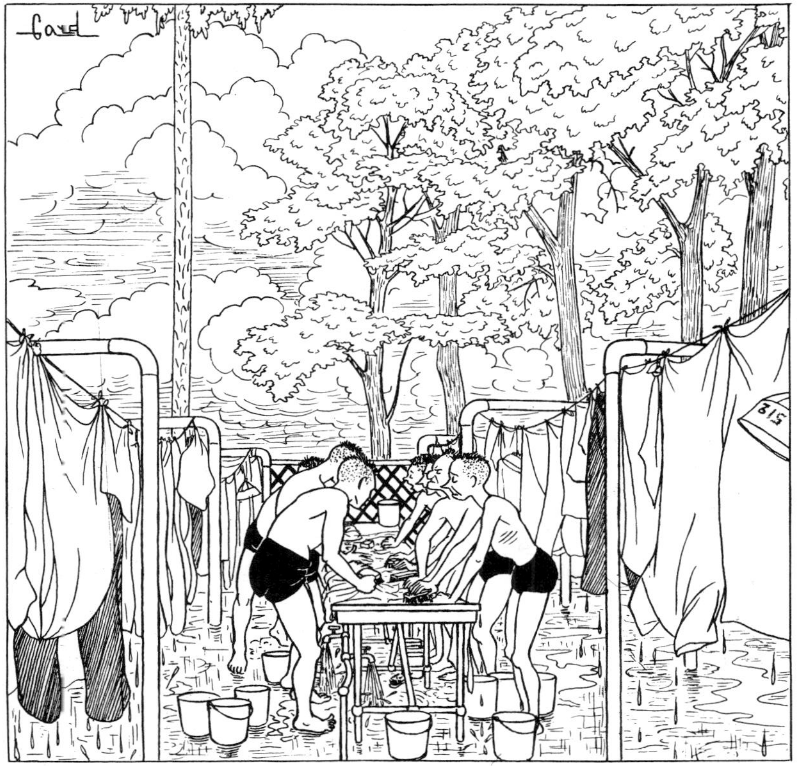

The sky, the trees and the water

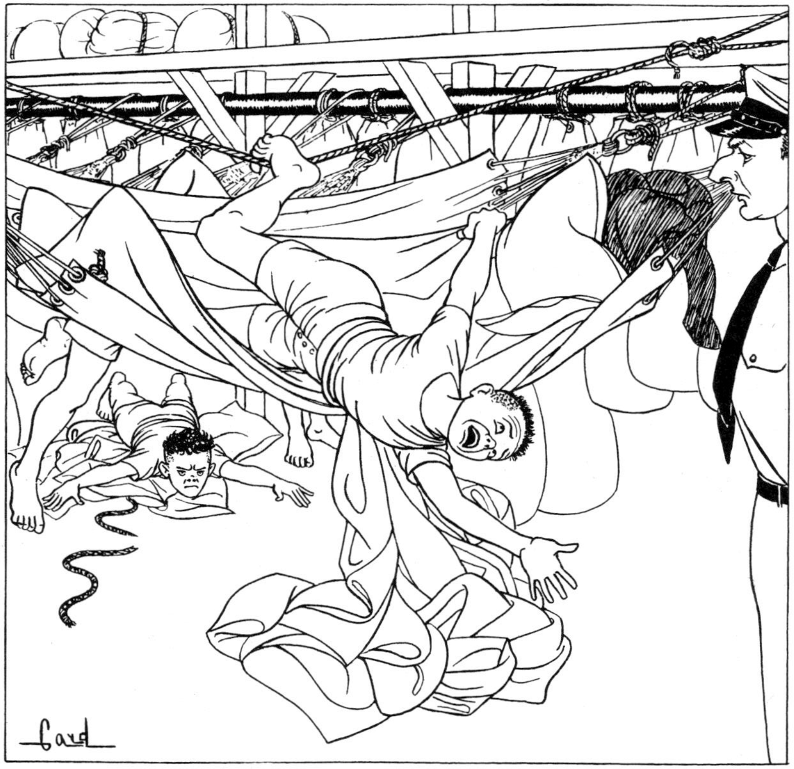

First night in Hammocks

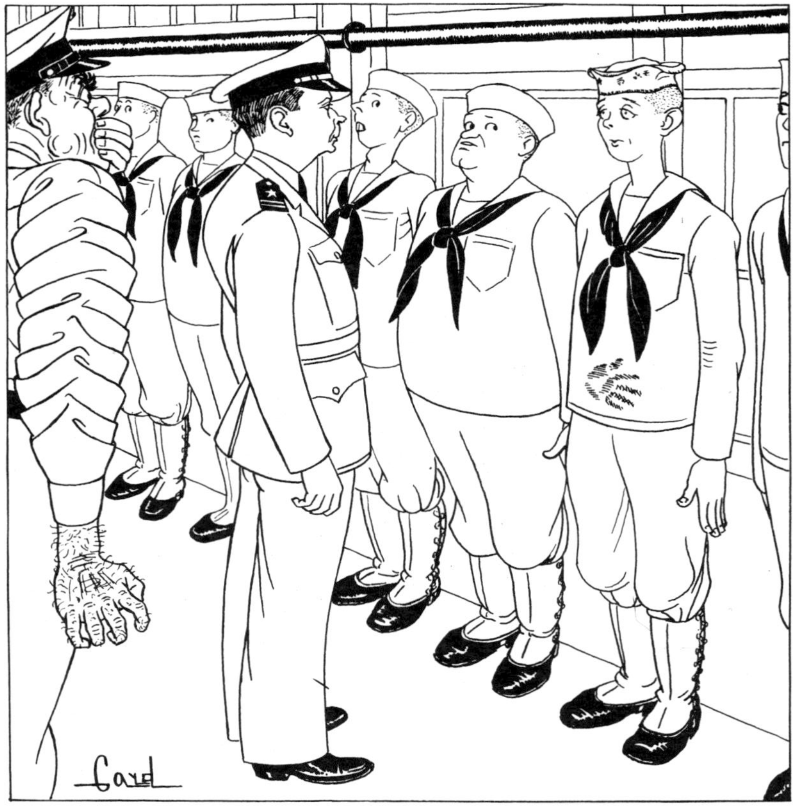
Gard

Barrack Inspection

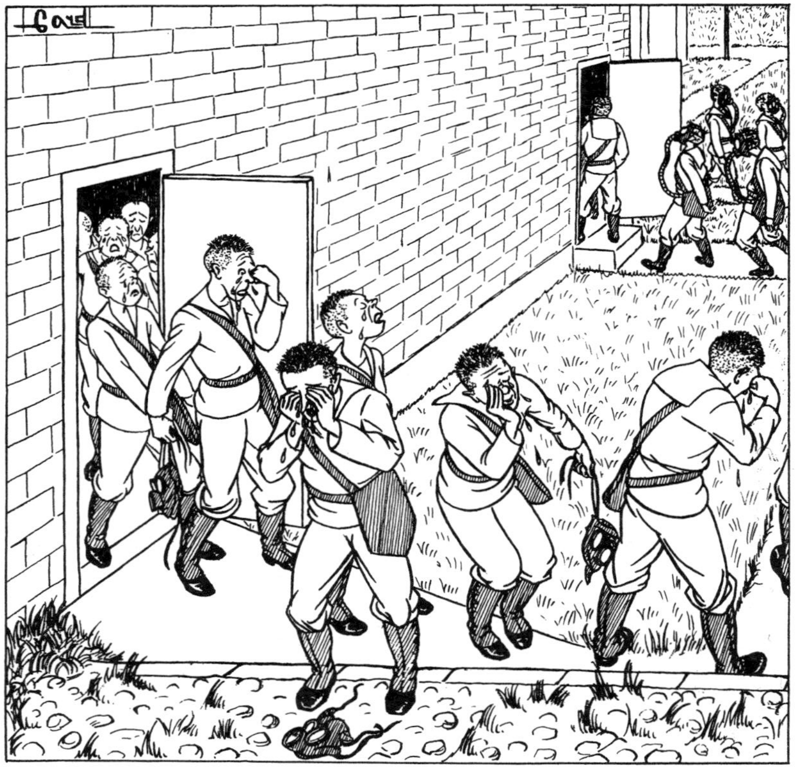
Gard

In and Out of Gas Chamber

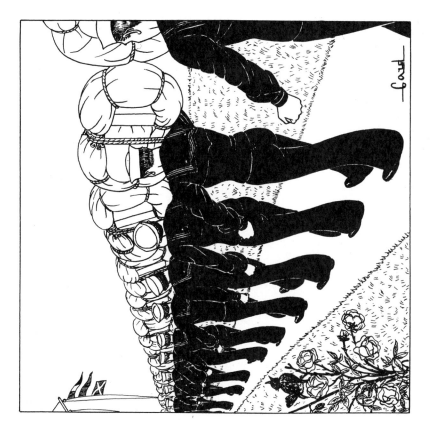

Diagnosis and Treatment

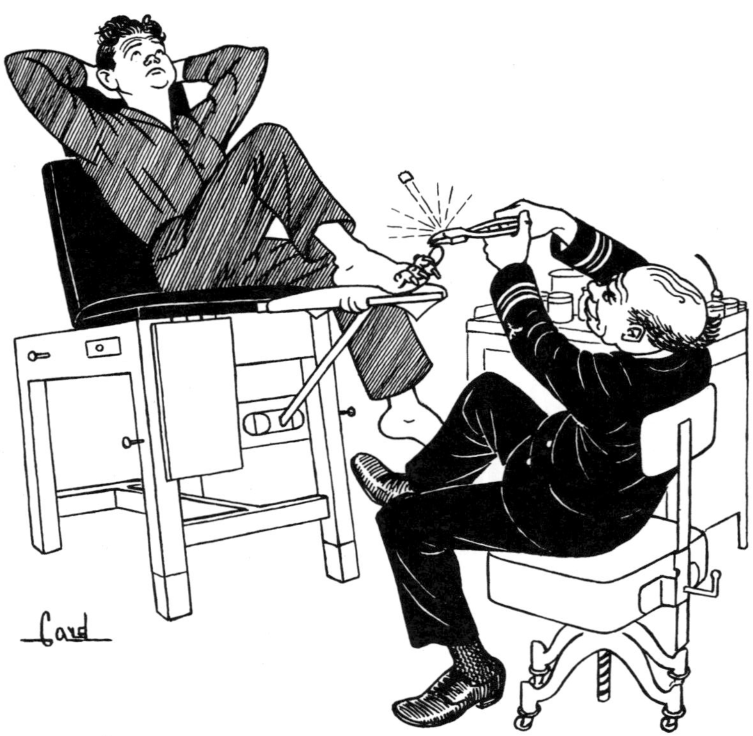
Gard

Pedicure de luxe

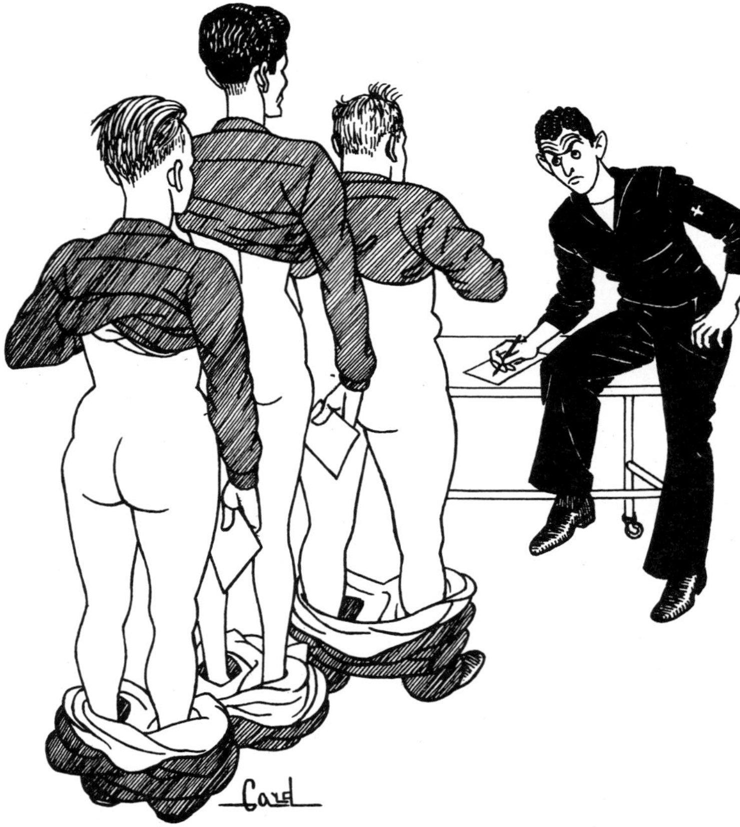
Gard

Routine physical

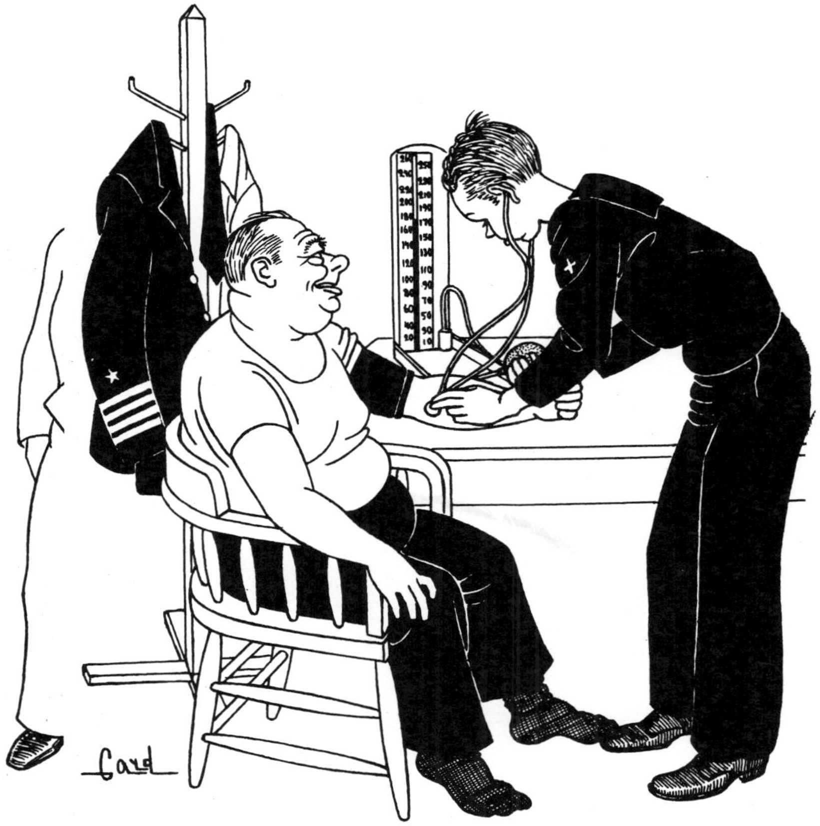

Special examination
(Promotion & Discharge)

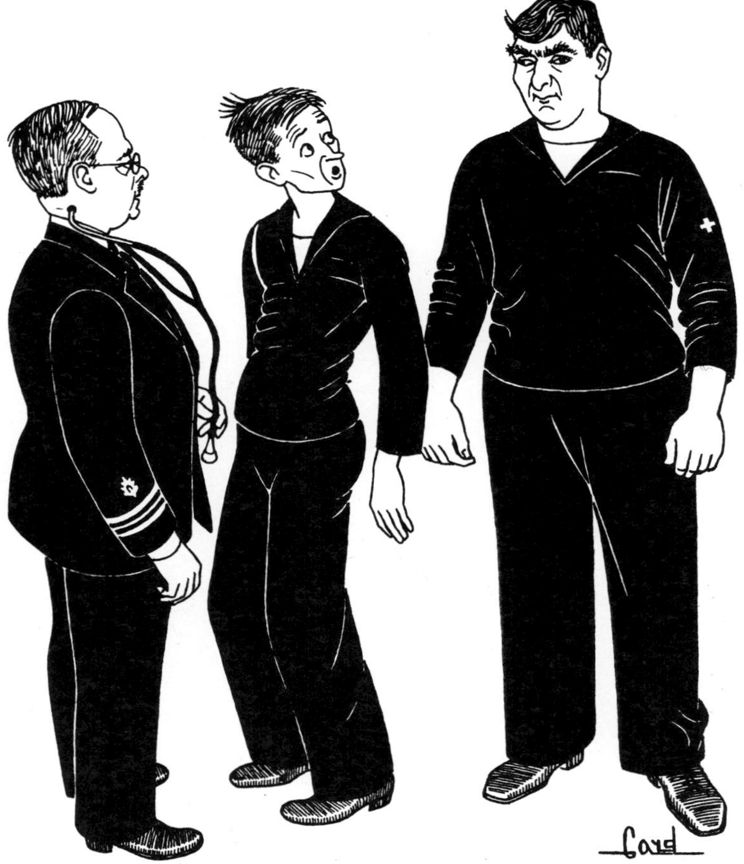

Medical Officer of a day
"O.K.-The corpsman will give you a good rub down..."

Gard

DETAILING UP-PATIENTS TO GO AFTER MORNING CHOW

Gard

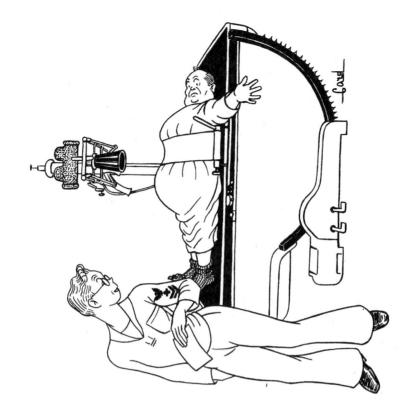

X-RAY

"TAKE A DEEP BREATH AND HOLD IT, CHIEF — I WILL BE BACK IN FIVE MINUTES."

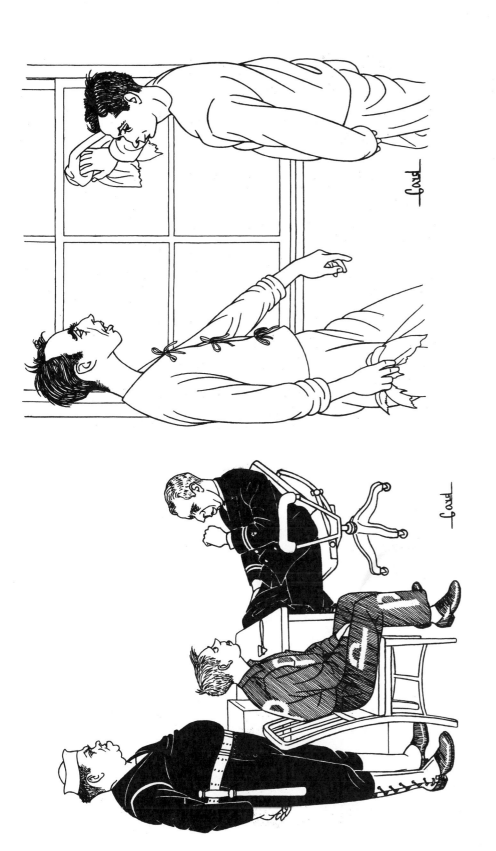

Card

Psychiatric interview

"...And suddenly my memory came back on the 29th day over leave..."

Card

Wednesday before Friday—Captain's inspection

"Three days I'm here with an ingrown toenail and they're just sticking thermometers in me twice a day for their records!!"

Gard

Day after Friday-Captain's Inspection

Gard

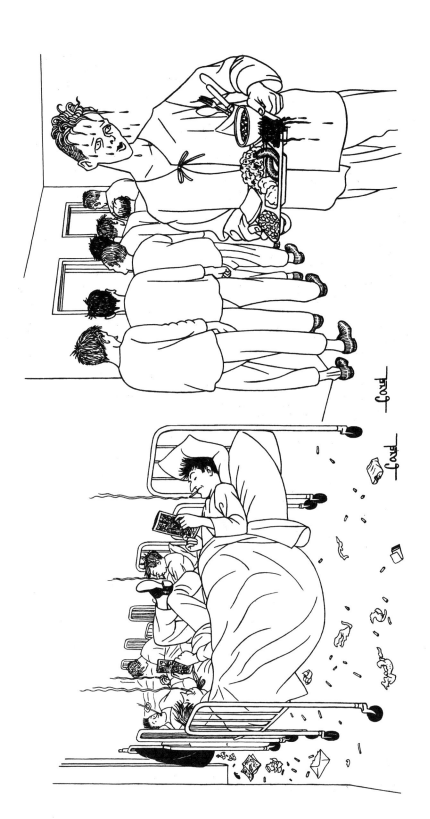

The Well-Balanced Chow

LOVE AND ROCKETS

BY GILBERT AND JAIME HERNANDEZ

The World's Greatest Comics Magazine, from the Publisher of the World's Greatest Cartoonists.
Three times per year from Fantagraphics Books.

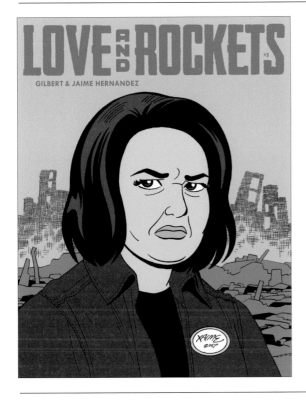

ALSO AVAILABLE: The Complete *Love and Rockets* Library, Vols. 1–14

Suehiro Maruo

Inés Estrada

嵐

LIKE ALMOST EVERYONE ELSE I know who is into comics, I can tell you that I've been fascinated with them since I was a kid. I grew up in Mexico City, where I would go to the market with my mom – and that was always my chance to get her to buy me some comics at the newsstand. The ones she would let me get were the ones that featured crudely drawn Mexican versions of Woody Woodpecker, Tom and Jerry and Droopy Dog. They looked like bootlegs, but they were actually official! But none of that mattered to me. I still asked my mom to buy me a new issue each weekend. While trying to decide which one to buy, my eyes would always drift off to the racks holding the *Libros Vaqueros* [Cowboy Books], these erotic – and sometimes straight-up – porn comics that are obviously not for kids. I managed to flip through them a few times, but of course, she would never buy them for me. There was something about them that really pulled me to them, even if I couldn't understand what it was yet. At age six, I was already on my way to becoming a pervert …

In the 2000s, when I was in high school, there weren't many more comics to find in Mexico City besides the ones I've mentioned already. It's funny that, even though Mexico has a strong cartooning history (especially in political cartoons), there isn't much of a comics culture. Luckily for me, the internet

LEFT: From *Mr. Arashi's Amazing Freak Show*, 1984.

was already fast enough that you could load an image in a couple of minutes – so that was my gateway to discovering new comics to read. Manga was the easiest to find, and it also had both of the things in comics that grabbed me from the beginning: funny cartoon characters and weird, sexy shit. I read through thousands of pages of irrelevant crap, until one day I found something that looked unlike any of the other manga I've seen before. That was the work of Suehiro Maruo.

I don't think anyone could argue that his work isn't visually impressive. Everything he draws (the anatomy, the backgrounds) is so perfectly rendered that it's a little intimidating to think that a human can draw like that, and in such volume. But the narratives … That's where I know some of you would disagree with me about liking his comics. Because, yeah, they're all about extremely fucked-up shit. All of his beautiful drawings serve to contrast his stories, which feature intense scenes of violence, nonconsensual sex and all sorts of other triggering, offensive acts. And that's why it's so hard to find his work in English – because who could venture to publish comics like that, and especially right now?! But aside from all the horrible things he chooses to depict, there is something very real and passionate about his comics. Maybe his early work was more about gratuitous violence and fetish porn, but after reading the Spanish edition of *The Smile of the Vampire*, I am convinced that there is a real thoughtfulness and depth behind his comics. It's a shame that more hasn't been published in English … I treasure all the titles I've managed to get. I look at them often for inspiration, even the ones that are in Japanese (which I can't read). His work is the best example that it is possible to create something that can be both beautiful and horrifying at the same time. The Japanese even have a name for it: *ero-guro*, which literally means "erotic grotesque." So, if you're a weirdo like me, and that sounds like something you would like, then you should definitely check out the work of Suehiro Maruo! But beware, no matter how ready you think you are, once you open one of his books you will enter a world so twisted and unlike any you've ever seen before in a western comic, or even in mainstream manga …

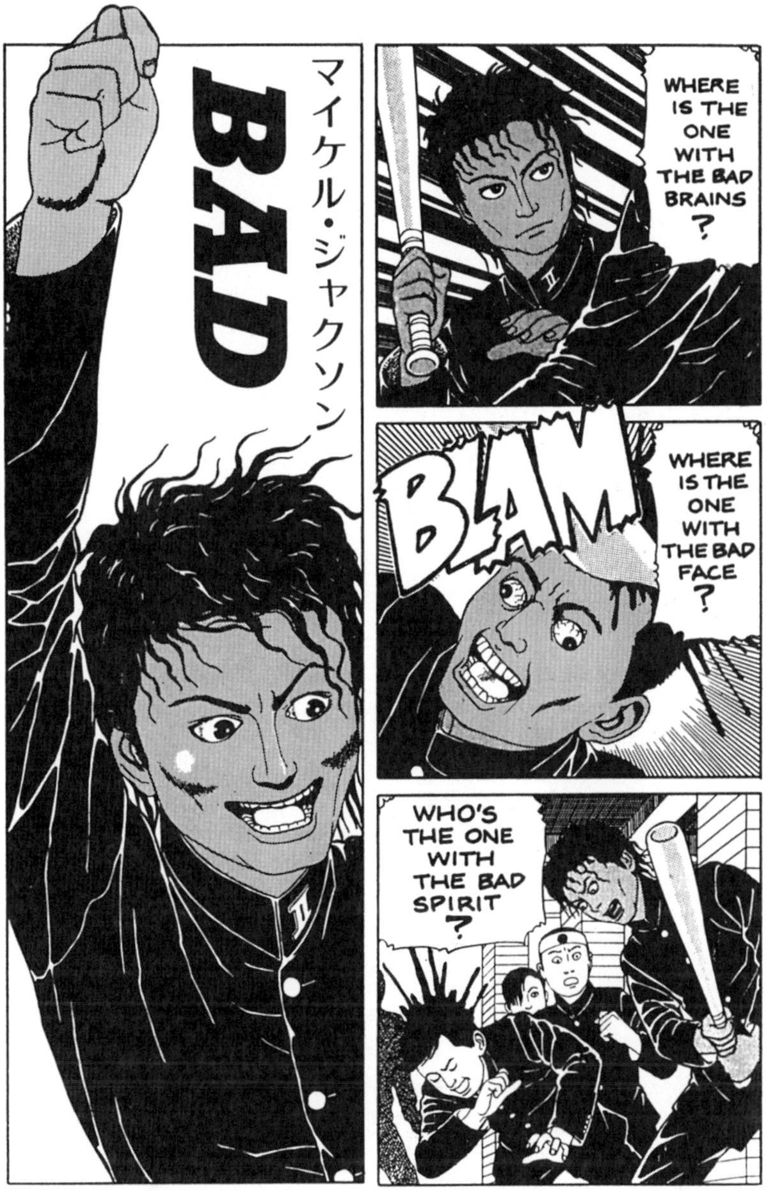
WHERE IS THE ONE WITH THE BAD BRAINS ?
BLAM
WHERE IS THE ONE WITH THE BAD FACE ?
WHO'S THE ONE WITH THE BAD SPIRIT ?
マイケル・ジャクソン
BAD

ABOVE: From Maruo's "Bad", 1991. Translated by Hiroshi Amano and lettered by Lea Hernandez.

In the next issue...

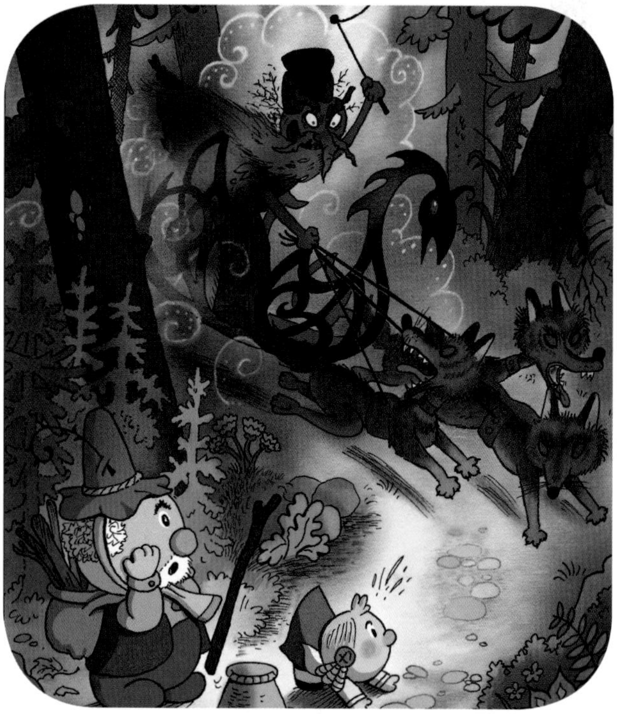

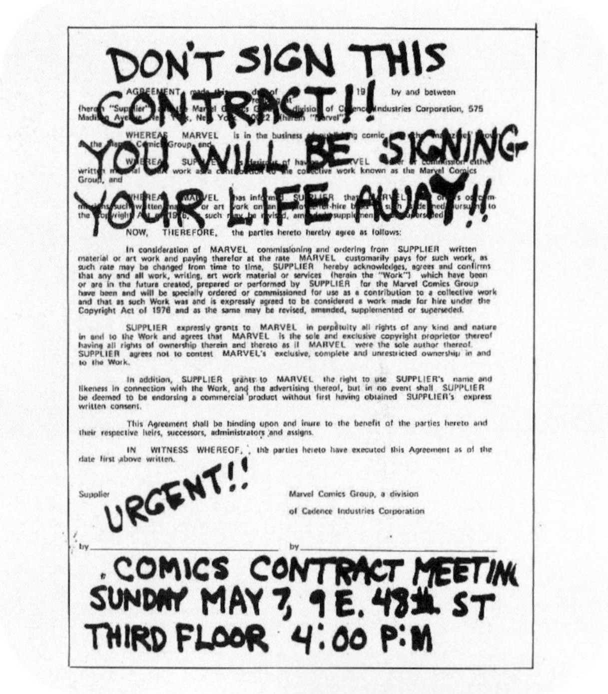
DON'T SIGN THIS CONTRACT!!
YOU WILL BE SIGNING YOUR LIFE AWAY!!
NOW, THEREFORE, the parties hereto hereby agree as follows:
In consideration of MARVEL commissioning and ordering from SUPPLIER written material or art work and paying therefor at the rate MARVEL customarily pays for such work, as such rate may be changed from time to time, SUPPLIER hereby acknowledges, agrees and confirms that any and all work, writing, art work material or services (herein the "Work") which have been or are in the future created, prepared or performed by SUPPLIER for the Marvel Comics Group have been and will be specially ordered or commissioned for use as a contribution to a collective work and that as such Work was and is expressly agreed to be considered a work made for hire under the Copyright Act of 1976 and as the same may be revised, amended, supplemented or superseded.
SUPPLIER expressly grants to MARVEL in perpetuity all rights of any kind and nature in and to the Work and agrees that MARVEL is the sole and exclusive copyright proprietor thereof having all rights of ownership therein and thereto as if MARVEL were the sole author thereof. SUPPLIER agrees not to contest MARVEL's exclusive, complete and unrestricted ownership in and to the Work.
In addition, SUPPLIER grants to MARVEL the right to use SUPPLIER's name and likeness in connection with the Work, and the advertising thereof, but in no event shall SUPPLIER be deemed to be endorsing a commercial product without first having obtained SUPPLIER's express written consent.
This Agreement shall be binding upon and inure to the benefit of the parties hereto and their respective heirs, successors, administrators and assigns.
IN WITNESS WHEREOF, the parties hereto have executed this Agreement as of the date first above written.
Supplier
URGENT!!
Marvel Comics Group, a division of Cadence Industries Corporation
by
by
COMICS CONTRACT MEETING
SUNDAY MAY 7, 9 E. 48th ST
THIRD FLOOR 4:00 P.M

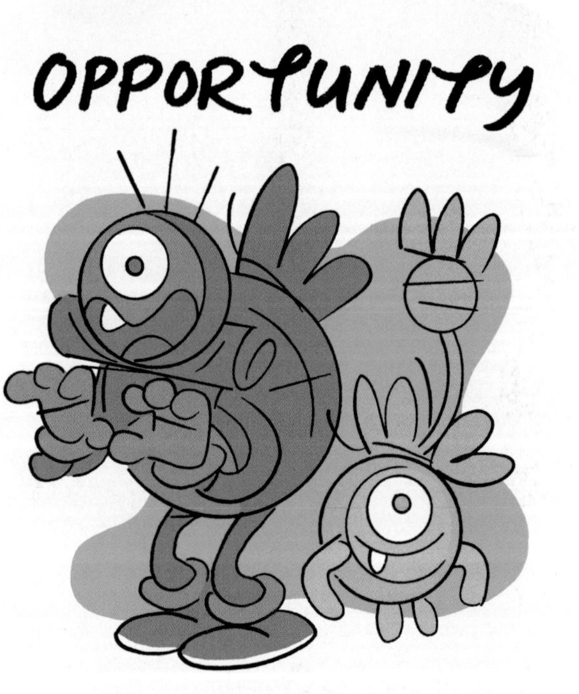
OPPORTUNITY

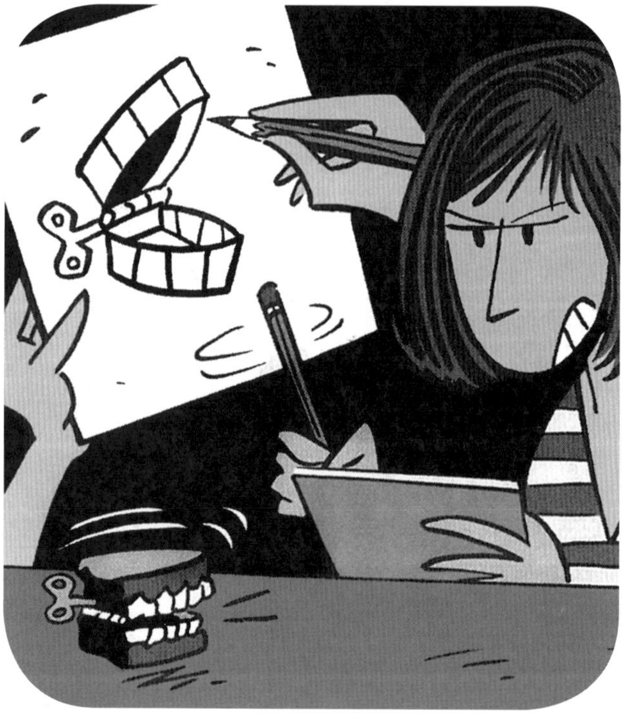